Genealogy and Literature

Genealogy and Literature

Lee Quinby, editor

University of Minnesota Press
Minneapolis
London

T

1002128650

Published by the University of Minnesota Press
111 Third Avenue South, Suite 290, Minneapolis, MN 55401-2520
Printed in the United States of America on acid-free paper

Library of Congress Cataloging-in-Publication Data

Genealogy and literature / Lee Quinby, editor.
p.   cm.
Includes bibliographical references and index.
ISBN 0-8166-2560-3 (hc). — ISBN 0-8166-2561-1 (pbk.)
1. Social structure in literature.   2. Canon (Literature)
I. Quinby, Lee, 1946–   .
PN56.S564G46   1995
809 — dc20
95-739

The University of Minnesota is an equal-opportunity educator and employer.

609831

For my sons,
Michael Miller and Paul Miller

Contents

Part III: Seeking the Limits of the Possible

Acknowledgments

I am grateful to the contributors to this collection: their generosity of spirit and remarkable punctuality deserve special notice. I also wish to thank the two anonymous reviewers for their encouraging, helpful recommendations and Laura Westlund for her skillful copyediting.

Financial assistance from Hobart and William Smith Colleges helped to allow me to draw on the good services of John D'Agata and Elizabeth Hoskins and to cover other expenses incurred in the process of gathering necessary materials.

Introduction
Genealogy and the Desacralization of Literature

Lee Quinby

Let us give the term *genealogy* to the union of erudite knowledge and local memories which allows us to establish a historical knowledge of struggles and to make use of this knowledge tactically today.

Michel Foucault[1]

Regimes of sacralized truth conceal the violences installed within their logic. Yet these violences are evident in their action on bodies and in bodily reactions, of those who collaborate as well as those who resist. As Foucault puts it, "the body manifests the stigmata of past experience and also gives rise to desires, failings, and errors."[2] Bodily "stigmata" or inscriptions of history are "traced by language and dissolved by ideas." Language's role in revealing, covering over, or erasing history's inscriptions on bodies is part of what makes literature and its criticism worthy of genealogical attention. Through its pursuit of "the accidents, the minute deviations—or, conversely, the complete reversals—the errors, the false appraisals, and the faulty calculations that gave birth to those things that continue to exist and have value for us," genealogical investigation makes visible the ordering of discourses into the prose and poetry forms that constitute the field of literature.[3] Genealogy seeks to demystify the pieties that continue to haunt literature by searching out the way "the literary" is delineated, how these texts are produced and distributed. It attends as well to the alterations of the field, highlighting modes of resistance within both literature and literary criticism and theory. Genealogical inquiry also exposes the means by which sacralized literature, literary criticism, and literary theory fortify a power/knowledge formation that justifies hierarchy, commits violences in the name of morality and truth, and defuses possibilities for social change.

This book is an effort to show genealogical analysis at work in the desacralization of literature. For upholders of literary tradition, desacralization might sound a bit like taking not only the lamb but also the priest to slaughter. This is not entirely wrong. A diminution of faith in literature as a revelation of universal truth and absolute morality does put an end to the priestly function still enjoyed by some academics and longed for by others. Desacralization also staves off the bestowal of blessings on avant-garde literature and the literature of authenticity, the forms through which resacralization processes are most likely to occur these days through claims of inherent subversiveness. Yet desacralization neither kills off literature nor exiles departments of literary studies. It does not sacrifice their "firstborn," their majors. Indeed, as the essays in this volume demonstrate, desacralization may not be literature's saving grace but rather its reinvigorator.

Desacralization is an effort to analyze the ways in which certain discourses, literature and philosophy in particular, emerge during the eighteenth century as discourses said to transcend and subsume all others.[4] Over the past two decades a number of critical approaches—feminist, deconstructive, and new historicist the most prominent—have advanced positions that desacralize these discourses. Feminists have demonstrated the masculinist construction of "universality," which privileges men over women by sanctioning forms of behavior and rationality cast as the special reserve of men and masculinity. Deconstructionists have shown how a metaphysics of presence functions within literature to represent a recaptured lack, the fullness of the logos, thereby exposing and dethroning the logic that lays claim to transcendence. And new historicists have debunked the autonomy of literary texts by relocating works both of literature and criticism in their historical, socioeconomic contexts. These modes have also enabled and been enabled by African American, ethnic, and lesbian and gay perspectives on literary studies. Yet the desacralization of literature requires both an extension of and a departure from each of these modes of criticism. Genealogical analysis is a way of undertaking such a task.

The links between genealogy and desacralization may be found in their shared tactical use of knowledge. When Foucault drew on Nietzsche's use of the term genealogy to challenge traditional history's search for origins, continuity, and coherence, he dealt a blow to a regime of truth that denies the ambiguous beginnings, vicissitudes, and incongruities of our existence. This important critique is now two decades old, and yet, despite having made significant inroads within such fields of study as history, literature, philosophy, psychology, and sociology, many of the totalizing and teleological assumptions that genealogy challenges remain entrenched. This is not unexpected: there was certainly no utopian prediction that genealogists would unite to seize the means of knowledge production. It does indicate that genealogy is to be an ongoing task — that a genealogical approach includes investigating how sacralization recurs, even within critical discourses such as feminism, deconstruction, and new historicism. Sacralization blunts the critical edge of feminism, for example, when feminism analyzes gender as a separable category distinct from race, class, and sexuality, or of deconstruction when it assumes the operation of specific binaries as always already there, or of new historicism when its predisposition toward the overdetermined blinds it to possibilities of transgression and social change.

In this sense, desacralization works in coalition with other critical methods that avoid and challenge claims of teleological and unified meaning, joining forces with deconstruction, carnivalization, and deterritorialization.[5] Just as deconstruction is an analytical tool for prying open the locks of binary systems of meaning, so too carnivalization and deterritorialization are oppositional reading strategies that disrupt the prime allegiances of valuation. Carnivalization, following Mikhail Bakhtin, aims to subvert the official meaning system by emphasizing, even exaggerating, certain moments in the dominant linguistic order so as to trope the excesses that have been concealed or suppressed.[6] Like carnivalization, deterritorialization privileges disruption. In the view of Gilles Deleuze and Félix Guattari, "deterritorialization of language" occurs through a nomadic stance in relation to a dominant or official language. Their celebration of Kafka as a "minor author" is an invocation to become minor readers, "to make use of the polylingualism of one's own language, to make a minor or intensive use of it, to oppose the oppressed quality of this language to its oppressive quality, to find points of nonculture or underdevelopment, linguistic Third World zones by which a language can escape, an animal enters into things, an assemblage comes into play."[7]

Genealogy consolidates this coalition of erudite knowledges by forging links through a critique of "ideology." Despite the secularization that typically (though often tacitly) accompanies the defense of ideology as a theoretical concept, its usage continues to bolster resacralization. Orthodox Marxism has been thoroughly criticized for the untenability of a base-and-superstructure model, by neo- and post-Marxists as well as by Foucault, Derrida, and others; thus the form that ideology as a concept most often takes in current analyses is less laden with overt declarations of the analyst's ability to ascertain scientific truth and expose "false consciousness." Nevertheless, the weight of the entrenched meaning of the term is still felt. As Michele Barrett observes, "The connotations of simplistic illusion or 'false consciousness,' however inaccurate, are difficult to shake off. The implication of an 'infra-structure' is always there. The 'explanation' in terms of class is never really forgotten." The greatest disservice, as Barrett points out, is that "the work undertaken by the concept of ideology is often too shallow and too easy, by virtue of the history of the usage of the concept."[8] Exploration of local history helps offset this return of totalizing meaning by establishing the partial against the universal, but excavation of buried events is not enough. Various methods of unmasking naturalized truth are crucial to a genealogical project, which is why deconstruction, deterritorialization, and carnivalization are all necessary for debunking the absolute truth claims that sacralize literature.

Genealogical Literary Studies and the History of the Present

The brief overview just given is meant to suggest what genealogical inquiry can do for literary studies, a task that can be carried out only through critical practice and thus better indicated in the chapters that follow. But what value does the study of literature have for genealogy? Despite derisive attitudes about academic self-indulgence and privilege, voiced both inside and outside educational institutions, literary studies is necessary for understanding the history of the present. The majority of people in the United States may read relatively few literary texts, even counting popular romance and detective fiction, yet the aura of "great works" remains sufficient to draw on them for everything from computer ads to new films.[9] This does not suggest that these works remain somehow "alive" or give us insight into "human nature," but it does indicate that modern subjectivity has been molded around sacralizing distinctions that divide the superior from the inferior, distinctions that not only sell products but also justify hierarchy. This in turn means that literary studies today can provide a way of clarifying the power dynamics that considered literature to be so necessary for civilization that it became central to modern educational institutions at every level and was used as a disciplinary technology of colonization.

Studying literature to understand the history of the present thus requires a shift in expectation about what literature can teach us. This is not an over-inflation of expectation for literary studies. It's not the belief that Stanley Fish has ridiculed as the illusion that literary criticism will "contribute to the toppling of patriarchy."[10] But it isn't a reduction in expectation either, of the sort favored by Fish in asserting that "literary interpretation, like virtue, is its own reward."[11] Fish may be right in pointing out the hyperbole of some critics (though he's given to some hyperbole himself in setting this up as widespread), but his own solution, which may well be exhilarating to him and something of a bravura performance, contributes to the trivialization of both literature and its criticism.

Genealogical literary analysis teaches a great deal about how given cultures engage with and deny their own local dispositions and practices toward such preeminent concerns of literature as death, sexuality, war, love, hatred, and madness. Approaching literature this way means engaging it as an involvement with important problems, the cultural sites that fuel uncertainties about conduct and call forth efforts to understand their meanings and consequences. Along with music, film, philosophy, law, news media, and the visual arts, literature is one of the fields designated by Western culture to take up key problems. As Simon During has observed, "Today the texts that are most worth reading, encouraging others to read, and most worth writing about are those that produce active engagement in these problems, a conscious sense of involvement in them."[12] During's own literary criticism focuses on death in terms of the rise of realism and modern medicine in such novels as *Madame Bovary* and *Middlemarch*; he also discusses the way that *An American Tragedy* incorporates issues of capital punishment that were being debated at the time of its writing.

It follows that such an approach is less interested in the question of a literary canon per se than it is in examining the ways that a canon of great works is deployed to construct a dominant regime of truth. Instead of formulating countercanons or expanding the existing canon, genealogical literary criticism takes as its focus of study those texts that most illuminate the problems with which societies grapple (a critic's own society or that of a particular text). Some of these problems recur or remain over long stretches; others fall out of the arena of concern. To think about and teach literature from this perspective implies a reorganization of literary studies away from great works, period, and genre courses toward courses and critical analyses focused on what Foucault called "problemizations by thought." Thought, as defined here, is "what allows one to step back from this way of acting or reacting and question it as to its meaning, its conditions, and its goals. Thought is free-dom in relation to what one does, the motion by which one detaches oneself from it, establishes it as an object, and reflects on it as a problem."[13] Prob-lemization by thought is also what motivates the way that cultural studies brings together literature, law, and popular culture. The juxtaposition of these varying discourses highlights the rules and regulations that define them as well as establishing points of intersection among them.

Although current critical understanding of genealogy remains primarily Foucauldian, a genealogical focus on practices in the present necessarily re-quires engagement with a number of post-Foucauldian concerns. One such concern follows from changes in the fields of knowledge that comprise the humanities. The postmodern era of electronic technology has altered knowl-edge production in dramatic ways since Foucault's formulations about ge-nealogy. The anonymity of electronic communications allows for virtual dis-sociation between communicator and text. Computer technology is fast transforming the modes of existence of a number of discourses, including lit-erature. Though still very much at an experimental stage, electronically pro-duced hyperfiction is an interactively constructed form in which plots twist and turn as they are erased or replicated through the additions and deletions of a possibly indeterminate number of people whose identities may or may not be known.[14] In this respect, electronic production of power/knowledge has given new meaning to Foucault's query at the end of "What Is an Au-thor?": "What matter who's speaking?"

A Baudrillardian response to this question might lead to proclamations about the end of literature: in the world of simulation, death is displaced and with it the moving force of art and literature. Although there is a kind of in-verse drama to such speculation, the judgment is simply premature. Rather than making that turn, a post-Foucauldian genealogical approach attends to the question of who is speaking with renewed interest. I do not mean to echo the antipoststructuralist accusation that has been made about a "con-venient" disappearance of the author at just the time that women and other marginalized authors are gaining recognition. This argument misses the dis-tinction Foucault makes between author and author-function. Foucault's questions about author-function are still the key ones for challenging pre-sumptions of originality, authenticity, unity, and core selfhood—the central tenets of sacralized literature and criticism. His analysis of the way that the notion of the author has functioned in modern Western society makes clear that focusing on the "author" as creator of meaning enables a disappearance to occur. The author must be "dead" in order to effect a "thrift in the prolif-eration of meanings." The notion of author as "genius" is the primary means by which this death and its ensuing immortality are achieved. Such a re-sacralizing stance toward an author claims literature as a source of inex-haustible meanings while shoring up certain meanings and excluding others.

Whereas the initial critique of the author-function called for a certain level of indifference to the issue of "who is speaking" as a way of offsetting presumptions of the author as sole authority, a post-Foucauldian genealogical approach prompts questions about authors in an effort to understand what I would call the "author-subject." Rather than indifference to authorial informa-tion, genealogical investigation is vitally interested in a specific author's gender, race, ethnicity, sexuality, friendships, family relations, religious affiliations, social class, education, travel, readings, diaries, letters, as well as newspaper coverage and films of the time. These are the materials of a given author's processes of subjection and subjectification. Investigating them enhances our understanding not of the author's inner life or of the presumed unity of thought, text, and era, but of the multidiscursiveness of author-subject and the containments or dispersions of multiple meanings of a given text.[15]

Another post-Foucauldian feature of genealogy involves changes in repre-sentations of universality. These days, claims of universality are often explic-itly challenged by dominant systems of knowledge production. Multicultur-alism, far from being isolated in college and university curricula, or distinguishable as a rallying cry for radical democracy, has become a cam-paign strategy for politicians and multinational CEOs. This is not to say that assumptions of universality, teleology, and progress have been cast off. On the contrary, they have been readorned through new articulations. The post-Foucauldian task of genealogy is to target these intricately patterned masks of abusive power/knowledge as well as to ascertain how this particular trans-lation of universality in the name of difference promotes, perhaps inadver-tently, new forms of subjectivity.

Genealogical Fiction

Literary artists themselves can help direct genealogical efforts to desacralize literature. One of the boldest examples of what I call "genealogical fiction" is Toni Morrison's novel *Jazz*, published in 1992. Bringing together the terms "genealogical" and "fiction" to describe Morrison's novel is a way of marking its break with the two other strands of literary tradition most often drawn on in critical responses to *Jazz*: historical and postmodern fiction.

One reason to make this distinction is to address some of the negative criticisms that the novel received upon publication from a number of reviewers who either disparaged it for unconvincing character motivation or dismissed it as pretentiously postmodern. Such criticisms either assume or promote a goal of historical realism and then lay blame on Morrison for not living up to their definition of good fiction. This is the thrust of David Mason's comments when he states that his impression "on finishing Toni Morrison's latest historical fiction was that here was a short story inflated by literary style." He echoes the sentiment expressed by several mainstream literary reviewers when he goes on to say that "Morrison's narrator is merely an anonymous literary presence who has studied postmodernism."[16]

Mason's reading seems to me equally inadequate in his attribution of postmodernism to Morrison's narrator. The narrative voice of *Jazz* may well have studied postmodernism but is better understood as the voice of one who has studied the past, acknowledged its inconsistencies, and speculated on the consequences of everyday events — the matter of history — on the lives of those in the present. The narrator's stance toward the past and present enacts a defining trait of what I mean by genealogical fiction. Genealogical fiction focuses on history but does not adhere to the assumptions and narrative conventions of a historical novel. And even though genealogical fiction may employ postmodern narrative techniques in order to break with the narrative coherence of conventional historical fiction, it does not promulgate a postmodernist sense of crisis.

In its performance of history, genealogical fiction (or poetry or drama) breaks the hold of official truth and the metaphysics of memory, putting in their place the truth of countermemory. *Jazz* is an exemplar of this type of literature because its story of beginnings reopens a door barred by the concealments of the official, white supremacist narrative of the past. The question of genealogy as a study of the descent of family lines is one of the problematics on which *Jazz* specifically focuses. The story of the character Golden Gray, for example, the son of the "whitelady" Vera Louise Gray and "a Negro boy from out Vienna way" is the kind of subjugated truth that dispels the truth recorded in the "family tree" histories of white slaveowners.[17] In this sense *Jazz* performs the task of genealogy that Foucault calls "descent" by studying the "numberless beginnings whose faint traces and hints of color are readily seen by an historical eye. The analysis of descent permits the dissociation of the self, its recognition and displacement as an empty synthesis, in liberating a profusion of lost events."[18]

It has become axiomatic to point out that traditional history consecrates itself by polarizing truth and fiction. I do not want to rehearse that critique of historical narrative here, for it has been well circulated, if not established in practice, that history is fiction in the sense that it is representation. The point I do want to stress is that, even though both disciplinary history and genealogy are necessarily fiction, they are different kinds of fiction in several important ways. Whereas disciplinary history denies its own masquerade by insisting on monumental history as the sole story, genealogy pushes "the masquerade to its limit."[19] And while standard history — and some revisionist history — strives to establish the "roots of our identity," genealogy "commit[s] itself to its dissipation."[20] Finally, while the motor of disciplinary history ensures that it rush past judgment of the will to knowledge, genealogy demands that "the critique of the injustices of the past by a truth held by men in the present becomes the destruction of the man who maintains knowledge by the injustice proper to the will to knowledge."[21]

All genealogy is fiction, then, but by no means is all fiction genealogical. Genealogical fiction focuses on the rogue events, people, and places that are excised from conventional historical and literary narratives so as to problematize the founding tenets of accepted ("acceptable") history: the tracing of origin as the singular, miraculous moment from which all meaning and privilege derive; the insistence on continuity and influence; and the disavowal of contingency, accident, and novelty in the dispersion of events that have impact on our lives. Fiction that is genealogical challenges the will to knowledge that freezes the past by claiming its injustices and cruelties to be ordained or inevitable. The value of such fiction for the history of the present resides in its effects. As Foucault observed, it is possible "to make fiction work within truth, to induce truth-effects within a fictional discourse, and in some way to make the discourse of truth arouse, 'fabricate' something which does not yet exist, thus 'fiction' something. One 'fictions' history starting from the political reality that renders it true, one 'fictions' a politics that doesn't yet exist starting from an historical truth."[22] As a work like *Jazz* so amply illustrates, literary fiction can serve as a compelling fictioning of another truth of the past.

Genealogical Approaches to Literature

I have selected and organized the essays in this volume to emphasize the desacralization of literature, its relationship to death, and its potential for transfiguring truth. Part I, "To Know What Literature Is," gets its title and its first chapter from an interview that Roger-Pol Droit conducted with Michel Foucault in 1975. The excerpt included here was part of a longer dialogue edited by Pol Droit and first published in *Le Monde* in 1986. Like many of Foucault's interviews, this is a record of provocative observations. It is not to be taken as a theory of literature. Foucault's discrediting of the totalizing project of theory (in regard to the theory of the subject and a theory of power, for example) should be enough to discount that as a goal anyway.[23] Despite its brevity and elliptical pronouncements, this piece provides valuable methodological insights for genealogical literary studies. It joins hands with the controversial and far more discussed "What Is an Author?" in its effort to shift from an ontology of literature to an analysis of literature as a discursive practice.

Most crucially, by focusing attention on the boundaries erected between literary and nonliterary discourses, as well as the boundary crossings that occur, these remarks guide us to a better understanding of the way literature as a field of power/knowledge functions within specific cultural contexts. Foucault's own application of this approach during the interview is consonant with his remarks in the *History of Sexuality* about resistances as multiple, changing, sometimes necessary and at other times unpredictable. This emphasis on the plurality of resistances should not be taken, as it sometimes is, as a statement of either the impossibility of resistance or the impossibility of evaluation of resistances that have occurred. Quite the contrary: "It is in this sphere of force relations that we must try to analyze the mechanisms of power. In this way we will escape from the system of Law and Sovereign which has captivated political thought for such a long time."[24] I would add here that through such an approach we combat the system of Truth and Author that has captivated literary thought for so long. But resistance at one moment and in a particular context may not be resistance in another time and place. In the interview reprinted here, Foucault explicitly makes this point in regard to debates within the academy. Given the pervasive context in which literature was cast as a genius's expression of immortalized truth, he indicates that counterclaims of literature's intransitivity—the insistence that literature is preeminently about literature—were a way of challenging sacralization. But he then goes on to clarify the limitation of that stance too, notably its tendency to resacralize literature as inherently subversive. The message underscored here is that no discourse or practice can ever be *inherently* subversive.

If Foucault's remarks set the stage for a reformulation of literary studies, the subsequent chapters of this book put this reformulation into motion. In chapter 2, Lennard J. Davis argues that the construction of deafness was integral to the production of silently read texts in the eighteenth century. In "Universalizing Marginality: How Europe Became Deaf in the Eighteenth Century," Davis reveals how publications specifically on deafness and sign language were incorporated into both philosophical and literary discourses. Thinking about the emergence of literature within this context has far-reaching implications. Davis's account of the eighteenth-century debates about language, reading, and human capacities resituates current debates about the relations between speech and writing. His analysis of the simultaneous marginalization and universalization of deafness during this period also puts a new light on class power dynamics by demonstrating how social inequities were structured through the emergence of the category of deafness. Finally, he offers new ways to think about literature as, literally and often thematically, an incorporation of sign language.

Chapter 3 turns to the question of momentous cultural changes on the order of those Foucault describes in *Discipline and Punish*, in which a society shifts from practices of public torture to technologies of disciplinary training. In "Monstrous Body, Tortured Soul: *Frankenstein* at the Juncture between Discourses," Ellen J. Goldner traces this shift by exploring Mary Shelley's novel as a site of contestation between the entrenched discourse of the public spectacle of bodily torture and the emerging discourse of the privatized soul of self-surveillance. Goldner's exploration of the relationships between the disciplinary discourses that comprise the narrative of *Frankenstein* and modern subject formation situates literature as productive of the shifts from sovereign to bio-power. She shows that the ambivalence expressed within the novel about the alienation effects of disciplinary power, an anguish felt by both Victor Frankenstein and the monster he creates, is part of the production of an interiorized, "deep self" subjectivity. Such a critique enables us to discern the subtle seductions of the discourse of the tortured soul, which was granted pride of place within the field of literature as the agonized imagination of the romantic artist.

Moving from techniques of individualization to the political technologies that totalize a society, chapter 4 focuses on mid-nineteenth-century discourses of colonialism, race classification, and literature. Malini Johar Schueller's "Indians, Polynesians, and Empire Making: The Case of Herman Melville" illuminates the ways that critique of and complicity in colonialism intersect in *Typee*, *Omoo*, and *Mardi*. By examining the race and gender representations in these works, Schueller underscores both the acuity of Melville's critique of colonialist discourse and the reappropriation of empire that emerges at narrative boundary-sites in which racial and gender demarcation occurs. Precisely because such reappropriation is not inevitable, as some modes of current criticism seem resigned to conclude, this kind of attention is especially valuable as a way of fostering resistance in the present.

The title of part II, "A Language Poised against Death," is drawn from "Language to Infinity" because all four of the chapters that comprise this part of the book address the signification of death that Foucault argues is central to the category of literature. But all four chapters also depart in important respects from the arguments advanced throughout that essay.[25] Written during the early sixties, "Language to Infinity" marks a shift in how Foucault addresses literature. It is less a paean to transgression than are his writings about Bataille, yet it opens with Blanchot's romantic evocation of "writing so as not to die." It contains startlingly ahistorical remarks, as in the following: "Death is undoubtedly the most essential of the accidents of language (its limit and its center): from the day that men began to speak toward death and against it, in order to grasp and imprison it, something was born, a murmuring which repeats, recounts, and redoubles itself endlessly, which has undergone an uncanny process of amplification and thickening, in which our language is today lodged and hidden."[26] Yet this essay historicizes literature in several crucial ways essential for genealogical analysis, not the least of which is its bold assertion that " 'literature' came into existence ... at the end of the eighteenth century."[27] The chapters of this section further Foucault's shift toward history by clarifying how death and transgression are always local events.

In *Foucault and Literature*, Simon During has explored more fully than anyone else the forms a genealogy of literature takes. His book demonstrates Foucault's contributions to American and European literary history by developing his claim for literature's relatively recent emergence. Chapter 5, "Post-Foucauldian Criticism: Government, Death, Mimesis," reprinted here from During's book, traces the entry of literature, literary criticism, and literary theory into English school systems in the nineteenth and twentieth centuries, indicating literature's relations with other operations of modern power. During then takes up the contributions and limitations of new historicism for genealogical literary analysis. By focusing on Stephen Greenblatt's *Shakespearean Negotiations*, he shows why Foucauldian analyses that pursue nonmimetic paradigms insufficiently address the complex and often concealed ways in which representations of death and violence function in literature. Genealogical analysis, he maintains, must take into account the "delirium of mimesis."

In chapter 6, "Cannibalizing the Humanist Subject: A Genealogy of Prospero," Tom Hayes explores how humanism represents death, sexuality, and madness as an alterity to be conquered. His genealogical investigation of Prospero, which ranges from Shakespeare's depiction in *The Tempest* to Peter Greenaway's 1991 film *Prospero's Books*, demonstrates humanism's masculinist and heterosexist construction of autonomous selfhood. But Hayes also presents possible views of Prospero as a subject in process. This emphasis on Prospero as a character willing to interrogate his own compulsions toward domination forwards him as a figure of genealogical self-criticism for white, heterosexual men. This approach illustrates genealogy's transformation of character study, which shifts focus from the internal structure of a given text (without disregarding those textual features) to the dynamics within the literary field.

That the literary field is fraught with political contestation is made even more clear in chapter 7, in Claudette Kemper Columbus's analysis of *The Foxes*, a novel written by the Peruvian José María Arguedas in 1971. *The Foxes* depicts complicities among Peruvian government officials and businessmen, international corporations, and the mafia, and also implicates the U.S. war in Vietnam and the moon shot; it prompted objection to Arguedas from both governments. The United States denied him a visa to attend a PEN conference in New York and, even though this and other works have been translated into almost all of the world's major languages and three of his other novels have been published in English, *The Foxes* has yet to be translated into English. In "Grounds for Decolonization: Arguedas's *Foxes*," Columbus shows how Arguedas's intertwining of ancient Andean myths, contemporary Peruvian social issues, and his personal diary contemplations of his own suicide form a narrative of resistance to modes of colonization. Against colonization, which she argues is a defining feature of power relations, are possibilities of decolonization, which *The Foxes* enacts by enfolding the violations of time and space under domination within myth's depictions of nonlinear time and sublime space. The juxtaposition of these conflicting modes of duration is posed dramatically around the novel's embrace of Arguedas's death, an act performed as political protest against the oppressive forces that prohibit or circumscribe individual and communal freedom, defined here as access to decolonizing options.

Chapter 8 shifts the focus from effects of colonization and resistance to failures of resistance against colonialist missionary culture. Imafedia Okhamafe's "Genealogical Determinism in Achebe's *Things Fall Apart*" shows how the patriarchal economy of power relations of the nine-village clan, Umuofia, is structured around dichotomies of manhood and womanhood that hierarchically divide and define everything from bodies to crops. His analysis of the village's *egwugwu* life practices demonstrates an internal crisis that diffuses efforts of resistance against Christian colonization. By focusing on the means by which clan genealogy disallows any questioning of its gender hierarchies, specifically through the plight of Okonkwo, Okhamafe suggests that Okonkwo's final act — a suicide that fundamentally violates the very tradition he had so fought to uphold — was in some respects already determined by the requirements of manliness defined in terms of physical strength and a blood economy.

Part III, "Seeking the Limits of the Possible," also draws its title from "Language to Infinity," but, again, these chapters take their focus more from the historical and political implications of that essay than from its moments of dramatic but ahistorical claims for language. This vacillation between the historical and the ahistorical congeals in the passage about the evocation to seek the "limits of the possible." Pointing to Sade's importance in establishing literature as necessarily "always excessive and deficient," Foucault writes:

> This language's claim to tell all is not simply that of breaking prohibitions, but of seeking the limits of the possible; the design, in a systematically transformed network, of all of the branches, insertions, and overlappings which are deduced from the human crystal in order to give birth to great, sparkling, mobile, and infinitely extendable configurations; the lengthy passage through the underground of nature to the double lightning flash of the spirit (the first, derisive and dramatic, which blasts Justine, and the second, invisible and absolutely slow, which — in the absence of a charnel house — causes Juliette to disappear into a kind of eternity asymptotic to death) — these elements designate the project of subjecting every possible language, every future language, to the actual sovereignty of this unique Discourse which no one, perhaps, will be able to hear.[28]

This is Foucault in a totalizing vein that his later works put under well-warranted scrutiny. Appeals to the "double lightning flash of the spirit," the lack of reflection on the gendered bodies of Justine and Juliette, and the claims for literature as a virtually mystical and presumably unified "unique Discourse" are precisely what genealogy challenges.

Nevertheless, the historical insights here are worth underscoring. The paradox that authorizes the field that we know as literature is starkly visible in the texts of Sade and gothic writers of terror. These works embody words with sensation through their emphasis on terror, pain, and pleasure. But any such writing is also "of so little density that it is fated to extend itself to infinity without ever acquiring the weight that might immobilize it."[29] This paradox is at work in literature's tendency to proliferate; the gaps and folds emerging from literature's excessiveness and deficiency spin out desire for more embodied, sensate images, which in turn produce more weightlessness. This understanding of literature also puts in relief certain works that self-reflexively comment on the paradox that demarcates the field. Such works seek "the limits of the possible" of the discursive field designated as literature. Whereas modernist writing preeminently reflects on literature as a narrative formation through extended experimentation with language, which pushes toward breakdown in syntactic and narrative form, postmodern literature risks evacuating the field itself by overtly bringing into it theoretical discourses that induce crisis over identity, perception, and knowledge.

Chapter 9, my own contribution to this collection, is an address I presented at Purdue University's Annual American Studies Symposium in 1994.[30] The symposium posed the question of which directions American studies might take in the nineties. In "Sex Matters: Genealogical Inquiries, Pedagogical Implications," I propose that American studies as an academic program should undertake the making of genealogists. (My focus for the symposium was American studies, but this is my view for democratic education overall.) In calling for a genealogical approach to the study of the Americas, I wanted in particular to emphasize the importance of partiality to cultural analysis. I mean this in two senses: as genealogists we are partial or committed to the democratic struggles we investigate, and our investigations will necessarily be partial rather than complete and absolute. The specific focus of the talk, sex matters, looks at relations between materiality of bodies and discourses and proposes a method of juxtaposing discrepant historical, literary, and current texts or events as a way of dislodging naturalized assumptions. Such juxtaposition, I argue, is a risk-taking in thought that helps prevent the takeover of orthodoxy, a tendency that plagues pedagogy as much as it does religion and politics.

The last three chapters focus on works that take genealogical kinds of risks. One of the important features of chapter 10, "The Real and the Marvelous in Charleston, South Carolina: Ntozake Shange's *Sassafrass, Cypress & Indigo*," by José David Saldivar, is its clarification that genealogical desacralization does not promote the elimination of myth in literature. As

Columbus indicates in her examination of *The Foxes*, literary incorporation of indigenous myths allows Arguedas to challenge official forms of knowledge. Saldivar extends this demonstration of subjugated myth knowledge to his study of Shange's 1982 novel. The first portion of his essay provides a genealogy of magic realism in the twentieth century, from its initial appearances in Europe in writings of the surrealists, through its applications in Latin America in the 1940s for describing *lo real maravilloso* (marvelous realism) and *el realismo mágico* (magic realism), and its continued formulations in the 1950s and 1960s. Saldivar argues that a "fourth phase," found in works by Shange and others, provides an expanded and more political version of magic realism, one in which imperialistic geographic divisions within the Americas are discursively reconstituted.

In chapter 11, Donald H. Mengay illustrates how global transvaluations, in this case the incorporation of Western notions of individualism within Japanese culture, may be played out through reconceptualizations of the body, identity, and eroticism. In "Body/Talk: Mishima, Masturbation, and Self-Performativity," Mengay argues that the clash of cultures following the Second World War created a cultural flux akin to what Western readers have come to know as the postmodern condition. Yukio Mishima's *Confessions of a Mask* (English translation, 1958) is particularly noteworthy in this regard because it converts that flux into issues of personal identity through tropes of fluidity and discreteness. Mengay shows how the convergence of sexuality, death, and writing in *Confessions of a Mask* is represented through masturbation and how selfhood is defined as a performative act consonant with Japanese stage performance. This discussion also illuminates Euro-American deployments of disciplinary power and normalization by showing Mishima's acceptance of certain practices of Western individualism and rejection of others in his attempts to resist compulsory heterosexuality.

Kate Mehuron's " 'Dreadful Dioramas': Guibert's Countermemories" closes this collection with an exploration of Hervé Guibert's fictionalized tributes to Michel Foucault and the place of death in their friendship. Mehuron argues that Guibert's novel *To the Friend Who Did Not Save My Life* and his short story "A Man's Secrets" stage scenes of the philosopher's death that comprise mimetic moments before the fact. In her view, Guibert's description of his philosopher friend's death is to be understood as a presentiment of his own that he too will soon encounter from AIDS. From this analytical perspective, Guibert's portrayals constitute countermemories in which truth is cast as a complex play of dioramic images, in which one is both spectator and participant. His artistic "theft" of his friend's secrets and his revelations of the details of his final hours make up a literary diorama that depicts the "limits of the possible" — the representation of the scene of one's own death.

To seek such limits through literature is also to transform what we know as literature and the ways in which literature is regarded. Over the past two centuries, literature has been seen as a revelation of transcendental Truth, as a lament over the loss of such Truth, and as a subversion of ideological and political dominance. Skeptical about all three of these sacralizing stances, genealogical literary studies is nonetheless vitally interested in how they came to be established in European and American societies and what the consequences of such power/knowledge relations have been and are now. This book is offered as a contribution to that ongoing and collective effort to establish a genealogy of literature.

Notes

I would like to thank members of a work-in-progress group at Hobart and William Smith Colleges for their comments and suggestions on this Introduction: Betty Bayer, Claudette Kemper Columbus, Maram Epstein, Maureen Flynn, and Susan Henking.

1. Michel Foucault, "Two Lectures," in Power/Knowledge: Selected Interviews and Other Writings, 1972–1977, ed. Colin Gordon (New York: Pantheon, 1980), 83.

2. Michel Foucault, "Nietzsche, Genealogy, History," in Language, Counter-Memory, Practice: Selected Essays and Interviews, ed. Donald F. Bouchard (Ithaca: Cornell University Press, 1977), 148.

3. Ibid., 146.

4. See Michel Foucault, "The Functions of Literature," reprinted as chapter 1 of this volume.

5. Although Foucault took issue with Derrida on the status of truth and methods of dismantling it, I think it is valuable to use methods of deconstruction to break down naturalized meaning while trying to establish through genealogy how that univocal meaning got entrenched within a culture. See my Anti-Apocalypse: Exercises in Genealogical Criticism (Minneapolis: University of Minnesota Press, 1994), in particular chapter 3, "Philosophy Today: Not-for-Prophet Thought." Similarly, I am not arguing that Foucauldian discourse analysis holds the same premises about language and literature as carnivalization and deterritorialization; I am suggesting that these modes of subversion should be put to genealogical purpose.

6. Mikhail Bakhtin, Rabelais and His World, trans. Helene Iswolsky (Cambridge, Mass.: MIT Press, 1968).

7. Gilles Deleuze and Félix Guattari, "What Is a Minor Literature?" in Kafka: Toward a Minor Literature, trans. Dana Polan (Minneapolis: University of Minnesota Press, 1986), 26–27. Todd May makes the point that despite the friendship between Foucault and Deleuze, their views of desire were decidedly different: "To found difference in a desire that is either unfettered or in a constant play of deterritorialization and reterritorialization requires the positing of an origin that Foucault explicitly rejected as early as The Archaeology of Knowledge" (May, Between Genealogy and Epistemology: Psychology, Politics, and Knowledge in the Thought of Michel Foucault [University Park: Pennsylvania State University Press, 1993], 5). Also see Caren Kaplan, "Deterritorializations: The Rewriting of Home and Exile in Western Feminist Discourse," Cultural

Critique 6 (Spring 1987): 187–98, in which she cautions against "theoretical tourism on the part of the first world critic."

8. Michele Barrett, *The Politics of Truth: From Marx to Foucault* (Stanford: Stanford University Press, 1991), 168.

9. According to studies jointly conducted by the American Booksellers Association, the Association of American Publishers, and the Book Industry Study Group, 60 percent of households in the United States did not buy a book during the whole of 1991. The study indicates that of the paperback books purchased, almost half were romance novels. Popular fiction accounted for two-thirds of all books purchased. See "Even Stephen King Might Get Scared by These Figures," *Wall Street Journal* (10 January 1992): B2.

10. Stanley Fish, "Why Literary Criticism Is Like Virtue," *London Review of Books* (10 June 1993): 15.

11. Ibid., 11.

12. Simon During, *Foucault and Literature: Towards a Genealogy of Writing* (New York: Routledge, 1992), 238.

13. Michel Foucault, "Polemics, Politics, and Problemizations: An Interview with Michel Foucault," in *The Foucault Reader*, ed. Paul Rabinow (New York: Pantheon, 1984), 388.

14. See, for example, Robert Coover, "Hyperfiction: Novels for the Computer," *New York Times Book Review* (29 August 1993): 1–2. For a sustained treatment, see George P. Landow, *Hypertext: The Convergence of Contemporary Critical Theory and Technology* (Baltimore: Johns Hopkins University Press, 1992).

15. Cheryl Walker has raised crucial questions about how feminist criticism might approach the author. Drawing partially from Foucault, but also taking issue with his gender naïveté, she stresses that it does make a difference who is speaking, precisely because of the politics of race, gender, and class difference. She offers the term "persona criticism" as a way of engaging issues of difference regarding readers as well as writers. See Cheryl Walker, "Feminist Literary Criticism and the Author," *Critical Inquiry* 16 (Spring 1990): 551–71. For an illuminating discussion of the significance of authorship and sexuality, as applied primarily to film, see Richard Dyer, "Believing in Fairies: The Author and the Homosexual," in *Inside/Out: Lesbian Theories, Gay Theories*, ed. Diana Fuss (New York: Routledge, 1991), 185–201.

16. David Mason, "Mythical Histories," *Hudson Review* (Winter 1993): 660–61.

17. Toni Morrison, *Jazz* (New York: Alfred Knopf, 1992), 139–40.

18. Foucault, "Nietzsche, Genealogy, History," 145–46.

19. Ibid., 160–61.

20. Ibid., 162.

21. Ibid., 164. Foucault argues that these three uses of genealogy "oppose and correspond to the three Platonic modalities of history" (160).

22. "Interview with Lucette Finas," in *Michel Foucault: Power, Truth, Strategy*, eds. Meaghan Morris and Paul Patton, trans. Paul Foss and Meaghan Morris (Sydney: Feral Publications, 1979), 74–75.

23. See in particular Michel Foucault, "Afterword: The Subject and Power," in Hubert Dreyfus and Paul Rabinow, *Michel Foucault: Beyond Structuralism and Hermeneutics*, 2d ed. (Chicago: University of Chicago Press, 1983), 209; and "Michel Foucault: Final Interview," *Raritan Review* 5, no. 1 (Summer 1985): 1–13 (interview conducted by Gilles Barbadette and André Scala).

24. Michel Foucault, *History of Sexuality*, trans. Robert Hurley (New York: Pantheon, 1978), 1:95–97.

25. Michel Foucault, "Language to Infinity," *Language, Counter-Memory, Practice: Selected Essays and Interviews*, ed. Donald F. Bouchard (Ithaca: Cornell University Press, 1977), 52–67.

26. Ibid., 55.

27. Ibid., 66. Timothy J. Reiss provides a detailed treatment of how literature as we know it emerged in the seventeenth century; see Timothy J. Reiss, *The Meaning of Literature* (Ithaca: Cornell University Press, 1992).

28. Ibid., 61. For the discussion on excess and deficiency, see p. 65.

29. Ibid., 65.

30. I wish to express appreciation to Harold Woodman and Leonard Neufeldt for inviting me to this conference and to Donald Pease for his insightful comments about my presentation.

Part I
To Know What Literature Is

1

The Functions of Literature

Michel Foucault

This dialogue on the nature of literature is a fragment of a longer interview conducted on June 20, 1975, with Roger-Pol Droit. It took place several months after the publication of *Surveiller et punir* (February 1975) and one year prior to the publication of *La Volonté de savoir* (December 1976). Roger-Pol Droit and Michel Foucault had decided to collaborate on a book of interviews—an ongoing dialogue—that would further develop some of Foucault's theoretical concepts and address other issues left unexplored in his previously published work. The project, however, was never completed. The following represents a small portion of the "sixth" tape that was subsequently edited by Roger-Pol Droit and published for the first time in *Le Monde*, September 16, 1986. The translation is by Alan Sheridan. The editorial notes are by Lawrence D. Kritzman.

ROGER-POL DROIT: What place, what status, have literary texts in your research?

MICHEL FOUCAULT: In *Histoire de la folie* and *Les Mots et les choses*, I merely indicated them, pointed them out in passing. I was the kind of stroller who says: "Well, when you see that, you cannot but talk about *Le Neveu de Rameau*." But I accorded them no role in the actual economy of the process.

For me literature was something I observed, not something I analyzed, or reduced, or integrated into the very field of analysis. It was a rest, a thought on the way, a badge, a flag.

3

R.-P. D.: You didn't want to make these texts express or reflect historical processes.

FOUCAULT: No. [Silence, thought.] We must approach the question at another level.

No one has ever really analyzed how, out of the mass of things said, out of the totality of actual discourse, a number of these discourses (literary discourse, philosophical discourse) are given a particular sacralization and function.

It would seem that traditionally literary or philosophical discourses could be made to function as substitutes or as a general envelope for all other discourses. Literature had to stand for the rest. People wrote the history of what was said in the eighteenth century, via Fontenelle, or Voltaire, or Diderot, or *La Nouvelle Héloïse*, and so forth. Or they regard these texts as the expression of something that, ultimately, could not be formulated at a more everyday level.

In this respect, I moved from the expectative (pointing literature out when I happened to encounter it, without indicating its relations with the rest) to a frankly negative position, trying to bring out positively all the nonliterary or parallel discourses that were actually produced at a given period, excluding literature itself. In *Surveiller et punir* I refer only to bad literature ...

R.-P. D.: How is one to distinguish between the good and the bad?

FOUCAULT: That is precisely the question that will have to be confronted one day. On the one hand, we shall have to ask ourselves what exactly is this activity that consists in circulating fiction, poems, stories ... in a society. We should also analyze a second operation: among all the narratives, why is it that a number of them are sacralized, made to function as "literature"? They are immediately taken up with an institution that was originally very different: the university institution. Now it is beginning to be identified with the literary institution.

There is a very visible slope in our culture. In the nineteenth century, the university was the element within which was constituted a so-called classical literature, and which was valued both as the sole basis of contemporary literature and as a criticism of that literature. Hence a very curious interplay occurs, in the nineteenth century, between literature and the university, between the writer and the professor.

And then, little by little, the two institutions, which, despite all their squabbles, were profoundly linked, tended to merge completely. We know perfectly well that today so-called avant-garde literature is read only by university teachers and their students. We know very well that nowadays a writer over thirty is surrounded by students writing their theses on his work. We know that writers live mainly by teaching and lecturing.

So here we already have the truth of something: the fact that literature functions as literature through an interplay of selection, sacralization, and institutional validation, of which the university is both the operator and the receiver.

R.-P. D.: Are there criteria internal to the texts, or is it simply a matter of sacralization by the university institution?

FOUCAULT: I don't know. I would simply like to say this: in order to break with a number of myths, including that of the expressive character of literature, it has been very important to pose this great principle that literature is concerned only with itself. If it is concerned with its author, it is so rather in terms of the death, silence, disappearance even of the person writing.

It does not matter whether one refers here to Blanchot or to Barthes. The main point is the importance of this principle: the intransitivity of literature. This was, indeed, the first step by which we were able to get rid of the idea that literature was the locus of every kind of traffic, or the point at which all traffic came to an end, the expression of totalities.

But it seems to me that this was still only a stage. For, by keeping analysis at this level, one runs this risk of not unraveling the totality of sacralizations of which literature has been the object. On the contrary, one runs the risk of sacralizing even more. And this is indeed what happened, right up until 1970. You will have seen how a number of themes originating in Blanchot or Barthes were used in a kind of exaltation, both ultralyrical and ultrarationalizing, of literature as a structure of language capable of being analyzed in itself and on its own terms.

Political implications were absent from this exaltation. Some people were even able to say that literature in itself was so emancipated from all determinations that the very fact of writing was in itself subversive, that the writer, in the very gesture of writing, had an inalienable right to subversion! The writer was, therefore, a revolutionary, and the more writing was writing, the more it sank into intransitivity, the more it produced, by that very fact, the movement of revolution! As you know, such things were, unfortunately, said . . .

In fact, the approach used by Blanchot and Barthes tended to a desacralization of literature, by breaking the links that placed it in a position of absolute expression. This rupture implied that the next movement would be to desacralize absolutely and to try to see how, in the general mass of what was said, it was possible at a given moment, in a particular mode, for that particular region of language to be constituted. It must not be asked to bear the decisions of a culture, but rather how it comes about that a culture decided to give it this very special, very strange position.

R.-P. D.: Why strange?

FOUCAULT: Our culture accords literature a place that in a sense is extra-ordinarily limited: how many people read literature? What place does it really have in the general expansion of discourses?

But this same culture forces all its children, as they move toward culture, to pass through a whole ideology, a whole ideology of literature during their studies. There is a kind of paradox here.

And it is not unconnected with the declaration that literature is subversive. The fact that someone declares it to be so, in this or that literary review, is of no importance and has no effect. But if at the same moment the entire teaching profession, from primary-school teachers to heads of university departments, tells you, explicitly or not, that if you are to find the great decisions of a culture, the points at which it changes direction, then you must turn to Diderot, or Sade, or Hegel, or Rabelais — and you'll find it all there. At this level, there is an effect of mutual reinforcement. The so-called avant-garde groups and the great mass of university teachers are in agreement. This has led to a very heavy political blocage.

R.-P. D.: How have you escaped from this blocage?

FOUCAULT: My way of taking up the problem was, first, the book on Raymond Roussel and, then, the book on Pierre Riviére.[1] Between the two, there is the same question: what is the threshold beyond which a discourse (whether that of a sick person, or a criminal, etc.) begins to function in the field known as literature?

In order to know what literature is, I would not want to study its internal structures. I would rather grasp the movement, the little process, by which a type of nonliterary discourse, neglected, forgotten as soon as it was made, enters the literary field. What happens? What is triggered off? How is this discourse modified in its efforts by the fact that it is recognized as literary?

R.-P. D.: Nevertheless you have devoted texts to literary works about which this question is not asked. I am thinking in particular of the articles you published in Critique on Blanchot, Klossowski, and Bataille.[2] If they were brought together in a single volume, they might provide an image of your itinerary very different from the one we are used to ...

FOUCAULT: Yes, but ... [Pause.] It would be fairly difficult to talk about them. Really, Blanchot, Klossowski, and Bataille, who were in the end the three authors who interested me particularly in the sixties, were for me much more than literary works or discourses within literature. They were discourses outside philosophy.

R.-P. D.: Meaning?

FOUCAULT: Let's take Nietzsche, if you like. In relation to academic philosophical discourse, which has constantly referred him back to himself, Nietzsche represents the outer frontier. Of course, a whole line of Western philosophy may be found in Nietzsche. Plato, Spinoza, the eighteenth-century philosophers, Hegel ... all this goes through Nietzsche. And yet, in relation to philosophy, Nietzsche has all the roughness, the rusticity, of the outsider, of the peasant from the mountains, that allows him, with a shrug of the shoulders and without it seeming in any way ridiculous, to say with a strength that one cannot ignore: "Come on, all that is rubbish ..."

Ridding oneself of philosophy necessarily implies a similar lack of deference. You will not get out of it by staying within philosophy, by refining it as much as you can, by circumventing it with one's own discourse. No. It is by opposing it with a sort of astonished, joyful stupidity, a sort of uncomprehending burst of laughter, which, in the end, understands, or, in any case, shatters. Yes ... it shatters rather than understands.

Insofar as I was, after all, an academic, a professor of philosophy, what remained of traditional philosophical discourse in the work that I had done on the subject of madness embarrassed me. There is a certain Hegelianism surviving there. It isn't necessarily enough to deal with such menial things as police reports, measures taken for confinement, the cries of madmen to escape from philosophy. For me Nietzsche, Bataille, Blanchot, and Klossowski were ways of escaping from philosophy.

In Bataille's violence, in Blanchot's insidious, disturbing sweetness, in Klossowski's spirals, there was something that, while setting out from philosophy, brought it into play and into question, emerged from it, then went back into it ... Something like Klossowski's theory of breathing is bound up by I know not how many threads, with the whole of Western philosophy. And then by the presentation, the formulation, the way in which it functions in Le Baphomet, it completely emerges from it.

These exits and entrances through the very wall of philosophy made permeable — therefore, in the end derisory — the frontier between the philosophical and the nonphilosophical.

Notes

1. Raymond Roussel (1877–1933) was an experimental French writer best known for Impressions d'Afrique (1910) and Locus Solus (1914). His work had an enormous impact on the surrealist movement because of his probing exploration of poetic language. Foucault's Raymond Roussel was published in 1963.

Pierre Riviére was a twenty-year-old Norman peasant convicted in 1836 of the murder of his pregnant mother, his younger sister, and his brother. On studying medical and legal documents Foucault discovered this case, organized a research seminar, and with the collaboration of others published a study, Moi, Pierre Riviére, ayant égorgé ma mére, ma soeur et mon frére (Paris: Gallimard-Juillard, 1973); this was translated into English by Frank Jellinek as I, Pierre Riviére, Having Slaughtered My Mother, My Sister, and My Brother . . . : A Case of Parricide in the Nineteenth Century, ed. Michel Foucault (New York: Pantheon, 1975). The centerpiece of this work was an untouched memoir transcribed by the murderer.

2. Critique, founded by Georges Bataille and Jean Piel in 1946, was a pioneering journal in the development of contemporary critical thought. In its early years it explored the relationship between art and religion, thereby contesting the narrow category in which literature had previously been assigned. More recently it has introduced sociological, thematic, and poststructural research.

Pierre Klossowski (born 1905) is an avant-garde French novelist whose works provoke anxiety from the staging of a violent desire that destroys prohibitions and liberates violent fantasies. Manifesting the influence of Georges Bataille, his most famous works are Sade mon Prochain (1947), La Vocation suspendue (1950), and Le Baphomet (1965). Michel Foucault is the author of an important article on Klossowski, "La prose d'Actéon," Nouvelle revue francaise 135 (March 1964).

2

Universalizing Marginality: How Europe Became Deaf in the Eighteenth Century

Lennard J. Davis

This [sign] language is so natural to mankind that despite the help we get
from spoken languages to express our thoughts and all their nuances, we still
make frequent use of it, especially when we are moved by some passion, and
we leave off using the cold and measured tone prescribed by our institutional
training, to bring us closer to the tone of nature.

Synthetic Essay on the Origin and Formation of Languages (1774)

The counterintuitive point of this essay is that deafness, far from being an
epiphenomenon of eighteenth-century cultural interests, was perhaps one of
the central areas of concern. I want to make a claim for the centrality of
what might appear to be extremely marginal. Further, I want to make the
somewhat preposterous suggestion that Europe became deaf during the eighteenth century. Although this statement seems patently false, I hope to show
how cultural deafness became one of the hallmarks of early modern ideas
about public symbolic and information production, and how the deaf person became an icon for complex intersections of subject, class position, and
the body.

My claim to the centrality of deafness needs to be broken down into separate smaller claims. The first of these is that deafness becomes of interest to
European culture in the eighteenth century, and the second and related claim
is that this interest is the reciprocal reaction to, or perhaps the cause of,

deafness becoming visible for the first time as an articulation in a set of discursive practices.

Michel Foucault in his classic *Madness and Civilization* shows how madhouses replaced leper colonies in Europe at the close of the Middle Ages. This switch from the confinement of defects of the body to defects of the mind signals a switch to an age of Reason and, by extension, madness, from an age that focused on the superficial disease of the body. Thus madness became visible, and the treatment of madness became a discourse. I would like to argue in a similar vein that deafness became visible in the Enlightenment and thus became the subject of a discourse of treatment by professionals while ironically also becoming symbolic of an aspect of the Enlightenment subject itself.

Before the late seventeenth and early eighteenth centuries, the deaf were not constructed as a group. There is almost no historical or literary record of the deaf as such. We may rarely read of a deaf person but there is no significant discourse constructed around deafness. The reason for this discursive nonexistence is that, then as now, most deaf people are born to hearing families, and therefore are isolated in their deafness. Without a sense of group solidarity and without a social category of disability, they were mainly seen as isolated deviations from a norm, as we now might consider, for example, people who are missing an arm. For these deaf, there were no schools, no teachers, no discourse, in effect, of deafness.

Likewise, the deaf themselves could not constitute themselves a subgroup, as might other outsiders like Jews, subalterns, even women, because they remained isolated from each other and were thus without a shared, complex language. The only deaf who fully attained sociability were deaf in urban areas or deaf people in families or groupings of hereditary deafness. Here the use of sign language, as it developed over time, allowed the deaf to consider themselves a group and to communicate with each other.[1] In saying that deafness did not "exist" before the eighteenth century, I do not mean that there were no deaf people before that time or that no one had yet written about deafness. We find early references to deafness in the Old and New Testaments and in writings by Aristotle, Augustine, Descartes, and others. But something qualitatively different happens during the eighteenth century. Consider that in the beginning of the century no deaf schools existed in England or on the Continent. By the end of the century, schools had been established in Amsterdam, Paris, Vienna, Karlsruhe, Prague, Munich, Waitzen, Fresing, Lenz, Rome, Naples, Malta, Goningen, Tarente, Madrid, Zurich, Portugal, Poland, Denmark, and Sweden. By 1789 a dozen schools had been founded in Europe and by 1822 there were sixty. Clearly, these data amount to something more than a statistical blip.

Of course, one might conclude that education, not deafness, was the central phenomenon. However, hospices for the blind had consistently been in existence since the third century. The blind were historically regarded as objects of charity, and the most famous hospice for the blind was the "Quinze-Vingts" founded by Saint Louis in 1260 in Paris, where it still exists (Paulson, *Enlightenment, Romanticism, and the Blind in France*, 8). Education for the blind began in a systematic way in the eighteenth century with the founding of the Institution des Enfans Aveugles in Paris in 1784, but they had been constituted as a group long before then. William Paulson argues that this process in turn involved a desacralization of the blind that accompanied a medicalization of the disability. Deafness as a phenomenon engaged the intellectual moment of this period in a way that blindness and other disabilities did not. Deafness, after all, was about language, about the essential human quality of verbal communication. Diderot wrote on both the blind and the deaf: the connection between blindness was more a fundamental question about the nature of perception, whereas deafness was more fundamentally about the existence and function of language. Citing Diderot, Paulson writes:

> What the blind man lacks is *denomination*, the ability to name visible objects, to put signs and referents together. Yet without that ability he is able to manipulate the signs as well as anyone else, creating an illusion of reference that is broken only when one remembers that he is blind. (48)

The relation of the blind to language is thus not as vexed as it is for those who are deaf.[2] An indication of how special a place the deaf held in the eighteenth-century imagination can be seen in the remarkable success of Jean Nicolas Bouilly's play about the abbé de l'Epée, the founder of the first deaf school. This theatrical piece had over one hundred performances in Paris at the end of the eighteenth century, making it the second-greatest dramatic success of the era, surpassed only by the *Marriage of Figaro*.[3]

The seventeenth and eighteenth centuries saw the first major publications of books relating to deafness. In Europe the works published during this period were a medical treatise by German physician Solomon Alberti, *Discourse on Deafness and Speechlessness* (1591), G. Bonifacio's treatise *Of the Art of Signs* (1616), and Juan Pablo Bonet's *A Method of Teaching Deaf Mutes to Speak* (1620). In England, the first book published was John Bulwer's *Philocophus [The Deaf Man's Friend]* (1648), followed by his *Chirologia; or, The*

Natural Language of the Hand (1654). Bulwer was a member of the Royal Society, as were a number of these early writers on deafness; George Delgarno's *Art of Communication* (1680), John Wallis's *De loquela* (1653) and "A Letter to Robert Boyle, Esq." (1670), and William Holder's *Elements of Speech* (1699) were all products of Royal Society members. George Sibscota's *Deaf and Dumb Man's Discourse* was published in 1670. The eighteenth century witnessed Johann Ammon's *Dissertatio de loquela* (1700), which had been preceded by his *Surdus Loquens [The Talking Deaf Man]* in 1694; Daniel Defoe's novel *Duncan Campbell* (1720); *Instruction of Deaf and Dumb by Means of Methodical Signs* by the abbé de l'Epée (1776); J. L. F. Arnoldi's *Practical Instructions for Teaching Deaf-Mute Persons to Speak and Write* (1777); and R. A. Sicard's *Theory of Signs* (1782), among others.

Starting in 1771 in Paris, the abbé de l'Epée held public displays of the ability of deaf students every Tuesday and Friday morning from 7:00 until noon, but the crowds increased so dramatically that he had to add another session in the evening. In 1772 printed programs warned that "because the assembly hall can hold only one hundred people, spectators are kindly requested not to remain more than two hours" (Lane, *When the Mind Hears*, 47). It is hard to imagine this kind of devotion to a cause that was in effect marginal. In 1794 the abbé Sicard held performances once a month for Parisians, in addition to special demonstrations for the various emperors of Europe, the pope, and even a command performance before the British Parliament. The monthly sessions began at noon and ended at 4:00 P.M., with three hundred to four hundred spectators assembled. Deaf people were asked abstract questions through interpreters, like "Why is baptism called the portal of the sacraments?" Deaf students replied in written French as well as in Latin, Italian, Spanish, German, and English. These public demonstrations were attended by many French intellectuals, including Condillac, the English philosophers James Burnett and Lord Monboddo, the papal nuncio, John Quincy Adams, and many others (Lane, *When the Mind Hears*, 46–47). In Scotland, Dr. Johnson made a special stop on his tour of the Hebrides to visit the deaf school run by Thomas Braidwood.

Deafness was for the eighteenth century an area of cultural fascination and a compelling focus for philosophical study. The logical question is, why? Some answers may be obvious. As Harlan Lane points out in his *Wild Boy of Aveyron*, philosophers of this period were obsessed with trying to define what made humans human. Aristotle's classic and elegant definition included upright gait, human appearance, and language. The investigation of "savages," orangutans, wild children, and the deaf allowed "scientific" observation as to what "natural man" might be like. Rousseau, Herder, Condillac, Monboddo, Locke, and others argued over how language began, how reason and thought intertwined into the human essence. The wild child and the deaf person provided living examples of the mind untouched by civilization. Here the questions could be put: Are there thoughts prior to language? Can a being be human without language? In his *Treatise on Sensations*, Condillac imagined a statue brought to life in stages illustrating the development of human from animal. How appropriate that Sicard presented a prelingual deaf child at one of his public events, saying, "I have been waiting to introduce you to a new subject, almost an infant, a little savage, a block of unchiseled marble or rather a statue, yet to be animated and endowed with intellect" (Lane, *When the Mind Hears*, 34). Sicard went on to give the child his very first lessons in language before the crowd. Here we see the new natural man sought by explorers and now by philosophers. These theatrical displays amounted to a Foucauldian panopticon to observe the primitive emerge into language, and into deafness.

The irony is that deafness, while an area of cultural fascination, had to be contained and controlled, as it still is, by the very hearing world that was fascinated by this phenomenon.[4] The panopticon created by Sicard put the deaf on display, but did not allow the deaf to control their own display except by the deviousness of subaltern strategies. We can get an idea of the somewhat sadistic probing by the hearing world and the competent but defiant replies of Jean Massieu at one of these sessions:

"What is a sense?" Massieu was asked.
"An idea-carrier," he answered.
"What is hearing?" asked some people trying to disconcert him.
"Hearing is auricular sight."
"What is gratitude?" asked the abbé Sicard.
"Gratitude is the memory of the heart," Massieu answered him.
"What is God?"
"The necessary Being—the sun of eternity."
"What is eternity?" someone asked.
"A day without yesterday or tomorrow," Massieu immediately replied. (Lane,
   The Deaf Experience, 78–79)

In response to being at the focal point of the clinical gaze, Massieu develops an almost aerobic response to these difficult mental exertions. His deafness is anatomized by examining his language abilities, a procedure to which he creates strategies of compliance.

These types of examinations and philosophical disquisitions help us to place deafness as an emergent, constructed category. Yet I would like to suggest that philosophical and even medical curiosity is only an epiphenomenon of another causality that brought deafness to cultural attention. The wild child/deaf-person scenario is based on the idea that deaf people are without a language, unless they learn either to write or to speak the language of the hearing majority. Dr. Johnson called deafness "one of the most desperate human calamities" for that reason. Johnson expresses one view of deafness as a limit to sociability, social intercourse, education, and, indeed, humanity and reason. But another, more powerful view of deafness is woven into eighteenth-century culture that considers the deaf person to be someone who reasons, feels, thinks, and uses language just as hearing people do, only the language used is different from that of the linguistic majority. The language is in fact the language of texts, of writing, of novels.

In *Duncan Campbell*, Daniel Defoe embodies this idea of the deaf man as textual master. Duncan Campbell is not merely equal to hearing people but is portrayed as a hyperbolically superior being, a godlike man of great intelligence, handsome looks, and supernatural powers. Far from being disabled, he is enabled with the gift of second sight, which allows him to write the name and foretell the future of another person at a first meeting. Although in actuality Campbell was a fraud—a hearing huckster pretending to be deaf, a common stereotype in the French theater—the fact that Defoe regards him as deaf permits us to learn something about attitudes toward the deaf, if not about Defoe's attitude to fact and fiction.[5] What is interesting about Defoe's account is that it rests on the assumption that Campbell has his own integral language. Defoe quotes extensively from John Wallis, who had published a book on educating the deaf (though he seems simply to have plagiarized the method from George Delgarno) and was, not uncoincidentally, Defoe's brother-in-law:

> It will be convenient all along to have pen, ink, and paper, ready at hand, to write down in a word what you signify to him by signs, and cause him to write, or show how to write what he signifies by signs, which way of signifying their mind by signs deaf persons are often very good at: and we must endeavor to learn their language, if I may so call it, in order to teach them ours, by showing what words answer to their signs. (31)

Wallis, and by extension Defoe, acknowledges that the deaf have their own preexisting language and that language is mediated to the hearing world through writing and textuality. Later when Duncan meets an old hearing friend, Defoe comments, "Here the reader must understand they discoursed on their fingers, and wrote by turns" (164).

In addition to making the point that the deaf possess a language, many writers, including Wallis, emphasize a connection between deafness and writing. For Defoe, writing seems the natural way for a deaf person to communicate, as natural as sign language. Defoe names other famous deaf people, including Sir John Gawdy, Sir Thomas Knotcliff, Sir — Gostwick, Sir Henry Lydall, and Mr. Richard Lyns of Oxford, who "were all of this number, and yet men eminent in their several capacities, for understanding many authors, and expressing themselves in writing with wonderful facility" (32). Here being deaf leads naturally to writing. This correlation is made clearly by trope when Duncan must tell a beautiful young woman that she will be disfigured by smallpox and then die: "he begged to be excused, and that his pen might remain as dumb and silent as his tongue on that affair." The metonymy of pen and tongue again connects writing to deafness. This link is made more explicit when Duncan "tells" a long story to a group of friars by writing it down:

> ... so taking up another piece of paper, Fathers, said he, shall I entertain you with a story of what passed upon this head, between two religious fathers, as all of you are, and a prince of Germany.... The story is somewhat long, but very much to the purpose and entertaining; I remember it perfectly by heart, and if you will have patience while I am writing it, I do not doubt but that I shall not only satisfy you, but please you and oblige you with the relation. (131)

Here Duncan acts in the manner of a novelist, translating experiential reality into textual signs, and his deafness melts away into the matrix of writing. It is no coincidence, then, that one of Duncan's favorite activities is walking in graveyards: "one would imagine he takes delight to stalk along by himself on that dumb silent ground, where the characters of the persons are only to be known, as his own meaning is, by writing and inscriptions on the marble" (154). The silent character of the dead and the ground, considered "dumb" and "silent," is given language in the graphic trace on the tombstones, and Duncan can read them as can any reader of novels who, of course, must get at character through decoding a cluster of signs.

Given a written text, there is little difference between a hearing person and a deaf one in the reading or writing process. The deaf can read and write: they only have to translate from sign language to the signs of written language. This point of connection, which may be thought fanciful, was recognized by at least one eighteenth-century reader who wrote to the *Spectator* (no. 474, September 3, 1712) seeking the whereabouts of Duncan Campbell:

... now hearing you are a dumb man too, I thought you might correspond and
be able to tell me something ..."

This reader sees the writer of the *Spectator* as "dumb" specifically because he
cannot speak except through writing! Authors are in fact mute *because* of
typography.

Writing is in effect sign language, a language of signs. Sicard emphasized
this connection when he said, "written language ... alone can replace speech"
(Lane, *When the Mind Hears*, 37). Saboureux de Fontenay, a deaf man writing in 1764, describes finger spelling as a language in which "the hand is
used like a pen" (Lane, *The Deaf Experience*, 26), and l'Epée described sign
language as a type of "writing in the air" (cited in Mirzoeff, "Body Talk,"
581). Rousseau acknowledges that writing as well as gesture are forms of sign
language virtually equal to speech. He says if humans could not speak,

> we would have been able to establish societies little different from those we
> have, or such as would have been better able to achieve their goals. We would
> have been able to institute laws, to choose leaders, to invent arts, to establish
> commerce, and to do, in a word, almost as many things as we do with the help
> of speech. (9)

Herder, too, acknowledges that speech is not necessary for language, and
notes that "the savage, the hermit living alone in the forest, would have had
to invent language for himself ... without the help of a mouth and without the
presence of a society" (118). Diderot in his *Letter on the Deaf and Dumb* says
that speech itself is just a representation of the state of the soul: "Ah sir, how
much our apprehension is modified by the signs we use! And how cold a copy
is even the most vivid speech of what takes place within us" (34). All of
these philosophers point to the notion that any sign system can be language.

So intertwined were the issues of writing and language with the issue of
deafness that they seemed inseparable. Tellingly, Sicard's career was deeply
interwoven with textual language. In 1795 he was appointed to the section
on grammar in the French Institute, which later became the French Academy.
He helped lay the groundwork for the Academy's dictionary of the French
language and was also a member of the Grammatical Society. Another dictionary maker, Dr. Johnson, is described by Boswell during a visit to Braidwood's school for the deaf in a "circumstance ... which was truly characteristic of our great Lexicographer. 'Pray,' said he, 'can they pronounce any *long*
words?' Mr. Braidwood informed him they could. Upon which Dr. Johnson
wrote one of his *sesquipedalia verba*, which was pronounced by the scholars,
and he was satisfied" (389). Johnson sees his visit to the deaf as an opportu-
nity to investigate from a lexicographical point of view.

Why, then, is deafness such an area of focused activity? Why the obsessive connection between deafness and writing? We need to recall that it was during the eighteenth century that reading became consolidated as an activity. J. Paul Hunter points to data suggesting that "literacy in the English-speaking world grew rapidly between 1600 and 1800 so that by the latter date a vast majority of adult males could read and write, whereas two centuries earlier only a select minority could do so" (65). Debates ensued during this period as to whether written or spoken language was the primary form of linguistic communication. David Bartine details the transition from an oral culture to a culture of silent reading in his *Early English Reading Theory: Origins of Current Debates*. These debates open the possibility that written language was the primary form of linguistic enterprise. Benjamin Smart, for example, "asserted more emphatically than his predecessors that writing is the original and primary language for all forms of reading. Even for an oral reader the nature of written language is the *first* consideration" (Bartine, *Early English Reading Theory*, 133). If this is the case, then the deaf are living examples of the ideology of the written text at work. As Oliver Sacks notes:

> The congenitally deaf, it should be added, may have the richest appreciation of (say) written English, of Shakespeare, even though it does not "speak" to them in an auditory way. It speaks to them, one must suppose, in an entirely visual way—they do not hear, they *see*, the "voice" of the words. (6, note 13)

As if designed by Roland Barthes, the text is experienced by the deaf at the degree zero of writing, as a text first and foremost. That is, to be deaf is to experience the written text in its most readerly incarnation. The text would not then be transformed into an auditory translation, but would be seen as language itself.

This point can be turned around somewhat as well. Because the eighteenth century was a period in which readers on a large scale first began to experience reality through text, they may be said to have had a different relation to reality and to texts.[6] Part of that difference has to do with the fact that in order to become readers, people in the eighteenth century had to become deaf, at least culturally so. To read requires muteness and attention to nonverbal signs. Writing and reading became the dominant form of using sign language, the language of printed signs, and thus hearing readers and deaf readers could merge as those who see the voice of the words. Elizabeth Eisenstein points out that the political world changed through the advent of print: "Printed materials encouraged silent adherence to causes whose advocates could not be located in any one parish and who addressed an invisible public

from afar" (42). The very nature of political assent, through the silent decoding of reading, became a newly "deafened" process that did not require
adherents to gather in a public place or rely on a vocal response to a rallying
cry (42). As the hearing person became deaf, the deaf person became the
totemic representation of the new reading public.

One can see this attention to deafness as part of a general transition from
a society that based its cultural production on performances to one that focused its cultural attention on texts. In a text-based society, the physical presence of an auditor or an audience is no longer necessary, as it would be in a
world based on performances. The cultural narrowness of a society in which
spoken language is paramount expands to include all users of language, spoken or not.[7]

This point may seem a strange one to grasp, but the fact that you are reading this essay without my physical presence proves that it is irrelevant whether
or not you are deaf, at least insofar as receiving and understanding my meaning. Further, if you consider that most of the knowledge you have about academic, discursive matters is almost entirely derived from nonhearing knowledge acquisition, then you can understand the import of this widespread shift
from performance to text-based knowledge.[8] As Foucault and others have
noticed, knowledge per se since the classical period is embedded in discursive structures, and for the past three hundred years such discursive forms as
described by Foucault are mainly of the type that are recorded in texts and
make up the ensemble of texts that constitute the archive.

In opposition to this archival knowledge, the eighteenth century's fascination with conversation can be seen as a kind of cultural nostalgia for a form
that was in the process of becoming anachronistic.[9] It is of course most telling
that our accounts of conversation, particularly the obsessive compiling of
Johnson's conversation by Boswell and the splenetic compendium of conver-
sational abuse by Swift in his *Polite Conversation* are themselves only known
in their typographic incarnation. The deaf, then, seen as readers and writers
par excellence, as fellow creatures who existed first and foremost in semiology, were the first totemic citizens in the new age of textuality.

Yet, as with any good totem, the deaf person was both universalized and
marginalized, held up as an object of admiration and patronized as an object
of pity. Like contemporary African-Americans and Chicanos, who are celebrated as the upholders of multiculturality and made visible as such by the
media, but who are in reality reviled and oppressed by an economic system
that relies on their impoverishment, so the deaf in the eighteenth century
had this polysemous interpretation imposed on them. Their subject positions

are, in this sense, overdetermined. Here the issue of class comes into syn-chretic combination with the issues of otherness and of disability. As is still the case, unless a deaf person happened to be born into a wealthy or noble family, he or she would occupy the lowest economic rungs of society. In fam-ilies in which deafness is hereditary, that economic position will be passed along to the next generation as well. The majority of deaf in the eighteenth century had jobs as menial workers. They may therefore be described as necessarily part of a working class, and their disability is made complex and multifaceted by its connection with issues of class, as well as linguistic domination.[10]

The testimony of Pierre Desloges, a student of l'Epée, may illustrate some of the themes I have been describing in this essay. Fittingly, most of what we know about Desloges comes from a pamphlet he wrote in 1779 entitled *Ob-servations d'un sourd et muet sur 'Un Cours élémenataire d'éducation des sourds et muets' publié en 1779 par M. l'abbé Deschamps.*[11] The marginality of this man, like the majority of deaf in his moment, is universalized through print that articulates him as part of an official discursive practice, removing him from the marginality of the streets. He becomes a representation of a group, yet, as Ernesto Laclau and Chantal Mouffe point out, "every relation of rep-resentation is founded on a fiction: that of the presence at a certain level of something which is absent from it" (119). In this sense, what is absent from any account by Desloges is the physical presence of his deafness. Ironically, that feature of his existence is under erasure because of the very existence of print and Desloges's writerly existence.[12]

These are the facts of his life presented by the writer. Desloges was born in 1747 in the town of Le Grand-Pressigny in the Loire Valley. After an attack of childhood smallpox, he became deaf and mute. His education ended with his disability, but he had acquired some skills in reading and writing. At the age of twenty-one he went to Paris and took up the trades of bookbinding and paperhanging. Only at the age of twenty-seven did he learn the sign language used by the Paris deaf community.

The first significant aspect about this publication is its very existence. Had there not been an interest in deafness, it is hard to imagine that an obscure paperhanger in Paris could have been launched into print. Moreover, his purpose in writing is not mainly autobiographical but rather his attempt to defend deaf education based on sign language, as practiced by l'Epée, against the attack made by the abbé Deschamps, who in turn was influenced by the first "oralist" Jacob Pereire. That a publisher was willing to print a commentary on this debate indicates the cultural relevance of the subject.

Desloges's marginality is signaled initially by the hearing editor who first highlights the dubious status of the work by insisting on its not being a fiction. By now, such assertions of factuality only serve to fictionalize a work.[13] Further, the editor stresses that the writing is authentic, although the editor

> corrected the young man's quite faulty spelling. I pruned some repetitions and softened a few words that could have given offense. Aside from these minor emendations, the essay is entirely the work of the deaf Desloges. (Lane, *The Deaf Experience*, 29)

These words immediately contextualize the otherness of Desloges, who must be linguistically sanitized and standardized. His deafness is seen as a mark of difference that separates him from normal readers whose spelling does not have to be corrected and whose usage will not offend. Yet, at the same time, the entrance of the deaf consciousness into the realm of the textual is celebrated: "I felt the chief interest of this essay would come from its author, that perhaps for the first time a deaf-mute had the honor of being published" (29). This doubleness of attitude toward Desloges's marginality will play out in much more complex ways as well.

Desloges begins his essay constructing a subject position from his own marginality. He notes immediately that he is of the lower classes, saying, "My line of work obliges me to go into many homes," and adds that "the whole of my subsistence comes from my daily work, while my writing must be done during the time I have for sleeping" (30). He is speaking both as a deaf man and, even more tellingly, as a working man. His writing is seen as occupying a space other than the time a man of letters devotes to it; writing time is in fact stolen from a very full workday. Although there certainly was a tradition of working-class characters in fiction, it was much rarer to have an actual member of that class appear in print. The otherness of Desloges's deafness, like the blackness of Equiano's skin, permits the class element to be overridden and permitted through the gate of print. Body always effaces class in the sphere of bourgeois narrative, as Pamela's body erases her class lines.

Desloges is writing out of a profound marginalization. His contact with the hearing world is based on misunderstanding, and through writing, that is, using the nonhearing text, he is hoping to eliminate such miscommunication: "I am invariably questioned about the deaf. But most often the questions are laughable as they are absurd; they merely prove that almost everyone has gotten the falsest possible ideas about us" (30). Here too we see that he is not simply questioned about being deaf, but about "the deaf," clearly indicating that the category of deafness has emerged as an area of cultural curiosity. Further, he notes that he is writing this work to correct the public's errors, particularly "the last straw" (30) of misunderstanding accomplished by Deschamps's book against the use of sign language as an instructional medium. One of the advantages of a text-based society is that individual voices and minority opinions can be more easily heard, if indeed they are permitted access, and Desloges recognizes this empowerment provided by print. In the same way that print culture was involved in the development of nationalism, print also created some version of solidarity for marginalized groups.[14] Thus Desloges can write:

> As would a Frenchman seeing his language disparaged by a German who knew at most a few words of French, I too felt obliged to defend my own language from the false charges leveled against it by Deschamps. (30)

Here we can see that perhaps some aspect of the emergence of the deaf is linked to their defining themselves as a linguistic subgroup. Like other races, nationalities, ethnic groups, and nations, their redefinition as a political entity is linked to larger issues about the growth of nationalism in the eighteenth and nineteenth centuries.[15]

Like other writers translating from a foreign language, Desloges will have problems explaining the subtleties of his own language. He can write in French, but to try to convey the sense of sign language may be an insurmountable problem. A single sign "made in the twinkling of an eye would require entire pages" to describe, and such detail would "soon become boring to the delicate ears accustomed to the winsome sounds of speech." Desloges is looking across a cultural divide between speech and sign language. The fact that Desloges sees this transaction as audible rather than textual, referring to the readers' "ears" rather than eyes as the recipient of his text, points to a curious structuring of languages. Sign language for Desloges is actually a text, but one performed rather than printed. Speech is a "winsome sound," more ethereal and less text-based, less semiological than sign. At the same time, the performative nature of sign gives it "so much strength and energy" that it can lose its muscular verve only when translated into written language. Here we see the mediating role of sign language as a middle term between speech and writing.

For Desloges, spoken language has a double impossibility. Most deaf people are mute only because they cannot hear, but Desloges has an additional impairment that he attributes to smallpox but which is clearly part of a larger neurological problem. When he developed smallpox at seven years of age, he then suffered some profound illness for two years that caused him to lose all his teeth and develop a strokelike dysfunction of his lips, so that "my lips became so slack that I can close them only with great effort or the assistance of my hand.... One can reproduce my speech fairly accurately by trying to speak with the mouth open, without closing lips or teeth" (31). This double impossibility, being both deaf and physiologically mute, makes speech seem quite arbitrary to Desloges. He feels acutely that spoken language is privileged over textual language. This privileging of one sense over another is arbitrary, not natural, as Rousseau has pointed out. As Desloges writes, sign language is the "most natural means for leading the deaf to an understanding of languages, nature having given them this language to substitute for the other languages of which they are deprived" (35). Some of the cognitive dissonance one experiences in reading Desloges's work may arise from the fact that he is writing about his deafness and mutism in the most logical, coherent, and elegant language. The arbitrariness of hearing language over nonspoken language, and the consequent marginalization of those who do not participate in this linguistic majority, emerges as a force of power.

The strength to overcome this linguistic domination arises by chance when Desloges is twenty-seven years old. He gains the power of sign language — a power linked to the power of seeing himself as belonging to an oppressed group, the deaf. Before this period, "for as long as I was living apart from other deaf people, my only resource for self-expression was writing or my poor pronunciation" (32). But it is only through contact with the other deaf in Paris, who are themselves working class, that Desloges finds power in his marginal status. Fatefully, Desloges meets a deaf, illiterate Italian servant who teaches him signing; that the man is described as illiterate is fascinating given that he was linguistically competent enough to teach Desloges an entire language system.

At this point in the book, it is frustrating that Desloges abruptly announces, "I think this is enough about me and that a longer treatment of such a minor subject would try my readers' patience" (32). One can speculate that Desloges's entrance into sign language leads him to the subject of l'Epée, in whose defense he spends the rest of the book. Truly marginalizing himself, confining his own story to the margins of the text, Desloges only exists insofar as he is a successful example of a teaching method. But, like subalterns and slaves, Desloges is able to exist by tactics of submission that are in fact defensive. After all, he does narrate his own life and present a textual representation of his language and therefore of himself.

Without mentioning his own life story again, he inserts his deaf existence and working-class perspective into the text. Desloges attacks indirectly the power of the hearing world over the deaf when he notes that "deaf people who are abandoned in asylums or isolated somewhere in the provinces" (16) do not learn sign language. When deaf people are united, as they are in major urban areas like Paris, they can organize linguistic power. He gives himself as an example of someone whose signs had been "unordered and unconnected" coming into contact with "deaf people more highly educated" than himself. When this synergistic meeting occurs, language happens through the regulation of a subaltern community.

This critical mass of deaf people, a kind of liminal community, is uniquely both deaf and underclass. In Desloges's tones one can hear a will to power that perhaps reflects republican sentiments of the time.

> There are congenitally deaf people, Parisian laborers, who are illiterate and who have never attended the abbé de l'Epée's lessons, who have been found so well instructed about their religion, simply by means of signs, that they have been judged worthy of admittance to the holy sacraments, even those of the eucharist and marriage [which had been previously denied to the deaf]. No event— in Paris, in France, or in the four corners of the world—lies outside the scope of our discussion. We express ourselves on all subjects with as much order, precision, and rapidity as if we enjoyed the faculty of speech and hearing. (36)

The matter of class and the matter of deafness merge into a kind of empowerment founded on community and communication. Desloges makes the argument that deafness and sign actually reconfigure the disabled into the category of specially abled. He says that "our ideas concentrated in ourselves, so to speak, necessarily incline us toward reflectiveness and meditation" (37). That is, ideas seem not to need a semiology; the deaf experience ideas in themselves. To further bolster this point, Desloges echoes Hobbes's lament that modern languages have fallen away from original ideas when he says that sign language is "a faithful image of the object expressed" (37). The metonymic nature of sign anchors the deaf to the signified rather than the signifier. As such, sign can better express emotions and sentiments, and Desloges goes so far as to claim that "no other language is more appropriate for conveying great and strong emotion" (37). The romantic aspirations for sign language, a physical form of poetry, are balanced by an Enlightenment concern for rationality. Desloges thus claims that sign is more efficient than speech: "The phrase *le mos qui vient* contains four words; nevertheless I use only two signs for it, one for the month and one for the future" (38).

The very nature of sign language, as a language of the underclass, is impregnated with class markers. In Desloges's words: "When necessity or expressive clarity demands, we always mention the social class of the person we are speaking about or wish to introduce" (41). To designate a close acquaintance one needs only three signs: first gender, then class, then profession. In designating nobility, there are signs for upper and lower nobility, which are followed by occupation, coat of arms, or livery. Manufacturers are distinguished from tradesmen, "for the deaf have the good sense not to confuse these two occupations." The sensitivity of the deaf as marginalized underclass is reflected in their minute gradations of the harms of class. The sign for tradesman is made as follows: "With the thumb and index finger, we take the hem of a garment or some other object and present it the way a tradesman offers his merchandise; we then make the movement for counting money with our hands, and cross our arms like someone resting" (41). This gestural rebus combines the ideas of capital, trade, money, and leisure, painting a picture of the essence of the bourgeois cash nexus. The same subtlety of class analysis is included in the sign for "working" that applies to "manufacturers, artisans, and laborers." An additional sign indicates who is supervising and who is obeying: "We raise the index finger and lower it in a commanding way—that is the sign common to all supervisors" (41). The same sign distinguishes a shopkeeper from a street vendor.

Sign language organizes the nuances of class power. This language is most universally a language of the laboring classes. It contains within its very structure the strategies and tactics of conformity and transgressivity typical of a subaltern group. Yet at the same time, sign language offers, by virtue of its marginality, a kind of universality. Desloges notes that "several famous scholars have worn themselves out in the vain search for the elements of a universal language as a point of unification for all the people of the world. How did they fail to perceive that it had already been discovered, that it existed naturally as sign language" (45). Citing Condillac and Court de Gébelin, who praise sign language as a kind of universal language, Desloges goes on to say that "I cannot understand how a language like sign language—the richest in expressions, the most energetic, the most incalculably advantageous in its universal intelligibility—is still so neglected and that only the deaf speak it" (45–46).

That Desloges would even consider recommending that sign language be used by the hearing world indicates the extent to which universal language schemes, and the notion of internationality that was very much a part of the revolutionary period at the end of the eighteenth century, could be applied to universalizing of the marginality of deafness. Yet his idea is not so wild. In many ways, sign language provides us with a language that opens many doors. Critically, its existence as a third term mediating between text and speech opens the possibility for mediating that theoretically troubling divide. The age-old and now current debates between those who see literature as primarily a text and those who see it primarily as an expression of the body, of reality, can perhaps find a complex intersection by admitting the "literature" of sign language into the debate.

But precisely because sign language will never actually become a universal language, we must stop and consider how truly hegemonic and controlling a concept is the notion of writing and speech as a "hearing" phenomenon. The argument I have tried to make is that the deafness of textuality is one of the best-kept secrets of the Enlightenment and beyond. It is not so much that convention has ruled here, but that there has been an active suppression of the insight I have proposed. After all, the body is political. Its form and function have been the energetic site of powerful control and management. An able body is the body of a citizen; deformed, deafened, amputated, obese, female, perverse, crippled, maimed, blinded bodies do not make up the body politic. Utterances must all be able ones produced by conformed, ideal forms of humanity. In effect, there cannot be a complete analysis of early modern, modern, and postmodern culture without bringing the disabled body and the disabled utterance into line. Such a correction would only be one part of the process of resituating the universalizing of marginality.

Notes

1. Deafness did not "exist" before the eighteenth century for two reasons. First, the isolated deaf person was simply seen as an aberration in the particular town or family, considered first and foremost a nonperson. The deaf person in an extended group of deaf, however, might not be thought of as deaf because the deaf individual was part of a functioning system. Nora Ellen Groce's marvelous book *Everyone Here Spoke Sign Language: Hereditary Deafness on Martha's Vineyard* (Cambridge, Mass.: Harvard University Press, 1985) relates how an inherited trait brought to the island in 1633 resulted in the deafness of a substantial minority of people living on Martha's Vineyard until quite recently. Because the minority made up a significant number, the deaf were actually not visible as deaf. One resident responded to the author's question about what the hearing thought of the deaf by saying, "Oh, they didn't think anything of them, they were just like everyone else," and then went on to describe to the author's amazement how everyone on Martha's Vineyard spoke sign language.

2. It is telling, too, that the language of the deaf, sign language, was an indigenous language that arose spontaneously where groups of deaf people formed a community. The language taught in deaf schools was more or less a standardization of that autochthonous language. Braille was a system invented by a seeing man, Charles Barbier, who had invented this form of writing during wartime to enable messages to be read at night without the use of light, which would betray position to the enemy. In 1830, Barbier brought the system to the Institution des Enfans Aveugles in Paris, where a blind student, Louis Braille, developed and promulgated Barbier's plan. In this sense, deaf language is a special issue, whereas Braille is actually a system not exclusively "blind" in its applications.

3. Nicholas Mirzoeff points out in his article "Body Talk: Deafness, Sign and Visual Language in the Ancien Régime" that the portrayal of deaf characters was a long-standing tradition in French theater. He refers to the appearance of Le Sourd as early as the sixteenth century. But as he also notes, "these 'deaf' characters normally spoke and often were pretending to be deaf in order to deceive others in pursuit of a love affair" (570). We can assume, then, that these depictions were not of the deaf per se, but of comic imitators of deafness.

4. See Harlan Lane, *The Mask of Benevolence: Disabling the Deaf Community* (New York: Alfred A. Knopf, 1992), as well as my review of this book in *The Nation* 253, no. 1 (July 6, 1992): 26–27.

5. That Duncan Campbell was a huckster who only pretended to be deaf and who made his money by duping people has little bearing on the attitudes toward the deaf that Defoe espouses. Defoe is always a writer whose ambivalence to fact and fiction only makes his work more interesting to a modern reader. For more on this ambivalence, see my *Factual Fictions: Origins of the English Novel* (New York: Columbia University Press, 1983), 154–73.

6. For examples of this shift to textual forms of experiencing ideology, see Joseph Allen Boone, *Tradition Counter Tradition: Love and the Form of Fiction* (Chicago: University of Chicago Press, 1987) and Nancy Armstrong, *Desire and Domestic Fiction: A Political History of the Novel* (Oxford: Oxford University Press, 1987), along with my *Resisting Novels: Fiction and Ideology* (New York: Routledge, 1987).

7. Martin Jay, in his *Downcast Eyes: The Denigration of Vision in Twentieth-Century French Thought* (Berkeley: University of California Press, 1993), details a general historical trend that conceives of the Middle Ages as biased toward hearing or touch, and the Enlightenment as favoring sight. Roland Barthes in *Sade, Fourier, Loyola*, trans. Richard Miller (New York: Hill and Wang, 1976), wrote concerning Ignatius Loyola that "in the Middle Ages, historians tell us, the most refined sense, the perceptive sense, *par excellence*, the one that established the richest contact with the world, was hearing: sight came in only third, after touch. Then we have a reversal: the eye becomes the prime organ of perception (Baroque, art of the thing seen, attests to it)" (46). Jay questions this simplifying tendency on the part of writers like Barthes, although he does end up affirming that something happens in European culture to the question of vision. One of the areas he pinpoints is the separation of the visual and the textual—what he calls "the secular autonomization of the visual as a realm unto itself" (44). This point fits well into the idea that the eighteenth-century text, though requiring vision, is actually more about the issue of hearing. The vision of reading, then, is not necessarily the vision of seeing. Indeed, the vision of reading is in effect one that is more about incorporating hearing language through the eyes than it is about seeing objects.

8. Further technological advances like those provided by computer networks, fiber optics, and other advanced forms of communications have completely shifted the ground from spoken language to semiological representations. As electronic mail, computer bulletin boards, and other computer-based forums for communication develop, we will find ourselves less and less reliant on spoken language. Computer literacy has already become a valuable, if not indispensable, skill in many areas of culture.

9. See Leland Warren, "Turning Reality round Together: Guides to Conversation in Eighteenth-Century England," *Eighteenth Century Life* 8 (May 1983): 65–87.

10. The connection between deafness and class was put in its most extreme form when Jane Elizabeth Groom, a deaf activist, proposed in the 1880s that the deaf leave England and found a deaf state in Canada. Groom's reasoning was particularly related to class: her argument was that the deaf in England were poor and could not compete with the hearing in a tight labor market. The answer could not be revolution, but secession.

11. I cite all further quotations of Desloges's text from Harlan Lane, *The Deaf Experience*.

12. Jacques Derrida deals with a similar phenomenon in his book *Memoirs of the Blind*. He says the following of the work of Antoine Coypel and others who draw the blind: "The opera-

tion of drawing would have something to do with blindness, would in some way regard blindness.... Every time a draftsman lets himself be fascinated by the blind, every time he makes the blind a *theme* of his drawing, he projects, dreams, or hallucinates a figure of a draftsman, or sometimes, more precisely, some draftswoman" (2). Drawing blindness involves blindness in the process of drawing and points to the blindness in drawing as well as the sightedness in the concept of blindness. In a similar vein, writing from the deaf point of view reveals the deafness in writing, while concealing the deafness of the writer.

13. See my *Factual Fictions: Origins of the English Novel*, 11–24, for a discussion of this notion of denial as a hallmark of fictional ambivalence.

14. See Benedict Anderson, *Imagined Communities: Reflections on the Origin and Spread of Nationalism* (London: Verso, 1983).

15. I devote a chapter to this subject in the forthcoming book *Theorizing Disability: Embodiment and the Realm of the Senses* (to be published by Verso in 1996), of which this essay is a part.

Works Cited

Bartine, David. *Early English Reading Theory: Origins of Current Debates*. Columbia: University of South Carolina Press, 1989.

Boswell, James. *Journey to the Hebrides*. London: 1785.

Defoe, Daniel. *Duncan Campbell* (1720). In *The History and the Life and Adventures of Mr. Duncan Campbell*, ed. G.A. Aitken. 1895. Rpt. New York: AMS, 1974.

Derrida, Jacques. *Memoirs of the Blind: The Self-Portrait and Other Ruins*. Trans. Pascale-Anne Brault and Michael Naas. Chicago: University of Chicago Press, 1993.

Diderot, Denis. *Letter on the Deaf and Dumb* (1751). In *Selected Writings*, ed. and trans. D. Coltman. New York: Macmillan, 1966.

Eisenstein, Elizabeth. "Some Conjectures about the Impact of Printing on Western Society and Thought: A Preliminary Report." *Journal of Modern History* 40, no. 1 (March 1968): 1–56.

Foucault, Michel. *Madness and Civilization*. New York: Random House, 1967.

Herder, Johann Gottfried. "Essay on the Origin of Language." In *On the Origin of Language: Two Essays by Jean-Jacques Rousseau and Johann Gottfried Herder*. Trans. John H. Moran and Alexander Gode. New York: Unger, 1966.

Hunter, J. Paul. *Before Novels: The Cultural Contexts of Eighteenth Century English Fiction*. New York: Norton, 1990.

Laclau, Ernesto, and Chantal Mouffe. *Hegemony and Socialist Strategy*. New York and London: Verso, 1985, rpt. 1989.

Lane, Harlan. *The Wild Boy of Aveyron*. Cambridge: Harvard University Press, 1976.

———. *When the Mind Hears: A History of the Deaf*. New York: Random House, 1984.

———, ed. *The Deaf Experience: Classics in Language and Education*. Trans. Franklin Philip. Cambridge, Mass.: Harvard University Press, 1984.

Mirzoeff, Nicholas. "Body Talk: Deafness, Sign and Visual Language in the Ancien Régime." *Eighteenth Century Studies* 25, no. 4 (Summer 1992): 561–86.

Paulson, William R. *Enlightenment, Romanticism, and the Blind in France*. Princeton: Princeton University Press, 1987.

Rousseau, Jean-Jacques. "Essay on the Origin of Languages." In *On the Origin of Language: Two Essays by Jean-Jacques Rousseau and Johann Gottfried Herder*. Trans. John H. Moran and Alexander Gode. New York: Unger, 1966.

Sacks, Oliver. *Seeing Voices: A Journey into the World of the Deaf*. New York: HarperCollins, 1989.

Van Cleve, John Vickrey, and Barry A. Crouch. *A Place of Their Own: Creating the Deaf Community in America*. Washington, D.C.: Gallaudet University Press, 1989.

3

Monstrous Body, Tortured Soul: *Frankenstein* at the Juncture between Discourses

Ellen J. Goldner

In *Discipline and Punish,* Michel Foucault probes two different discourses: a discourse of the public spectacle of the body, which, in 1757 in France, is active at the scene of public torture, and a discourse of discipline, which, near the end of the eighteenth century, abandons the public display of the body in order to produce, to articulate, and to place under surveillance the internal soul or psyche of the prisoner. In the shift between the old discourse and the new, the public spectacle of the body gives way to a highly individuated soul—one that is meticulously documented even as it is privatized. In the same shift between discourses, the power to determine events and their meanings passes out of its visible locus in the feudal sovereign, and comes to circulate invisibly through persons, their activities, and their gazes. Foucault insists that within a few decades the nature of crime and criminality and, concomitantly, the nature of power and the person are altered.[1]

In this essay I seek to add to current discussions prompted by Foucault a question that he seldom poses: how does a culture undergo so thorough a change between discourses in so short a time?[2] Mary Shelley's *Frankenstein* offers a valuable site of investigation because it dramatizes the wrenching shift between a discourse of the body as public spectacle and a discourse of the soul as a site of discipline, and it does so repeatedly. Foucault's "The Functions of Literature" (see chapter 1 of this volume) suggests that we stop treating literature as a sacralized object that stands separate from and above the politics of culture, and that instead we treat literature as part of a cultural/

political field. Literature then becomes available as a tool for examining cultural and political processes. When considered in this light, a novel such as *Frankenstein*, which is set at a juncture between discourses, can help us to examine the dynamic of cultural revision as it changes the nature of power/ knowledge and the distribution of its features. Once we treat literature as enmeshed within a political field, acts of cultural revision acquire meanings different from those attributed to them by the romantics and modernists who played significant roles in the sacralizing of literature. A text's reworking of a discourse need not imply that it functions as either a radical or a transcendent (re)vision of cultural norms. The text may now be seen as simultaneously producing and (re)producing through a mass press the practices that constitute an emerging discourse.

The cultural revisions that take place in texts like *Frankenstein* can be understood in part through Philip Fisher's definition of culture: "what the present does in the face of itself for itself."[3] Texts that help to mediate the shift between discourses often misrepresent the old discourse, stripping it of its authority. At the same time they construct recognizable representations of the chief requisites of the emerging discourse in order that they may be recognized and practiced repeatedly by readers in a mass literary market. As Fisher suggests, the emergent cultural understanding is finally set in place through mystification: a forgetting of the work that produced it.[4] Hence, when we retrace the processes by which a literary text revises a discourse, we can both see how the text relays and produces the terms of understanding, and work to demystify the text and the mode of understanding in which it participates.

Readers and critics in the late twentieth century can find a twofold value in retracing the processes of discourse in a text such as *Frankenstein*. Lee Quinby suggests in her Introduction to this volume that desacralizing readings provide us with the history of the present — a crucial history if we are to understand the discourses within which we live and think. I would add that the use of literary texts for this purpose is especially important under the postmodern conditions of late capitalism. In *Discipline and Punish*, Foucault traces a shift in the source of meaning production from a sovereign to the diffuse distribution of "bodies, surfaces, lights, (and) gazes" that he finds at the end of the eighteenth century in Bentham's plan for the panopticon.[5] We, at the end of the twentieth century, live amid postmodern information exchange that entails a much wider diffusion of the elements of power/ knowledge. Quinby rightly calls attention to the features of electronic communication that introduce post-Foucauldian problems and require new questions, but the acceleration of information exchange in other ways intensifies

the very problems Foucault raises. Our own discourse is so diffuse and pervasive, and involves the continually shifting (hence discontinuous) interactions
of so many variables, that, as Jameson notes, it is extremely difficult to trace.[6]
This dynamic accounts for the density of the prose of postmodern writers like
Foucault. Just as Shelley's *Frankenstein* is enmeshed within the discourses of
its time, Foucault's writing and my own writing are enmeshed within a late-
capitalist postmodern discourse that, while enabling us to recognize the fluid
properties of power, also drives features of our writing, such as the need to articulate one local milieu after another amid densely interactive textual fields.

When we read texts as sites in which cultural understandings are at once
relayed and produced, we practice reading and articulating the dynamics by
which intricate and wide-reaching discourses work, a skill crucial to any contemporary politicocultural project. Even as the literary text generates and
distributes the terms of a discourse, it can also serve to open the discourse to
critical inquiry.

I turn to Mary Shelley's *Frankenstein* to explore how a culture undergoes a
rapid shift between discourses because Shelley's novel offers a particularly
interesting version of the process of discourse revision and distribution that
occurs in many nineteenth-century texts in the United States and Europe.
The change in emphasis from public body to private soul, for example, characterizes Hawthorne's *Scarlet Letter* as the novel turns its attention from Hester Prynne to Arthur Dimmesdale. The figure of the double (two characters
who, like Victor and the monster, form a representation of a single self or
soul that circles back upon itself) characterizes Poe's "William Wilson" and
Dostoyevsky's *The Double*.[7] Whereas many nineteenth-century texts seem
driven to produce and expand representations of the isolated individualized
soul, *Frankenstein* obsessively repeats the displacement of the old discourse of
the body by the emerging discourse of the soul, as it spins out multiple variations of the problem. I discuss here scenes in which *Frankenstein* marginal-
izes the older discourse's image of the body; other scenes in which it empties
the body of specific sensations; yet other scenes in which it separates the
body like a husk from the soul; and other scenes still in which it disciplines
the body. In all of these scenes the novel regulates bodies and inscribes them
in a disciplinary network by pressing them into the service of the soul. The
novel casts the body as the Other both out of which and against which it
forms the soul. The text's production of a conspicuous body as monstrous
and unnatural stimulates the development of Victor's tortured soul, which is
constituted by self-reflexive language that circles round and round the dead
bodies provided by the plot.

Shelley's text is subtle and mobile as it stages and restages the shift between a discourse of the body in public and a discourse of the isolated soul.
In its variations on the problem, Frankenstein gives its readers repeated practice in the general activity of abandoning one discourse for another, as well
as practice in the specific act of installing discipline in myriad locations.
The numerous variations on the theme of abandoning the body for the soul
help to produce the densely interwoven fabric of language and imagery that
constitutes and spreads the emergent discourse across readers in a mass literary market. As it dramatizes the cultural shift in so many representations
and at so many different sites, Frankenstein helps to fortify the new discourse
against disruptions. The fledgling soul thus comes well armed to the various
sites of contestation between the old discourse and new, where the text finds
discipline either painful or unworkable.

From Body to Soul

Discipline and Punish opens with a scene of torture from the older discourse
in which the sovereign — through his agent, the executioner — beats down
on, marks, and dismembers the body of the condemned who has dared to
break the law of the prince. The sovereign takes public revenge on the body
of the condemned and marks that body so that the public may clearly read
upon it the signs of the sovereign's power. After European spectacles of public torture have disappeared, Frankenstein presents us with its monster — the
pieced-together remains of dismembered bodies — that returns from the grave
in order to give birth to the isolated soul.

Shelley's monster makes its appearance at a time when the old discourse
of the marked and public body lingers, but mainly in a misunderstood form,
to be exhausted and rejected. In Shelley's novel, situated near the beginning of a new discourse, discipline takes hold of the signs of the older discourse, revises their meaning, and inverts their value. Shelley's monster figures both the primary text of the older discourse and the public conditions
of its readership: it is at once a huge spectacle of a body and an undisciplined
mixture of many bodies.[8] In Frankenstein, discipline appropriates the conspicuous body, redefining it as hideous; it makes of that body a mere (pre)text
for the painful production of the private soul. The monster's enormous body
briefly appears in Frankenstein both as a public spectacle and as a multiplicity
of physical sensations. Yet the novel introduces the striking body of the
older discourse only in order to privatize it, to diminish it, and even to
negate it.

Mary Shelley's text first revises the meaning of the conspicuous body by metonymically linking its sheer size and power with deformity. When Victor Frankenstein encounters the monster in the Alps, he responds to "its gigantic stature and the deformity of its aspect" (73).⁹ Later, when he again sees the monster, he exclaims, "Sight tremendous and abhorred!" (94). *Frankenstein* not only presents the conspicuous body as Other (a deformity), but also inverts the significance of the body in public. When the monster makes his only public appearance, the plot attributes violence to the spectators, who drive the monster away: "The whole village was roused; some fled, some attacked me, until, grievously bruised by stones and many other kinds of missile weapons, I escaped ... and fearfully took refuge in a low hovel" (101). Shelley's novel briefly presents the body in its old role as public spectacle, but it does so in order to revise public life into an evil and the spectacle of the body into a (pre)text for hiding the body.

As the monster takes refuge in the hut where he will isolate himself to live in privacy for more than a year, he escapes the public display of the body as well as the sensations of the body. Shelley's *Frankenstein* subjects the huge body of the monster to severe deprivation, casting the monster outdoors in winter, where food and warmth are scarce. In the spare winter setting, which the monster opposes to Adam's paradise, the sensations of the body become, like the scene of public life, a painful burden to be escaped. The monster begins life thoroughly immersed in the undisciplined physical senses that were important to the older discourse: "A strange multiplicity of sensations seized me and I saw, felt, heard and smelt at the same time" (98). However, amid the deprivations of winter, where almost all sensations are painful, the monster learns to discipline his senses, carefully accounting for each one so that he might escape first thirst, then hunger, and finally, in his hut, the cold.

The scene of the monster in winter helps us add to Foucault's analysis of critics who gradually began to condemn public torture as an inhumane practice. Foucault comments that those who came to see public torture simply as a mode of inhumane barbarism failed to recognize the meticulous ceremony of the prince's power in the spectacle.¹⁰ Reading *Frankenstein* helps us to recognize how such critics also may have fueled the transition to a discourse of discipline. Shelley's novel, which surely calls for the reader's humane response to the monster, focuses on the body in pain for reasons different from those of the newspaper accounts with which Foucault documents the scene of torture in *Discipline and Punish*. *Frankenstein* highlights the body in pain while avoiding all scenes of the body in pleasure so that the humane appeal for less suffering might become the rationale for suppressing the body and instituting a discourse of discipline.

As soon as the monster takes refuge in the hut, his body's shelter becomes the source of its subjection. The hut, that "shelter ... from the inclemency of the season, and still more from the barbarity of man" (102), forces the monster to diminish his enormous body and its movements: the hovel is "so low that [he can] barely sit upright in it" (102). In the monster's hovel, Shelley's text dramatizes the transition between discourses. It imprisons and disciplines the enormous body and its movements so that in their stead it can expand the scope of the monster's soul, as he learns language and turns inward to contemplate his own isolated condition.

Much as the hut provides small space for the huge body, Mary Shelley's text provides small space for its description. When Victor creates the monster, the novel devotes only two sentences to its specific description (56), after which the novel offers no specific description of the monstrous body until the closing chapter (207). Even at moments when the monstrous body is crucial the novel elides it. When the monster beholds his reflection in a pool and suffers the shock of recognition of his body's difference from others, we do not see the body: "But how was I terrified when I viewed myself in a transparent pool! At first I stared back, unable to believe that it was indeed I who was reflected in the mirror; and when I became fully convinced that I was in reality the monster that I am, I was filled with ... despondence" (108). Later, the monster tells us that "[hope] vanished when [he] beheld [his] person reflected in water or [his] shadow in the moonshine" (125). At these moments, the text diminishes the huge body to almost nothing in order to make room for a mind that contemplates its own condition.

When the monster escapes the primary conditions of the old discourse (the scene of public life and the powerful sensations of his own body), the monster's hut becomes the novel's chief disciplinary site. In the hut the presence of the monstrous body gives way to its absence and the body in the present gives way to a soul that dwells on the future.

The hut is a transitional structure between the dungeon of the older discourse, which encloses, deprives of light, and confines, and Bentham's panopticon, which sets in motion pervasive mechanisms of surveillance.[11] Once the monster fills the crevices in the walls of the hut to hide himself, he, like the prisoner in the old dungeon, is isolated, hidden, and generally deprived of light. He does leave "a small and almost imperceptible chink through which the eye [can] just penetrate" (103), through which he spies on the De Laceys.

The powerful element of surveillance enters the monster's life through the peephole and (re)forms him. Although he watches the De Lacey family without being watched (his invisibility is a residual condition of the dungeon), the De Laceys nonetheless become the monster's supervisors. They provide him with a model of language and discourse that he will internalize and by which he will come to measure his own behavior.

Spying on the cottagers through the peephole leads the monster to regulate his body. After taking careful account of the De Laceys' schedule — when they leave the cottage, when they remain at home, and when they sleep — the monster places his own body and its movements on a schedule that complements theirs. Because the very presence of his enormous body is a threat to the cottagers, he must regulate it carefully, making certain that he leaves the hut only when they are asleep. Like a prisoner under the new penal system, the monster in the hut lives disciplined to a timetable, which makes "[his] mode of life in [his] hovel ... very uniform" (109). The peephole also leads the monster to discipline his physical desires. Through it, he learns that when he fully satisfies his hunger, he robs the cottagers of food. In response, the monster restricts his diet to berries and nuts. When he sees through the peephole that Felix cuts wood every day, the monster even disciplines his enormous body by putting it to work cutting wood for the De Laceys.

The restrictions the monster places on his body (his timetable, his limited diet, his cramped quarters, and his isolation) are all placed in the service of his developing soul. Earlier, the monster had been so fully present in his painful physical sensations that he might well remind a reader of *Discipline and Punish* of the condemned man at the scene of torture: "I felt *tormented* by hunger and thirst ... I was a poor helpless, miserable wretch. I ... could distinguish nothing; but feeling pain invade me on all sides, I sat down and wept" (98–99; my emphasis). In the hut, the monster learns to subordinate the present sensations of the body to a future trial in which others will pass judgment on his soul.

Once the monster enters the hut, he succumbs so fully to discipline that almost immediately he views the De Laceys as judges, who will perform actions appropriate to trials, like those that Foucault places at the heart of a disciplinary discourse. The monster plans to tell his life story to the cottagers in the hope that they will judge him a worthy companion. As he prepares himself to meet the De Laceys he says, "I endeavored to fortify myself for the trial, which in a few months I resolved to undergo" (125). All the discipline of the monster's present life in the hut is placed in the service of his future trial where, before the De Laceys, he plans to prove himself a worthy soul.[12]

In the monster's upcoming trial, as in all trials Foucault finds in a disciplinary society, the soul is to be judged. Shelley's novel, in the transition between the old discourse and the new, highlights the difficulty of suppressing the conspicuous body in order that the soul might be produced for judgment. The monster can display his soul to the De Laceys only if the whole family, like the blind father, can entirely overlook his body. Even as the plot shows the difficulty of subduing the conspicuous body, the text—through the monster's story—appeals to the reader to do exactly that. The novel may censure inhuman characters who reject the enormous body as hideous, but Shelley's humane text doubles the rejection of that body. The text dismisses it, huge and imposing though it is, as unimportant.

The monster's hut is an intricate mechanism of surveillance. The monster not only prepares for the De Laceys to judge his life as he resides there, but he also gives a full account of the development of his soul in the hut to Victor, who in turn gives it to Walton, who in turn lays it before the reader for judgment. In his initiation into a discourse of discipline, the monster learns both to place himself under the surveillance of others and to place others under his surveillance so that he might also judge them. While in the hut, the monster reads Victor's journal. He also carefully watches the De Laceys, noting their acts of kindness so that he might judge their character and hence their likely reception of him. He correctly judges blind old De Lacey to be the most approachable member of the family.

Amid all the discipline of the hut the monster's body is regulated and diminished in order to make room for his growing soul. In the hut, the monster is initiated into language and the culture's discourse, which includes a great-books course in Western literature. As the monster reads Plutarch, Milton, and Goethe, he is initiated into a discourse, at once romantic and disciplinary, that views reading chiefly as a spur for the reader to contemplate his or her own feelings and isolated condition (123).

After three seasons in the hut, the monster himself all but forgets the body that was so crucial to the older discourse. When he finds in the woods a portmanteau containing books and clothing, only the books are of interest to him. Once the monster learns to read, he retrieves the papers that earlier he had found but ignored in the clothes he took from Victor's laboratory. The papers—Victor's diary—reveal the story of the monster's origin (124). Here, the novel inverts the meaning of the clothing that once provided warmth and comfort to the monstrous body. As the monster retrieves the diary from the pockets of the clothing, the cover of the body becomes important only as a hiding place for the story of the soul.

Frankenstein defines the enormous body as a produced and unnatural body, as the body of the old discourse—or of any discourse—necessarily is. At the same time, however, the novel attempts to naturalize the chief elements of the new discourse: the disciplined body and the disciplined soul. The monster submits so easily and thoroughly to discipline that Shelley's "humane" novel implies that he is naturally inclined to discipline. He rejects it only after other characters fail to pay adequate attention to his discipline and hence fail to reward it. The novel tries to naturalize discipline even as it fears its failure. Rejected by Felix De Lacey, the monster abandons his hut and reverts to the conditions of the old discourse. He gives vent to a raging passion for revenge, which he flaunts in violent physical acts. Like the sovereign of the old discourse, as *Discipline and Punish* describes it, the monster now breaks and marks bodies.[13] The bodies of little William and Clerval are found dead, each with a fingerprint of the murderer on its neck.

Expanding the Soul

As the monster casts off his discipline and breaks into violence, Shelley's novel repeats the displacement of body by soul. The monster's newly undisciplined physical life, like his initial physical life, is placed in the service of producing a soul, but this time it is Victor's soul. *Frankenstein* enacts its most forceful transition between the old discourse and the new across the characters of the monster and Victor. In the murders that bind the two characters, the novel once again places physical life in the service of mental life by inverting the significance and value of the signs of the older discourse that had privileged the body in public.

Frankenstein privatizes the signs produced on marked bodies of the monster's victims. The fingerprints the monster leaves on the necks of his victims become private texts addressed to Victor alone, and Victor alone can read them. At the same time, the physical torture of the older discourse is revised into mental torture. The monster's murders reduce physical torture to its zero degree—the victims are killed in an instant—but those same murders produce in Victor prolonged mental torture. In Foucault's reading, the scene of torture in the old discourse relied on a careful calculus of pain.[14] The monster's murders also come to rely on a careful calculus of pain, but the pain has been displaced from the dying body to the still-living soul of the spectator. Standing over the dead body of William, the monster says, "This death will carry despair to [Victor] and a thousand other miseries shall torment and destroy him" (136).

Frankenstein dramatizes the transition between discourses by recasting the physical acts of the monster (the figure of the old discourse of the body) as mental acts in Victor (the figure of the romantic soul). The monster hides his body physically (he secludes himself in the hut) and as a result he gives birth to a soul. Victor hides the monstrous body mentally (he keeps it a secret) and as a result he develops a far more extreme version of the soul: the isolated and involuted soul of the madman. In revising physical life into psychological life, Mary Shelley's text forges in Victor mental actions that loom as large or larger than the monster's physical acts. In Victor's contest with his physical double, the romantic's soul grows to monstrous size.

Frankenstein produces the romantic soul in the very act of forcing the enormous body into secrecy. When Victor makes of the monstrous body a secret, he produces a rift between his own knowledge and the knowledge held by all other characters. From then on, the inside of his mind is inaccessible to every other character. With the monster's violence, the secret becomes the most important aspect of Victor's life. Hence, he grows increasingly isolated and comes to focus more and more on his own tortured and tortuous mental processes. After the deaths of William and Justine, Victor silently addresses his family: "Frankenstein, your son, your kinsman, your early much-loved friend,... he who would fill the air with blessings and spend his life in serving you—he bids you weep, to shed countless tears ... Thus spoke my prophetic soul ... torn by remorse, horror and despair" (85).

The body of the old discourse, which in *Frankenstein* appears as Other and thus deformed, is mirrored in Victor's soul, but with a difference. Whereas the text represents the monster's body as a *hideous* deformity upon which it can barely look, it represents Victor's soul as an *interesting* deformity upon which it dwells in chapter after chapter, and into which it invites the reader to look. In the difference between the unspeakable deformity of the body and the incessantly articulated deformity of the mind, Shelley's novel sets up the terms of a disciplinary discourse.

Frankenstein practices one of its most effective strategies for forgetting the body and memorializing the soul as it exploits the gap between signifier and signified: between language and body. In "Language to Infinity," Foucault discusses the gap between language and body in late-eighteenth-century sensation writing, especially the works of Sade. Foucault finds that language seeks to make itself thin in order to produce the body and the physical sensation of terror. However, because writing is unable finally to realize the body and its sensations, it gives rise instead to an endless chain of language, which emerges in tandem with the growing importance of a discourse of the library, in which fragmentary languages refer only to other fragmentary languages.[15]

Frankenstein sheds light on a major historical function of such a chain of language: Shelley's novel uses the chain of language to produce the space of the soul, especially the space of Victor's soul. As *Frankenstein* produces Victor's soul, language does not seek to make itself thin, as in the writing of Sade. On the contrary, Shelley's novel seeks out the inevitable disparity between language and body in order to prize it open, to widen it, and then to appropriate the newly enlarged space as the space of the life story: a space constituted by language that moves obsessively back and forth between the past history of the isolated individual and the future moment of his death. Shelley's novel uses language fraught with repetition to produce an enormous echo chamber of the soul that dissociates itself repeatedly from the body, its actions, and its sensations.

When Victor is arrested for Clerval's murder, *Frankenstein* seeks out extreme sensations in order to call attention to the gap between language and body and to widen it. Victor's physical sensations grow to a peak of terror when he is shown the dead body of Clerval. His terror is clearly beyond the capacity of language: "How can I describe my sensations on beholding it? I feel yet parched with terror, nor can I reflect on that moment without shuddering in agony" (169). Yet, if such physical sensation is too much for language, it is also too much for the body: "The human frame could no longer support the agonies I endured" (169). Overwhelmed by the extremity of his own sensations, Victor loses consciousness for a period of two months. He then (re)awakens to consciousness in a scene that serves as an emblem of the novel's own action, as it works to extend the language of consciousness backward through memory and forward through foreboding in a space self-consciously marked out by language.

After two months, Victor "finds (him)self as awaking from a dream" (169). Whatever physical agonies he endured are thus enveloped in the haze of the subconscious mind. He learns of them only now, over a distance of time and indirectly from Mr. Kerwin, the magistrate. The gap between Victor's awareness and his body's approach to death emphasizes and extends his soul, as Victor's lost months of consciousness lead to scenes that highlight the recovery and active extension of memory. Here, Victor as narrator displays his own heightened awareness of the act of coming to consciousness. "It was morning, *I remember* when I thus *awoke to understanding*. I had forgotten the particulars of what had happened ... but when I looked around and saw the barred windows and squalidness of the room ... *all flashed across my memory*"

(169–70; my emphasis). Victor also regains an awareness of his body; the plot, however, repeatedly stills his physical sensations through fatigue, enforced isolation, or drugs as the narration focuses on memory.

Because of Victor's lost consciousness, language is necessary to produce his soul out of its own forgetfulness. Through Kerwin's language, Victor learns not only about his own illness, but also about a chain of language that has produced Victor's soul for Kerwin's perusal, and which now (re)produces it for Victor himself. During Victor's illness, Kerwin has examined his ailing prisoner's papers; locating among them a letter from Victor's father, Kerwin has written to him and received a response. This chain of language, calling attention to its nature as language in the form of letters, has given Kerwin astonishing knowledge of the newly conscious Victor. When Kerwin's conversation with Victor circles back to the letters he has exchanged with Alphonse Frankenstein, it revives Victor's soul by stimulating his memory: Victor recalls both the murders and the monster so powerfully that he imagines the monster present at the jail (172).

As Victor recuperates, *Frankenstein* uses letters to produce not only the past of his soul but also its future. Victor does not regain full consciousness of his life story until he receives a letter from Elizabeth on his trip back to Geneva. Elizabeth's letter leads him to recall the monster's threat: " '*I shall be with you on your wedding night!*' " (179; emphasis in the original). Memory immediately sends his mind careening forward to the opposite pole of his biography, as he interprets the monster's words as a threat of his own fated death. Victor thus recovers consciousness in the space opened up by language, a space that becomes that of the anxious autobiography, within which the mind moves incessantly backward and forward in the frenzied act of writing the soul.[16]

Many times Victor expresses the desire to die so that he can find rest for his driven soul: "Why did I not die and sink into forgetfulness?" (167). Yet exactly matching his desire for death is the "unceasing ... vigilance" required to keep him from suicide (174). In the tension between Victor's longing for death and the vigilance that blocks it, Shelley's novel routes desire away from death (the end to which Victor's ailing body had been moving) toward a language that doubles back upon itself in obsessive acts of memory and forboding in order to produce the endless murmuring of the soul. Hence Victor, as narrator, introduces the scenes in which he comes to consciousness with a self-awareness so exhaustive and exhausting that all his physical energy must be placed in its service through language that thrives on redundancy: "I must pause here, for it requires all my fortitude to recall the memory of the frightful events which I am about to relate, in proper detail, to my recollection" (166).

Victor's language is characterized by a variation on the novel's strategy of repetition. Here, repetition in self-reflexive language extends the soul as it keeps death at bay.[17] And in *Frankenstein*, death must be kept at a distance in order for unceasing self-surveillance to produce a particularly modern version of the soul: one that having dispensed with divinity must rely that much more fully on self-policing.

Even beyond Victor's narration, Shelley's novel produces language that aims to reverberate endlessly. Just as letters produce the anxiety-ridden space of the life story in the scenes where Victor (re)gains consciousness, letters (Walton's correspondence with his sister) create an endless circulation of language within the novel's structure. *Frankenstein* is constructed as an echo chamber of voices: Walton's fragmentary letters quote the voices of Victor and the monster; Victor's voice also quotes the monster's voice; and finally the monster speaks to Walton about Victor. *Frankenstein* thus exemplifies the self-reflection that Foucault in "Language to Infinity" attributes to the principle of the library: "Within itself it finds the possibility of its own division, of its own repetition, the power to create a system of mirrors, self-images, analogies."[18]

Language not only echoes within the novel, it also reverberates endlessly beyond the narrative frame, defying the monster's claim that "the remembrance of [him and Victor] will speedily vanish" (211). The frame provided by Walton's letters is fissured in significant ways. Walton begins his final letter with a grave doubt over whether he will ever get free of the ice to deliver it. Although the ice breaks and a channel opens to the south, we watch the ice shift so suddenly and unpredictably that we must retain some doubt over whether he and his letter will arrive safely home. Shelley's novel, offering no responses to Walton from Margaret Saville, presents the letters as if they were undelivered. Walton's last letter, written under the reverberating strain of death (Walton's fear of his own death, his witnessing of Victor's death, and his hearing of the monster's impending death), appears to the reader increasingly as a series of private journal entries in which Walton bares his soul to no one in particular. On September 5, September 7, and September 12, we read only entries with dates, as in a journal. Furthermore, Walton's last letter remains unfinished, bearing neither closing nor signature.

When *Frankenstein* raises our doubts over whether Walton has completed his letter or whether his sister will receive it, the novel briefly yet finally imagines his letter as suspended in transit. Because Walton's letters comprise a novel, they are not merely suspended, but intercepted by a mass press that sets the voices of Victor and the monster in virtually endless circulation.

The monster's last speech supplies the final thrust to a reverberating language that can outdistance all bodies. At the very moment that it seems impossible to avoid the death of the soul in the death of the body, *Franken-stein* dramatizes even more insistently the pattern of infinite repetition in language in the monster's announcement of his own death: "I shall col-lect my funeral pile and consume to ashes this miserable frame.... I shall die. I shall no longer feel.... I shall be no more. I shall no longer see.... I shall die.... Soon these burning miseries will be extinct. I shall ascend my funeral pile" (210–11). Amid the voices that everywhere echo each other, the sustained repetition in Shelley's prose, and the interception of Walton's letters by a mass press that circulates the echoing voices outward across many readers, *Frankenstein* helps to produce a discourse of the soul that needs no body, a discourse whose only body is a language that at once produces and records souls who place themselves and each other under surveillance.

The proliferation of private and repetitive language of self-surveillance in Shelley's novel accompanies an important shift in the nature of power. *Frankenstein* drains power from its earlier locus in a person (the sovereign) and begins to articulate a new mode of power that traverses characters through the language of guilt and confession. When Victor Frankenstein creates the monster, he enacts the role of a seriously flawed sovereign, and not simply in the terms that Shelley suggests when the monster compares Victor to the Sovereign Creator in *Paradise Lost*. Victor's act of creation erodes the power of the sovereign that was so important to the old discourse that Foucault de-scribes in *Discipline and Punish* at the scene of torture.

Under the ancien régime, the sovereign publicly displayed his power on the marked and scarred body of the condemned. Victor Frankenstein, like the old sovereign, produces a marked body that bears the signs of his power. But as Shelley's text enacts the transition to a discourse of discipline, it abandons the public spectacle of power. Other characters fail to recognize the stamp of Victor's power on the monster's body. Only the reader in the private act of reading recognizes the signs of Victor's activity on the (de)-formed body. Equally important, the novel revises the meaning of the signs that the marked body bears. Because Victor has set out not to break a body but to make one, the markings that render the body monstrous register the would-be sovereign's failure more than his power. Victor himself says, "I had selected his features as beautiful. Beautiful! Great God!" (56).

As the power lodged in the single and visible person of the sovereign wanes in *Frankenstein*, the diffuse power that *Discipline and Punish* attributes to the new discourse emerges. The new mode of circulating power requires repetitive language both in the form of confession and in the form of inadequate explanations for the cause of events. We see disciplinary power at work across characters in *Frankenstein* as, one by one, a series of characters falsely proclaims his or her guilt as the murderer of little William. Justine falsely confesses to the murder and hangs for it; even Elizabeth declares that she is William's murderer (70); and Victor tells the reader that he is the true murderer of William. In its many confessions, *Frankenstein* dramatizes the diffusion of guilt and the repeated acts of confession appropriate to a disciplinary discourse. The false confessions also register confusion over where to locate the power behind a significant event, and they begin to trace a power whose path is indirect and circular.

When Justine, Elizabeth, or Victor confesses to the murder, each individual's claim to be the power behind the event is false or inadequate. Hence, the novel must qualify the confessions with further explanations that sweep across several characters. Justine confesses because the jury has convicted her of the murder and she wants her confessor to grant her absolution; her guilt then circles back upon her when she realizes she has confessed a lie. Elizabeth claims responsibility for William's death because she granted his request for the locket, which she presumes enticed the murderer. Victor's confession makes sense only when the reader recognizes that a power that once was Victor's has passed into the monster and out of Victor's control. At the same time the monster—the actual murderer—claims a more diffuse cause for his actions: his rejections by Victor, the villagers, and the De Laceys. In the confessions that so widely distribute guilt and the language of explanation, Shelley's novel begins to dramatize a power to cause significant events that circulates across individual characters. As the novel itself circulates through the literary market, it disseminates its confessions across many readers. *Frankenstein*'s diffusing language relays the power that causes events in the very act of tracing it.

(Re)inforcing the Emergent Discourse

The repetition of confessional language that everywhere produces souls is matched in *Frankenstein* by the repetition of denied and dissipated bodies. Because the bodies in Shelley's novel have stimulated so many discussions of gender, I would like briefly to set *Frankenstein*'s strategies for installing and spreading discipline in relation to those discussions. Most critics have understood bodies in the novel primarily as female. Homans discusses the dominant Western cultural myth that associates the body with "woman," though she reads the monster as the product of a solipsistic attempt by the male to bypass the female body. Collings offers a Lacanian reading of the monster. He understands it as Victor's reconstruction of the body of the Imaginary Mother that is displaced by the Symbolic language of the Father. He argues that the monster's appearance as a male indicates that the language of the Father cannot adequately represent the bodily Mother. Irigaray finds the female body to be represented in Western culture as fragmented in the margins of the hegemonic image of a whole male body; she also argues that the female body is in itself multiple or plural. Her work suggests a reading of the monstrous body comprised of fragments in *Frankenstein* as a female body.[19]

I would argue that in the historical shift away from a discourse of the body in public to a discourse of the privatized soul, representations of female bodies endure special hardships because of the long-standing cultural association between the body and "woman." Women's bodies are rigorously privatized in Shelley's novel: they are all set within the domestic "sphere" of the Frankenstein household. As many critics have noted, all the major female characters in *Frankenstein* demonstrate a passivity that denies physical action and finally requires their deaths.[20] Certainly, Victor is appalled at the thought of a female monster through whose body "a race of devils would be *propagated* on the earth" (158; my emphasis). Victor destroys the female monster, and Shelley's novel replaces that threatened proliferation of bodies with a proliferation of language that constitutes souls.

All of the denials, displacements, and destructions of female bodies — aligned with a reading of the monstrous body as female — do not, however, preclude similar outcomes for male bodies. London traces a notable disintegration of the male body in *Frankenstein* that undermines patriarchal myths of the self-possessed body of the man. She calls attention to the lack of self-containment of Victor's body: "Frankenstein's body becomes a notable site of hysterical self-display. For in Clerval's presence, Frankenstein finds that he cannot 'contain' himself—that he cannot be stilled: 'I was unable to remain for a single instant in the same place; I jumped over the chairs, clapped my hands, and laughed aloud.'" London finds that fragmentation, disintegration, and finally the prone posture of death are all staged on the male body.[21]

Frankenstein deploys its strategy of repetition and variation in order everywhere to subject bodies to souls. The novel inflicts on many different kinds of bodies (female and male, child and adult) many variations of denial, displacement, or disintegration in order that bodies, so important in the older discourse, might everywhere be placed in service to souls. In London's passage, for example, Victor's body becomes unstable and fragmented precisely as it becomes an analogue of his hyperactive soul.

In *Frankenstein*, strategies of repetition and variation characterize not only the displacement of body by soul, but also the revision of resistance to discipline into the confirmation of discipline. Situated at the juncture between discourses, *Frankenstein* is ambivalent about the new discourse it implements. Its protests against discipline, however, repeatedly produce its preconditions. Again and again the novel registers the pain of the newly isolated subject, as Victor and the monster express anguish over their alienation. Yet, their anguish produces both characters as subjects whose consciousness of separation is the most salient feature of their mental lives. *Frankenstein* defies the separated subjecthood of its characters as unrestrained longing breaks out of bounds, and passes through the various characters — the monster, Victor, and Walton — as they tell their tales. At the same time, the tales frame one another (Walton's narrative of longing frames Victor's narrative of longing, which in turn frames the monster's). Thus, the very tales that relay passion across characters also configure depth. They thereby indicate increasingly secret and inner selves, which the reader is invited to penetrate.

The narrative's plot is as ambiguous as its structure. When the monster is rejected by the De Lacey family, undisciplined passion — initially a quality of Victor — infects the monster as a relentless desire for revenge. The monster, rejected from his hut (the cell that kept him in his place) now circulates freely until his rebellion destroys all that is valued in private life. Yet, because the text presents the monster's indiscipline as the murder of the innocent, it triggers in the reader a disciplinary eye that tracks the monster wherever he goes.

Like its plot and structure, *Frankenstein*'s gothic settings are ambiguous. Nonetheless, they too are pressed into the service of the new discourse. The novel's bleak gothic settings, amid which Victor wanders, confuse the landscape and his soul, defying the boundary of the subject. Yet at the level of sentences *Frankenstein* teaches us how we are to read its landscapes. Repeatedly the novel shows us that soul and landscape are not equal and exchangeable entities, but tenor and vehicle of a metaphor, in which the landscape serves as the visible image of the soul. Of his own mental state Victor says, "I could give no expression to my sensations — they weighed on me with a mountain's weight" (42). Of Elizabeth's soul he says, "her grief was the misery of innocence which, like a cloud that passes over the fair moon, for a while hides but cannot tarnish its brightness" (84). Finally, he says of himself, "I am a blasted tree; the bolt has entered my soul" (153). If the gothic settings of *Frankenstein* confuse inner soul and outer landscape, Victor's narration reveals that they do so in order to project the psychologized soul outward that it might be writ large, and that readers new to a regime of discipline might become practiced in reading the psyche.[22]

Amid the circulation of texts in a mass press, *Frankenstein* prepares its readers to participate in the emergent discourse of discipline. Shelley's novel acts in conjunction with several other nineteenth-century novels in England, Europe, and the United States that send the self in pursuit of itself as they write the private soul. *Frankenstein's* particular potency in stimulating a rapid transformation between discourses lies in the obsessive repetitions and variations with which it performs its tasks.

Frankenstein inverts and revalues the signs of the old discourse of the body in public, stripping it of its authority and making its once-recognizable terms incomprehensible and monstrous, that it might become the Other against which the soul of the new discourse establishes its identity. At the same time, *Frankenstein* produces the new discourse by spinning out multiple variations of the soul and installing discipline in myriad and densely interactive locations within the text. The novel produces and reproduces the anxious soul through the proliferation of language as the soul's memory, which everywhere echoes itself in the reverberating voices of Victor, the monster, and Walton. In the repetition that characterizes *Frankenstein*—both in its structure and in its prose—the language of the soul in extremity demonstrates its omnipresence at the very moment that it displaces the body in extremity.

Through its repeated revaluations and displacements, *Frankenstein* fosters a stunning transformation. It revises the conspicuous body into the hidden soul, even as it makes the "hidden" soul an object of continual surveillance. It reimagines the body as unnatural, even as it renders natural and familiar the "unnatural" mind of a madman: in the construction of the monster, the novel transforms natural bodies into an unnatural body; in the articulation of Victor's near madness, it writes the soul conspicuously, making it visible and recognizable to readers in a wide-reaching literary market. *Frankenstein* thus helps to make available the "unique" soul of the madman as a model for the soul of everyman. As Shelley's novel inscribes the isolated soul in numerous locations, it requires its readers to install discipline at many different sites of their reading. It engages its readers in the practice of redefining resistance to discipline into the perfection of discipline. In its rebellion against a regime of discipline, Mary Shelley's novel condemns Victor Frankenstein's effort to perfect a science of man. Yet *Frankenstein* fosters the discourse that, according to Foucault, produces nothing other than "the science of man."[23]

Notes

1. Michel Foucault, *Discipline and Punish: The Birth of the Prison*, trans. Alan Sheridan (New York: Random House, Vintage Books, 1979). I summarize arguments that appear in several sections of *Discipline and Punish*; see especially 7–23, 187–94.

2. Amid postmodern explorations that trace discursive practices across multiple cultural spaces, this essay (re)turns to the temporal cultural processes that help to spread and legitimate those practices. I respond here to some of the concerns over loss of temporality and historicity raised in Fredric Jameson, *Postmodernism; or, The Cultural Logic of Late Capitalism* (Durham: Duke University Press, 1991), 6, 25, 39.

3. Philip Fisher, *Hard Facts: Setting and Form in the American Novel* (New York: Oxford University Press, 1985), 3.

4. Ibid., 4.

5. Foucault, *Discipline and Punish*, 202.

6. Jameson, *Postmodernism*, 54. David Harvey, *The Condition of Postmodernity: An Enquiry into the Origins of Cultural Change* (Oxford: Basil Blackwell, 1989) also understands causation in contemporary life to be a network of continuously shifting and interactive factors. Harvey describes a postmodern crisis of representation that he traces to changes in the nature of global capitalism that have been accelerating since the midnineteenth century; see especially 240, 260–65.

7. I am indebted to Lee Quinby for pointing out to me the shift in attention from body to soul in *The Scarlet Letter*. For a discussion of the monster in *Frankenstein* as the agent of Victor's desire, see Mary Poovey, "My Hideous Progeny: Mary Shelley and the Feminization of Romanticism," *PMLA* 95 (1980): 336.

8. My understanding of the public nature of the monster's body was stimulated by Warren Montag's Marxian reading of *Frankenstein*, in which he observes that "the monster is a totality assembled from ... a multitude of different individuals"; see Warren Montag, "'The Workshop of Filthy Creation': A Marxist Reading of *Frankenstein*," in *Frankenstein*, by Mary Shelley, ed. Johanna M. Smith, Case Studies in Contemporary Criticism (Boston: St. Martin's Press, Bedford Books, 1992), 303.

9. Mary Shelley, *Frankenstein; or, The Modern Prometheus* (New York: Signet, New American Library, 1965). All references to *Frankenstein* are from this text (the 1816 edition) and are cited parenthetically.

10. Foucault, *Discipline and Punish*, 33.

11. See ibid., 200.

12. I wish to thank a student of mine, Marianne Smith, for her valuable insights about the monster's schedule and his internalizing of the De Laceys as his judges.

13. Foucault, *Discipline and Punish*, 33–34.

14. Ibid., 33.

15. Michel Foucault, "Language to Infinity," in *Language, Counter-Memory, Practice: Selected Essays and Interviews*, trans. Donald F. Bouchard and Sherry Simon, ed. Donald F. Bouchard (Ithaca: Cornell University Press, 1977), 65–67.

16. Nancy Armstrong, *Desire and Domestic Fiction* (New York: Oxford University Press, 1987), 109–23, interprets letters and language in Richardson's *Pamela* as replacing the physical body of the woman with a representation of rational, well-disciplined, and female emotion sanctioned

by the middle class. In *Frankenstein*, in which masculine desire ravages domesticity, the soul is neither rational nor domestic. Nonetheless, language and letters produce the soul in place of the body in order that we may track all the motions of that maddened soul in our reading of the life story.

17. Foucault in "Language to Infinity," 59, discusses the use of repetition as a strategy of writing that arises in the late eighteenth century to keep death at a distance.

18. Ibid., 67.

19. For discussions relevant to the connection between *Frankenstein* and women's bodies, see Margaret Homans, *Bearing the Word: Language and Female Experience in Nineteenth-Century Women's Writing* (Chicago: University of Chicago Press, 1986), 1–5, 106; David Collings, "The Monster and the Imaginary Mother: A Lacanian Reading of *Frankenstein*," in *Frankenstein*, by Mary Shelley, ed. Johanna M. Smith, 248–49; Luce Irigaray, *This Sex Which Is Not One*, trans. Catherine Porter with Carolyn Burke (Ithaca: Cornell University Press, 1985), 28–30.

20. See especially Kate Ellis, "Monsters in the Garden: Mary Shelley and the Bourgeois Family," in *The Endurance of Frankenstein*, ed. George Levine and U. C. Knoepflmacher (Berkeley: University of California Press, 1974), 130–33; U. C. Knoepflmacher, "Thoughts on the Aggression of Daughters," in *The Endurance of Frankenstein*, ed. George Levine and U. C. Knoepflmacher, 108.

21. Bette London, "Mary Shelley, *Frankenstein* and the Spectacle of Masculinity," *PMLA* 108 (1993): 262.

22. Robert Donald Spector, *The English Gothic: A Bibliographic Guide to Writers from Horace Walpole to Mary Shelley* (Westport, Conn.: Greenwood Press, 1984), 244, notes the plethora of psychoanalytic interpretations of *Frankenstein*. Fred Botting, *Making Monstrous: "Frankenstein," Criticism, Theory* (Manchester: Manchester University Press, 1991), deconstructs a series of Freudian psychoanalytic readings of Shelley's novel. Botting comments on the powerful allure of *Frankenstein* for such readings, noting its family romance, its images of death and desire, and its central relationship of the double. Even as Botting warns against it, he calls attention to "the powerful conjunction of *Frankenstein* and psychoanalysis [which] seems too potent a mixture for critics to escape its intoxicating effects" (90).

23. Michel Foucault, *The Order of Things: An Archaeology of the Human Sciences* (New York: Random House, Vintage Books, 1973), 307–28.

4

Indians, Polynesians, and Empire Making: The Case of Herman Melville

Malini Johar Schueller

That Herman Melville dedicated the supposedly autobiographical account of his stay among the Typees to Lemuel Shaw, chief justice of the Commonwealth of Massachusetts, is surely curious. Melville was seemingly all but contemptuous of missionary activity in *Typee*, and Lemuel Shaw had belonged for many years to the Society for Propagating the Gospel among the Indians. In fact, two months after receiving his inscribed copy of *Typee*, Shaw solicited funds for the conversion of the Montapec Indians.[1] In one sense, we can see the dedication as Melville's attempt to sensitize his father-in-law to the destructive consequences of missionary activity. If we read the text as a literary event within the macropolitics of the period, however, we can see that it links together two important aspects of U.S. national identity: the internal colonization of Indians and external empire building.

By the end of the 1830s, as a result of Jackson's policies, Indians had been pushed west of the Mississippi and in effect posed no threat to the New England states. When Melville's literary contemporaries mourned the passing away of the Indian, their treatment of the Indians in the past tense constituted a complex gesture of consent to and guilt about policies that had decimated many Indian nations. William Cullen Bryant sought to explain the forcible dislocation of Indians, their leaving "the blooming wilds [they] ranged so long" as a "change [in] the forms of being."[2] Henry David Thoreau in *A Week on the Concord and Merrimack Rivers* recorded his pleasure at finding old Indian arrowheads, the material evidence of Indian culture. In *Walden*, however, Thoreau dramatized the breakdown of Indian cultures as an inevitability. The Indian was in a continuum with other "savage" races "degraded by contact with the civilized man."[3] In a similar manner, Melville used his narratives of the South Seas to deal both with the issue of Indian decimation at home and with colonial politics abroad. *Typee,* and also to an extent *Omoo* and *Mardi,* is a text in which the Melvillean narrator, although critical of colonialism, nonetheless situates himself within the discourse as colonist in order to maintain the separation between himself and the natives, a separation on which his racial and cultural identity depends.

Such racial separations and distinctions were an integral part of the discourses of colonialism and empire that were well entrenched in the United States in the midnineteenth century and of which imaginative literature was a part. Cultural critics such as Robert Drinnon and Richard Slotkin have brought to attention the importance of the idea of conquering racial Others for conceptions of national identity.[4] David S. Shields has shown how until the mideighteenth century the poetry of the United States featured a discourse of empire. After 1750, this myth was simply shorn of its British imperial frame and applied to the "republican glory of the rising glory of America."[5] From the beginning, therefore, the literary nationalism of the United States included the idea of a colonizing nationalism. When Crèvecoeur had formulated his queries about "What is an American," he had simply used the unquestioned designation linking nation and continent. By the nineteenth century, the appellation "America" was consciously preserved by many precisely because of its colonial connotations. "The whole continent of North America," wrote John Quincy Adams, "appears to be *destined by Divine Providence* to be peopled by one *nation,* speaking one language."[6]

In Melville's time, as Wai-chee Dimock has shown, the idea of the United States as empire had gained wide and acceptable currency. Jefferson praised the United States as an "empire for liberty," and Jackson used the phrase "extending the area of freedom" to justify the annexation of Texas.[7] When Melville published *Typee* in 1844, U.S. rhetoric on empire making was well established, and the Marquesan islands themselves had a key position within this rhetoric. The islands had been subject to a long history of colonization beginning in 1774 with James Cook.[8] In 1791 the French staked their claim over the islands. Two decades later, during the British-U.S. war of 1812, Capt. David Porter took possession of the Marquesas Islands in the name of the United States; in 1813, therefore, the Marquesas became the first colony of the United States.[9] The islands became a pawn in European power brokering, fought over by the British and then annexed by the French in 1842, all this leading to a decimation of the local population.[10] The politics of the islands were thus particularly important to the United States as an emergent imperial power.

Just as the rhetoric of the United States as empire was being strengthened in the political and cultural arenas, studies on the classification of races were consolidating. The beginnings of such studies were seen in the eighteenth century. In 1721, Richard Bradley identified "five sorts of men" according to their color.[11] In 1800 Georges Cuvier produced his theory of races, which classified humans into three groups in a descending scale of whites, yellows, and blacks. Such interests continued into the nineteenth century with S. G. Morton's publications about the skulls of American Indians and several other works on the "types" of humankind.[12] By the midnineteenth century, the Enlightenment valorization of reason was being used by proponents of polygenesis such as Charles Caldwell to distinguish between the Caucasians who had made "all the great and important discoveries, inventions, and improvements" and other races that were animalistic.[13] The absence and presence of reason to question the humanity of people of color was thus well entrenched in the nineteenth century.

Melville's narratives of the South Seas are intimately linked with these different scientific, political, and literary interests. *Typee*, the most politicized of the three narratives, is a complex cultural representation of Euro-American colonial aspiration articulated through what Homi K. Bhabha calls a "strategy of disavowal." As Bhabha explains, "the discourse of cultural colonialism" does not operate through a simple discrimination between the colonial and colonized cultures. Rather, the discourse is "produced through the strategy of disavowal" where "the trace of what is disavowed is not repressed but repeated as something *different*."[14] Melville's narratives of the South Seas are replete with overt disavowals of Euro-American colonial prerogative at the same time as they repeat cultural colonialism through strategies of difference: creating racial boundary situations and describing natives through the scientific schemata of classification. Indeed, what we may think of as strategies of "difference" from colonialism were, in fact, part of the technologies of biopower that were part of the hegemonic discourse of nineteenth-century Europe. As Michel Foucault points out in *History of Sexuality*, beginning in the seventeenth century, techniques for regulating the population into different groups and the dramatic proliferation of studies in housing, birthrate, and so on, served the purposes of segregation and social hierarchization.[15] Although Foucault's compelling analysis of the disciplining of the body and techniques of biopower omits any mention of colonialism and slavery, it is clear that the same disciplining strategies were also available for the discourses of colonialism in which Melville anxiously participated.

Typee records the adventures of Tommo and Toby's escape from a tyrannical whaling ship, their mistaken foray into cannibal territory and subsequent captivity by the natives, Tommo's growing fondness of the natives, and his final escape from the valley. Melville takes pains to distance himself from the colonial mission of civilizing savages. The narrator of *Typee* constantly attributes the felicity of the Typees (and we can assume that this is in contrast to the position of North American Indians) to their freedom from the corruption of European influence; in *Omoo* he presents an almost schematic correlation between the degeneration of the natives and colonization. He constantly attacks the misguided machinations and the self-evident cruelty of the missionaries. In *Typee* there are endless comparisons between the goodness, warmth, and simplicity of the natives and the cruelty, overintellectualization, and cunning of the European. This overt content level is so persuasive that one can almost read *Typee* simply as a repudiation of Western racial hierarchies. But such a reading assumes that ideologies work only in a primitive manner — overtly and by repression. As Foucault has shown us, such readings ignore the generative workings of power. Foucault upsets the vertical model of power and suggests, first, that power is something that circulates and, second, that it is a "productive network which runs through the whole social body" and "induces pleasure."[16] It is perhaps in the most benign of cultural situations, then, that we can see the most effective workings of the cultural discourses of colonialism.

Typee is ostensibly a record of Melville's stay at the island of Nukuheva from July to August 1842 after deserting his ship, the *Acushnet*.[17] Melville's arrival at Nukuheva coincided with the French acquisition of the Marquesas Islands and the French takeover of Tahiti. The young writer joined the public outrage at the takeover. Melville begins his narrative with a condemnation of this French appropriation. He describes the French occupation of the Marquesas as a "signal infraction of the rights of humanity" and decries the subterfuge whereby the French place their puppet, Mowanna, as the King of Nukuheva.[18] He uses the occasion to question France's claim to a civilized and humane culture. To this point the narrative seems highly critical of the colonial imperative, but as the description continues a much more ambiguous stance begins to develop. Melville directs his attention to the French takeover of Tahiti: "Under cover of a similar pretence, have the outrages and massacres at Tahiti the beautiful, the queen of the South Seas, been perpetrated" (23). At its didactic level, this statement obviously questions the violence of French occupation. At the level of metaphor, there are glimpses of the epistemic violence to follow. The feminization of Tahiti participates in, even as it questions, the axioms of colonialism that stake out territory by envisioning it as female body, either unruly and in need of male control or incapable of self-rule and in need of a male helping hand.

As the narrative continues, it becomes increasingly fraught with such moments of colonial inscription. In Euro-American colonial discourse space counts only as the imprint of empire building. (Thus we have the familiar phrase "X was 'discovered' in ..." as if a place and a people did not exist prior to colonization.) Such is the case with Melville's dramatization of the French takeover of Tahiti. The description begins with a critique of empire building. On the one side we have the arrogance of Du Petit Thouars, who "as an indemnity for alleged insults offered to the flag of his country ... demanded some twenty or thirty thousand dollars to be placed in his hands forthwith, and in default of payment, threatened to land and take possession of the place" (23). On the other side we have the Tahitians, who although "at first disposed to resort to arms, and drive the invaders from their shores," decide otherwise: "The unfortunate queen, Pomare, incapable of averting the impending calamity, terrified at the arrogance of the insolent Frenchman" flees the island (23).

Into this narrative of aggression and disempowerment, of which he is highly critical, Melville inserts an instance of feminine heroism. The episode concerns the bravery of the wife of the British missionary consul who keeps the British flag flying despite the French invasion. Often we see the repressed colonial subtext repeated as difference in seemingly irrelevant digressions, such as this one: "The consular flag of Britain waved as usual during the day, from a lofty staff planted within a few yards of the beach, and in full view of the frigate" (23). The exchange between a French soldier and the missionary wife is martial: "'The admiral desired the flag to be hauled down — hoped it would be perfectly agreeable — and his men stood ready to perform the duty.' 'Tell the pirate, your master,' replied the spirited Englishwoman, pointing to the staff, 'that if he wishes to strike those colors, he must come and perform the act himself; I will suffer no one else to do it.' ... Was that flag hauled down? Mrs. Pritchard thinks not; and Rear-Admiral Du Petit Thouars is believed to be of the same opinion" (24). Here the innocuous occasion of female heroism becomes the site of a troubled colonial identification. We note the facility with which this digression provides the narrator an occasion to unabashedly admire the British flag flying high over the Tahitian harbor. Interestingly enough, at this point the narrator does not excoriate the cultural dominance of the missionaries. Instead, the people of Tahiti become an exorbitant concern as Tahiti is conceptualized as a space to be fought over by rival European powers. The overarching question becomes one of rightful ownership; what gets negated is the ethical issue of dominance.

In the context of the cultural politics of the time, the issue of ownership of native property is highly crucial. As is well known, one means by which North American Indians were deprived of their lands was the argument that because the Indians refused to acknowledge private property, they had no rights to their lands. The important *Johnson v. M'Intosh* ruling of 1823 upheld Indian rights to property but insisted on the "preemptive" rights of the U.S. government over such property.[19] Melville could not have been totally unaware of the political questions ranging around questions of Indian land titles when he was writing *Typee*. Indeed, *Typee* follows a similar logic: while the narrative acknowledges the problem of native expropriation by dramatizing alien ownership, it also affirms Euro-American power over the natives by disallowing the native any voice at all.

After the initial chapters about the political maneuvering in Tahiti and the Marquesan islands, the narrative develops in ways that challenge the assumptions of colonial ideology. If the colonial world is, as Frantz Fanon describes it, a "Manichean" one in which the settler physically delimits the place of the native and "paints the native as a sort of quintessence of evil," Melville's narrative seems to subvert this colonial ideology.[20] Our narrator, the source of authority, is not a missionary, official, or settler, but one who himself has chosen to transgress "civilized" laws. He has jumped ship and escaped into a valley of Nukuheva island, where natives, because of their reputed ferocity, have been free of colonial influence. The narrator is not given the colonial privilege of conquering or exploring and naming "new" territory, but is instead named "Tommo" by the Typees. During his stay he is held prisoner by the natives. Unlike the traditional captivity narrative, however, where captivity reinforced the captor's morality and the antagonist's brutality, Tommo in his gentle imprisonment by the Typees discovers their superiority over the "civilized" world.[21] He forms a substitute family among the Typees with the father figure Marheyo, his son Kory-Kory, and the beautiful paramour Fayaway. And in what seems like a complete transvaluation of values, the narrator decides that cannibalism is not, after all, an absolute evil. He is perfectly content to stay with the natives and finally decides to escape only after he is convinced that he will be forced to undergo a total submission to the Typee culture through the ritual of tattooing.

Melville, that is, undermines the presumed racial hierarchies of his readers. But the narrative also continues to retain an urgent discourse of colonial

imperatives. It is this discourse and its sociocultural context that critics suppress, and thereby proliferate, when they universalize or dehistoricize Melville's
treatment of racial and social difference.[22] Edward S. Grejda's study is typical
of the failure of critics to come to terms with racial analysis. Grejda's explicit
purpose is to clarify Melville's judgments and attitudes to the "dark-skinned
races,"[23] but this purpose is immediately undermined by Grejda's assumption
of an ahistorical and asocial humanism he applies to Melville. Grejda assesses
Melville's achievement as one of recognizing the "fundamental sameness of
all human kind" (9). *Typee* continues to attract criticism of the universal
and symbolic school, some of which has its own obvious racial agenda. It has
been seen as a symbolic "descent into the canyon of the past" (Arvin), a
symbolic exploration into the Typee or "murderous part of all men" (Stern),
a discovery about the "fundamental enigmas of all mythology and all theol-
ogy" (Franklin), and "an apprentice version of Melville's horror at the rela-
tivity of values" (Oliviero).[24] Undoubtedly it is always possible to read symbol-
ism, universal values, and irony in each text, but these strategies too often
ignore the cultural complexities in which a text is engaged and through which
it participates in cultural discourses. The colonial subtext of *Typee* is one such
important cultural complex.

The various titles of the book indicate an awareness of issues of power, authority, and subjective positioning implicated in writing about cultural Others. The original title page of the English edition of *Typee* read, *Narrative of a
Four Months' Residence among the Natives of a Valley of the Marquesas Islands;
or, A Peep at Polynesian Life*. The revised U.S. edition was simply *Typee: A
Peep at Polynesian Life*. The shift from balancing the role of narrator-partici-
pant and narrator-observer in the original version to privileging the latter
suggests more than an acquiescence of the censorship to which Melville submitted.[25] As Melville wrote to his British publisher John Murray, he had always wanted the book to be titled *Typee*, partly because of the "very strange-
ness and novelty" evoked therein.[26] In the revised title Melville distances his
narrator from the native subject but also intimates a desire to be less than
authoritative. The narrator is cast as furtive voyeur peeping at the lives of
the natives; yet the changed title still maintains the natives as objects of
contemplation. Indeed, as the narrative continues, the anxiety about authority is often subsumed under more powerful forms of colonial representation
and classification.[27]

The introductory chapters of *Typee* describe Tommo's anticipation of the
Marquesas and are replete with fearful images of alterity. The Marquesas connote "strange visions of outlandish things ... savage woodlands guarded by

horrible idols—heathenish rites and human sacrifice" (11). These images co-exist with voluptuous images of native women. The women are "mermaids" and "nymphs" with "inexpressibly graceful figures" and "softly moulded limbs" (19–20). At this point in the text both sets of images—the fierce and the sensual—are supposedly purely imaginary for the narrator. As part of the imaginary, the images of sensual native women challenge the hegemonic regulations of Western white, middle-class male morality. Yet this form of resistance to social constructions at home also inadvertently becomes a form of oppression of the indigenous population. The very manner in which the islanders are described marks a difference between the narrator and the natives.

Whether dangerous or enticing, the natives belong to an unreal or fantasy world, one free of time, history, and presentness. Melville, of course, suggests that these images dramatize the näiveté of the narrator, who, at this early point, can speak only from his Euro-American perspective. However, the representation of natives, both within and without the United States, as free of historicity and conflict, was common in the culture at large and found its way into Melville's later works as well. In *Moby Dick*, for instance, Melville names Ahab's ship the *Pequod*, after "a celebrated tribe of Massachusetts Indians, now extinct as the ancient Medes."[28] The explanation, as Wai-chee Dimock points out, not only rewrites history by substituting extinction for extermination, but also places the Indians in the timeless past of the ancients.[29] Similarly, after Ahab's fiery injunction to wish death to Moby Dick, Tashtego, the only Indian onboard, has a response very much in keeping with the stereotype of the quiet, unsmiling (though ferocious) Indian and in stark contrast to the excitement of the rest of the crew. Tashtego smokes quietly as he reflects, "That's a white man; he calls that fun: humph! I save my sweat."[30]

In *Typee* Melville also seems to subvert Euro-American social and racial hierarchies. Before his arrival at the islands, the narrator thinks of the Marquesas through images of conquest, but it is he who is captured by the Marquesans and who begins to realize the moral superiority of the natives. Under the subject heading "Comparative wickedness of civilized and unenlightened people," the narrator concludes that given the "civilized barbarity" of the technologies of punishment in the United States, the term "savage" is grossly misapplied (121–22). It is particularly telling that the narrator reaches these conclusions after having sunk into a state of apathy, given himself "to the passing hour," and shrugged away all disagreeable thoughts (120). In other words, a deintellectualized narrator realizes the superiority of savages, and the manner in which the narrator presents his observations on the natives continues to empower him. In keeping with the nineteenth-century fetish for racial and ethnological categorization, Melville's narrator classifies the lives of the Typees. The narrative is here no longer a furtive "peep" at Polynesian life but a dramatization of a powerful will to know. Using the anthropological imperative of control, the narrator catalogs, labels, and judges Typee culture without doubt or hesitancy, asserting the powers of definition and control.

Definitive assessments of alien cultures strongly proclaim the simplicity of the latter, their easy interpretability. Thus it is significant that *Typee* purports to be an adventure story that is also presented as a comprehensive cultural study. Many of the later chapters are anthropologically arranged, from descriptions of the making of tappa and breadfruit to the "Natural History of the Valley," the "History of a Day as Usually Spent in the Typee Valley," the history of the "pi-pis," the religion of the Typees, the connection between tattooing and tabooing, the Typees' "Primitive Simplicity of Government," and "The Social Condition and General Character of the Typees." Such descriptive-anthropological moves are inherently acts of mastery because the anthropological imperative is only exclusively available: the so-called civilized people have the privilege of observing and recording the "habits" of so-called primitives; the position of the recorder is a position of power. In addition, as Aijaz Ahmad suggests, the classificatory mode in ethnology impoverishes the subject, forcing the multiplicity of the alien culture into a manageable hierarchy.[31]

One of the most striking revelations about the narrator's need for control is his impatience with the polyglossia of the Typee language. Its annoying peculiarity "is the different senses in which one and the same word is employed; its various meanings all have a certain connection, which only makes the matter more puzzling. So one brisk, lively little word is obliged, like a servant in a poor family, to perform all sorts of duties" (212). The versatility and richness of language should have been an inspiration to an aspiring writer (as it was with the complicated etymology of the whale and the different cultural meanings of the whale with which *Moby Dick* begins); but the linguistic prerogative traditionally belonged to the Euro-American colonizer. Further, for one striving for control over the subject, and attempting to define himself against an Other, such diversity threatened the simplicity and regularity that was necessary for control.

Melville's narrator thus tries to mold the reality of Typee culture into clear and simple categories: "Nothing can be more uniform and undiversified than the life of the Typees; one tranquil day of ease and happiness follows another in quiet succession; and with these unsophisticated savages the history of a day is the history of a life" (144). Tommo's own stay in the valley shows him that in fact days of feasting and warfare radically alter the time-space framework of the Typees. The entire community spends days preparing for "the feast of the calabashes," which is celebrated with dance and song. And as Marnoo's visit illustrates, the Typees continually react politically to the actions of the French at their harbors. Nevertheless, when engaged in the descriptive-anthropological mode, the narrator manages the Otherness of the natives by imposing a regularity, predictability, and stasis onto their culture.

In addition to its ethnological structure the text also perpetuates a racial hierarchy by having a narrator endowed with the symbols of European power. Tommo arrives at the valley with a meager set of possessions, but these are enough to ensure his cultural power over the natives. The novelty of Typee culture scarcely leaves Tommo at a loss. He soon becomes adept at making tappa, the traditional cloth of the natives; he begins to relish raw fish and learns to eat the slippery poee-poee deftly; and he gains mastery over all he encounters by classifying, assuming the role of the expert. The natives, in contrast, always stand in varying degrees of subordination to their captive. "Every article, however trivial, which belonged to me, the natives appeared to regard as sacred," writes the narrator (141). Tommo's weather-beaten shirts are used by the islanders on special festive days and render "the young islanders who [wear] them very distinguished characters" (176). We see how "civilized" possessions here signify more than their labor value. Simply put, the natives cannot measure the labor value of such items because, within the limits of the narrative, they can never produce them. Such possessions serve as signifiers of colonial power over the native. The native's delight at the mundane artifacts of culture and the incongruity between the savage's actions and civilized things emphasize the superiority of the Westerner and the inferiority of the savage.[32]

The Typees' interaction with Western artifacts typifies this hierarchical relationship. The ludicrous picture made by the aged warrior Marheyo as he wears the moldy shoes he has begged from Tommo is a traditional one symbolizing Euro-American colonial power:

> The venerable warrior approach[ed] the house, with a slow, stately gait, ear-rings in ears, and spear in hand, with this highly ornamental pair of shoes suspended from his neck by a strip of bark, and swinging backwards and forwards on his capacious chest. In the gala costume of the tasteful Marheyo, these calf-skin pendants ever after formed the most striking feature. (142)

Marheyo's (mis)use of Western artifacts works as a means of questioning any native access to power. Marheyo's status, signaled by words such as "venerable" and "stately," is immediately undermined and ridiculed as it is associated with his treating dirty, worn shoes as distinguished ornamental artifacts. Within the economy of colonial relations, Marheyo is equated with the value of his colonial possessions.

No less empowering to the narrator are his skills with the simple artifacts of civilization. The natives are amazed at the popgun Tommo carves for a child with a bamboo shoot and his pocketknife. The child "scamper[s] away with it, half delirious with ecstacy" and soon the entire Typee population becomes children. Tommo is "surrounded by a noisy crowd—venerable old graybeards—responsible fathers of families—valiant warriors—matrons— young men ... all holding in their hands bits of bamboo, and each clamoring to be served first" (141). Be it shoes or popguns, these artifacts of "civilization" serve to assert the childlike propensity of the natives despite their "venerable" and "responsible" demeanors.

In the context of colonialism and native extinction, the islanders' delight in weapons is particularly ominous. "Pop, Pop, Pop, Pop, now resounded all over the valley," the narrative proclaims (141). The weapons-turned-toys that the islanders avidly turn to implicate the islanders as willful participants in their own destruction. It is fitting, then, that Tommo's last gesture to the substitute family he has formed among the Typees is to give them some of the deadly artifacts he has saved for barter: a musket to Kory-Kory, rolls of cotton to Marheyo and Fayaway, and powder bags to the rest of the women.

The narrator's last contact with the Typees dramatizes two opposing pictures of the natives: the overly kind and the savagely fierce. Tommo leaves Typee after exchanging tearful good-byes with these childlike adults and also escaping the murderous intents of Mow-Mow, who follows his boat armed with a tomahawk. Such contrasting images of the "savage" as both childlike and cruel were commonplace in U.S. conceptions of Indians. As Richard Slotkin explains, the Indian was "alternately the symbol of humanity's childhood and of the Golden Age of man's solidarity with God and creation and the lustful, cruel violator of American pastoral peace."[33] What the Indian was not permitted to be was rational and intellectual. Melville's depiction of the Marquesans reflects a similar racial distinction.

The demarcation of the native as Other rests philosophically on binary thinking, which in Western metaphysics has operated destructively and hierarchically to separate male and female, white and nonwhite, self and other. Melville's works embody an important mode of resistance to this thinking because he constantly attempts to upset the hierarchy that privileges the first term over the second (white over native). Thus in *Typee* Melville's narrator admires the islanders—indeed, sees them as superior to Europeans—because of their simplicity, childishness, and instinctive behavior. But such criteria were long being used to reinforce a paternalistic epidermal alterity in the United States—by abolitionists who held that because blacks were simple and childlike (more moral if less intelligent than their white counterparts), they should be freed, and by proslavery believers who used the same criteria to argue that the blacks needed to be controlled. The criteria operated by what George M. Frederickson calls "romantic racialism," reinforcing the inferiority of the blacks but by invoking images of sympathy rather than hatred.[34]

Melville did not take to the lecture circuit to condemn slavery but, as Carolyn Karcher points out, dealt with some of the moral issues of slavery through his treatment of other people of color.[35] The colonial experience raised questions about the ethics of Euro-American dominance. Melville asserted the inherent moral superiority of the savage but only as long as the latter remained an identifiable savage. In fact, Melville takes care to justify his admiration of the Typees on racial grounds. Reflections on the beauty of the Typees are, in effect, reinforcements of European norms. It is striking how often the narrator refers to the fairness of the Typees, their almost-white complexions that differentiate them from the rest of the savages. In comparison to the Typees, "the dark-hued Hawaiians and the woolly-headed Feegees are immeasurably inferior. . . . The distinguishing characteristic of the Marquesan Islanders . . . is the European cast of their features—a peculiarity seldom observable among other uncivilized people" (176). In terms of the racial politics of antebellum United States, the Typees, we could say, could almost "pass" for white and therefore, it is implied, their being termed "savages" is a gross injustice.[36] The overt rhetoric about the beauty of the Typees serves as a guise to introduce a clear racial subtext that maintains strict hierarchical separations between European and native, white and nonwhite, civilized and savage. Melville attempts to keep these boundaries distinct, even as he introduces elements that question them, because to undo the binaries completely is to undermine the basis of Western-colonial self-definition.

Consequently the most interesting moments in Melville's texts are those in which he deals with what we might call boundary or transgressive situations. Such situations are numerous in any colonizing experience: the native who, like Caliban, learns the outsider's language and thus has the power to change it; the native who appropriates the powers of colonial signifiers; the colonial who "goes native" or participates ambivalently in both cultures. Melville's narratives of the South Seas present a complex approach to these moments of cultural crossing. The narratives permit increasingly radical trans-

gressive situations while at the same time they return these situations to binaristic representation.

Melville's interest in the ambiguous nature of cultural signifiers is signaled
early in the text in the description of the king and queen of Nukuheva who
have supposedly been "civilized" under the French. The queen of Nukuheva
walks regally beside her husband, attired in a silk dress and fancy turban hat.
Yet beneath the dress her body is imprinted with the tattooing that marks
her as a native. The cultural boundaries of the scene are complicated even further when the queen pushes aside the clothing of an old sailor and gazes in admiration at his similarly tattooed body (13–14). Within the rest of the narrative, Melville creates other characters that question cultural boundaries.

The most interesting transgressive representation is that of the anomalous
character Marnoo, who, unlike the rest of the Typees, is free to roam through
antagonistic tribes and communicate with the Europeans, and who speaks
colonial languages (French and English). Marnoo's acquisition of Western
culture clearly questions the traditional boundaries between civilized intellect and savage simplicity. Marnoo resists being classified as barbaric, simple,
or noble. But the racial ambiguity posed by this character is also explained
and thus settled in terms that reinforce racial binaries. Marnoo not only acts
differently from the natives, but looks different as well. He is a "Polynesian
Apollo" whose features remind the narrator of "an antique bust. But the marble repose of art [is] supplied by a warmth and liveliness of expression only to
be seen in the South Sea Islander under the most favorable developments of
nature" (131). Marnoo's uniqueness becomes the result of the fortuitous workings of culture over nature, of civilizing the savage. Yet soon we see that culture is identified in purely ethnological terms: "The natural quickness of the
savage had been wonderfully improved by his intercourse with the white
man" (136). Melville represents Marnoo as a singular character that questions stereotypes, but also simultaneously manages to use the language of
racial distinction to keep separate the savage and the civilized.

Although the intelligent and thinking native posed a problem for the easy
demarcation between the cognitive Westerner and the instinctive islander,
the Westerner who had chosen to live forever with the islanders (and with
no intention of proselytizing) was a more immediate threat to the idea of a
hegemonic Euro-American racial identity. The Westerner turned Other questioned what Edward Said has called the proprietary concept of culture that
"designates a boundary by which the concepts of what is extrinsic or intrin-
sic to the culture come into forceful play."[37] Such a person had given up access to culture and had thus repudiated the racial Manichaean ideology so

essential to colonialism. Melville found it increasingly difficult to accept without censure the lives of such people. We are introduced to one of these people at the end of *Typee*. Possibly as a result of pressure from his publisher, Melville appended to the narrative of his stay among the Typees "The Story of Toby: A Sequel to 'Typee.'" The ostensible purpose of the sequel is to provide a natural ending to the dramatic suspense about the whereabouts of Toby. But the sequel might well have been titled "The Moral of Jimmy: The Results of Savagery." Toby finds his way ashore partly with the help of Jimmy, an old sailor who lives with the islanders, has Marquesan wives, and acts as a translator between the French and the natives. The sequel details the treachery of Jimmy: Jimmy deceives Toby into thinking that the natives will fetch Tommo, plies him with a local liqueur, and cheats him of all his money. Such, it is implied, can only be expected from this "grizzled sailor" who lives a "devil-may-care life in the household of Mowanna the king," who is a "royal favorite, and [has] a good deal to say in his master's councils" (247).

Whatever Melville's motives may have been to write about racial transgression in *Typee*, he nonetheless continued to be troubled by such situations in *Omoo* and *Mardi*. In *Omoo* the Westerner turned savage presents a more threatening and destabilizing aspect. At the bay of Hannamanoo the crew of *Julia* is met by a delegation of islanders and the unnamed white man who shocks the narrator. The lone white is

> a renegado from Christendom and humanity a white man, in the South Sea girdle, and tattooed in the face. A broad blue band stretched across his face from ear to ear.... Some of us gazed upon this man with a feeling akin to horror, no ways abated when informed that he had voluntarily submitted to this embellishment of his countenance. What an impress! Far worse than Cain's.[38]

Tommo's desire to escape from Typee was precipitated not by his confirmation of cannibalism in the valley but by his fear of being tattooed by the zealous artist. Despite his reflections on the felicity of the islanders' lifestyle, Tommo could not submit to tattooing, the permanent visible impress of the Other on his whiteness. In *Omoo* the white sailor who has willingly submitted to tattooing and is therefore permanently inscribed by the native culture is profoundly disturbing. His presence questions the assumed superiority of Euro-American culture. However, the narrative solves this crisis by unambiguously valorizing racial and cultural hierarchies. We should not be surprised at Melville's censure of the sailor as a renegade "Christian." Melville, after all, did not question the ethics of the missionary enterprise, only its poor practical application.[39] But why is the sailor a renegade from "Christendom and humanity"? Are the islanders somehow less human than their Western counterparts? In provoking such a question, the text not only maintains cultural boundaries but also reflects a nineteenth-century anxiety about the status of the civilized Western subject. Thus the narrator, using a naturalistic logic, argues that only the most victimized could live happily with the savages. The anachronistic sailor is an unfortunate orphan who escaped the parish workhouse where he was scorned by all. "It is just this sort of men," the narrator surmises, "uncared for by a single soul, without ties, reckless, and impatient of the restraints of civilization, who are occasionally found quite at home upon the savage islands of the Pacific" (Omoo, 354).

The urgent political and philosophical questions posed by colonial ideology in Typee and Omoo might well have forced Melville to abandon all reference to particular historical situations and turn to philosophical and abstract narrative in Mardi—but Mardi continues to raise the political issues of Typee and Omoo. The hero of Mardi is a Prospero-like figure, unwillingly crowned king of the islanders; he is also the figure of colonial fantasy, the bearer of culture, rescuer of beauty (here symbolized by Yillah, a native beauty who mysteriously disappears). In fact, in this seemingly apolitical text, transgressive situations are more forcefully recuperated within Euro-American colonial hierarchies. Such is the case with the natives Samoa and Annatoo, who are in sole charge of the Parki after the crew's mutiny and murder of the captain. Even though there is no evidence to suggest Samoa and Annatoo's complicity with the mutineers, Melville, interestingly enough, focuses on the treachery and potential savagery of this couple. What is at issue is the act of appropriation by which the natives have assumed command, a situation that threatens the power relations between the whites and the natives.

Samoa is a native of the Navigator Islands, and Annatoo is a native of a "far-off anonymous island to the westward."[40] Although the couple is differentiated from the "half-breeds" who conducted the mutiny and who are "notorious for their unscrupulous villainy," they still present a threat to the narrator (729). Melville dramatizes this threat through a series of subversions of cultural and gender roles. The first appearance of Samoa suggests that the islander has acquired a fierce aspect because he has changed his attire, and therefore his character, by appropriating the signifiers of other cultures. Unlike Marheyo in Typee, who looks simply laughable as he wears Tommo's dirty shoes, Samoa, veritable captain of the Parki, looks dangerous: "He was a tall, dark Islander, a very devil to behold, theatrically arrayed in kilt and turban.... His neck was jingling with strings of beads" (726). Samoa and Annatoo resist being racially classified because they are given the agency to choose their own signifiers. Indeed, as they try on the clothing of the former crew, they are disdainful of the captain's clothes.

In an almost complete reversal of the dichotomy between Eurocentric individualism and native emphasis on community (a dichotomy that was used, as we have noted, to dispossess North American Indians), Annatoo appears as the archetypal individualist, assuming and demanding her rights to the ship's goods. In Annatoo Melville creates an anomalous character, one who is native and woman but not disempowered. But if Annatoo is strong and imposing, it is also made clear that the text invites us to read her as an aberrant woman. The narrative seems almost obsessively focused on the gendering of Annatoo. Samoa falls in love with Annatoo after her "first virgin bloom had departed, leaving nothing but a lusty frame and a lustier soul" (728). She is "sinewy of limb, and neither young, comely, nor amiable [and] exceedingly distasteful in my eyes. Besides, she was a tigress.... It was indispensable that she should at once be brought under prudent subjection; and made to know, once for all, that though conjugally a rebel, she must be nautically submissive" (750–51). Annatoo upsets both traditional gender construction and colonial relations that rely on such gender constructions. If, as George Mosse suggests, in modern European thought nation is perceived as exclusively male, Edward Said has shown how the colonized Orient was viewed as female territory ready for conquest.[41] The representation of Annatoo as the obverse of colonial fantasy is so powerful that simultaneous attempts to maintain a racial demarcation seem wishful. "Instances were known to me of half-civilized beings, like Samoa, forming part of the crews of ships in these seas, rising suddenly upon their white shipmates, and murdering them, for the sake of the wretched ship" (750). The narrative employs the familiar rhetoric of "us" and "them," "civilized" and "savage," in order to contain the power disruption occasioned by Samoa and Annatoo.

Melville's implications in the hierarchies of colonial discourse in his works of the South Seas and the narrative strategies of managing the native threat reveal the cultural significance of internal colonization and empire building to the literary imagination. This does not mean that Melville's texts were hopelessly captured by an overarching ideology that they could only replicate. My analysis here, in fact, has suggested how at several points Melville's texts do resist midnineteenth-century ideologies of racial and colonial thinking. Whereas Emerson confidently declared, "Cold and sea will train an imperial Saxon race ... All the bloods it shall absorb and domineer," Melville explored the consequences of such attempts at domination.[42] Yet to claim that

Melville's texts enact complete and absolute ruptures from colonial ideology would be to deny the very obvious traces of cultural colonialism in the texts.

Addressing the question of degrees of resistance, Foucault asks, "Are there no great radical ruptures ... Occasionally, yes. But more often one is dealing with mobile and transitory points of resistance."[43] What Foucault's analyses constantly reiterate is that there is no absolute resistance or absolute power. But to move from this formulation to the idea that power and resistance are fundamentally the same is to trivialize the issues.[44] Hegemonic constructions do exist. Too often, however, critics have seized Foucault's arguments to collapse all particular, historical distinctions between discourses of power and resistance, and to maintain an ahistorical belief in universal diffusion of power or the inherently subversive nature of all literature. Indeed, the current danger in postcolonial studies heavily influenced by Foucault is, as Ella Shohat has perceptively articulated, the fetishization of "hybridity," of universally calling attention to the "mutual imbrication" of center and periphery and the acceptance and privileging of such moves within academia. Simply celebrating hybridity without calling attention to questions of hegemony, Shohat suggests, "runs the risk of appearing to sanctify the fait accompli of colonial violence."[45] The violent traces of colonial ideology in Melville's texts are evident and need vigilant examination, just as do the resistances embodied in the representation of shifting racial boundaries.

Notes

1. Michael Rogin, *Subversive Genealogy: The Politics and Art of Herman Melville* (New York: Knopf, 1983), 45.

2. William Cullen Bryant, "The Prairie," in *The Norton Anthology of American Literature*, 3d ed. (New York: Norton, 1989), 1:896, lines 90, 86.

3. Henry David Thoreau, *Walden*, in *Walden and Civil Disobedience*, ed. Owen Thomas (New York: Norton, 1966), 23.

4. Drinnon and Slotkin both provide historical evidence to substantiate the mythology of conquest. Drinnon traces the continuity between the Puritans' view of the Indians as embodiments of instinct and sexuality and similar views of other races, culminating in the "Indianization" of the Vietnamese in the Vietnam war; see Robert Drinnon, *Facing West: The Metaphysics of Indian Hating and Empire Building* (Minneapolis: University of Minnesota Press, 1980). Slotkin examines the persistence of the Last Stand motif as developed around the figure of General Custer, and its relation to the definition of the frontier as an environment to be subdued; see Richard Slotkin, *The Fatal Environment: The Myth of the Frontier in the Age of Industrialization, 1800–1890* (New York: Atheneum, 1985). Curiously, neither author deals with *Typee, Omoo*, or *Mardi*. Drinnon sees Melville as one of the few counterculture figures, but he focuses mainly on *Confidence Man*.

5. David S. Shields, *Oracles of Empire: Poetry, Politics and Commerce in British America, 1690–1750* (Chicago: University of Chicago Press, 1990), 20.

6. Quoted in Reginald Horsman, *Race and Manifest Destiny: The Origins of American Racial Anglo-Saxonism* (Cambridge, Mass.: Harvard University Press, 1981), 87; emphasis in the original.

7. Wai-chee Dimock, *Empire for Liberty: Melville and the Poetics of Individualism* (Princeton: Princeton University Press, 1989), 9. In contrast to Dimock, Lawrence E. Buell views nineteenth-century U.S. literature as postcolonial. Buell suggests that Melville's writings reflect a postcolonial anxiety and consciousness of two audiences (the colonial and the native) similar to that of writers like Ngugi wa Thiong'O (228). Persuasive as this thesis is, it is problematic in that it minimizes the importance of the internal colonization of minorities in the United States. See Lawrence E. Buell, "Melville and American Decolonization," *American Literature* 64, no. 2 (June 1992): 215–38.

8. Greg Dening points out that although the first Europeans to invade the Marquesas Islands were the Spaniards in 1595, their settlement was brief and the islands were not invaded again until Cook's voyage; see Greg Dening, *Islands and Beaches: Discourse on a Silent Land, Marquesas 1774–1890* (Honolulu: University Press of Hawaii, 1980), 11, 16. I have relied on Dening's study for much of my information about the Marquesas.

9. See Walter T. Herbert Jr., *Marquesan Encounters: Melville and the Meaning of Civilization* (Cambridge, Mass.: Harvard University Press, 1980), 79.

10. During the nineteenth century, the population of the Marquesas Islands fell from an estimated 100,000 at its height to 4,865 in 1882; see ibid., 19.

11. Cited in Henry Louis Gates, "Critical Remarks," in David Theo Goldberg, ed., *Anatomy of Racism* (Minneapolis: University of Minnesota Press, 1990), 328.

12. Cited in Lucius Outlaw, "Toward a Critical Theory of Race," in Goldberg, ed., *Anatomy of Racism*, 63.

13. Charles Caldwell, *Thoughts on the Original Unity of the Human Race* (New York, 1830), 134–35; cited in Horsman, *Race and Manifest Destiny*, 119–20. Interest in the relationship between race and mental ability continued well into the end of the century. Melville himself was the subject of such a study by Havelock Ellis, who wished to prove the importance of ancestry for creative genius. Ellis wrote to Melville, "I am making some investigations into the ancestry of distinguished English and American poets and imaginative writers, with reference to the question of race. Will you kindly tell me to what races you trace yourself" (Ellis to Herman Melville, July 20, 1890, in *The Writings of Herman Melville: Correspondence*, ed. Lynn Horth [Evanston and Chicago: Northwestern University Press and The Newberry Library, 1993], 764).

14. Homi K. Bhabha, "Signs Taken for Wonders: Questions of Ambivalence and Authority under a Tree outside Delhi, May 1817," in Henry Louis Gates, ed., *"Race," Writing and Difference* (Chicago: University of Chicago Press, 1986), 172; emphasis in the original.

15. Michel Foucault, *The History of Sexuality*, trans. Robert Hurley (New York: Random House, 1980), 1:139–41.

16. Michel Foucault, *Power/Knowledge: Selected Interviews and Other Writings, 1972–1977*, trans. Colin Gordon et al. (New York: Pantheon, 1972), 98, 119.

17. In *Typee*, Melville gives the period of stay as four months. Charles Anderson, *Melville and the South Seas* (New York: Columbia University Press, 1949), 191–94, has determined the stay to be much shorter. Although grounded in racist assumptions, Anderson's book is useful for biographical verification and an analysis of Melville's reliance on previous books on the Marquesas.

18. Herman Melville, *Typee* (New York: Airmont, 1965), 22–23. Hereafter page references to *Typee* will be cited parenthetically in the text.

19. Quoted in Dimock, *Empire for Liberty*, 33. Dimock also shows how within American political discourse personhood and proprietorship were strategically equated (32).

20. Frantz Fanon, *The Wretched of the Earth* (New York: Grove Press, 1968), 41.

21. Michael Berthold examines *Typee* in the tradition of American captivity narratives. Puritan captivity narratives were "exemplary tales of piety and providence." With Cotton

Mather they became more propagandistic and by the early nineteenth century were sensationalized. These narratives were also popular in Melville's time. Reprints of Puritan and colonial captivity narratives continued to appear in the 1860s. See Michael Berthold, "'Portentous Somethings': Melville's *Typee* and the Language of Captivity," *New England Quarterly* 60 (1987): 549–67.

22. Walter Herbert's *Marquesan Encounters* provides an excellent political and historical background for *Typee*. Herbert examines the accounts of three widely different types of people who came to the Marquesas: Captain Porter, Reverend Charles Stewart, and Herman Melville. Analyzing the various types of Westerners who visited the islands, he situates Melville as a beachcomber whose ambiguous social status creates fruitful ambivalences in the text. Herbert studies Melville's attitudes to the Marquesans mainly by focusing on the characterization of Tommo and his changing views of the islanders. Thus he finds Melville's account emphasizes the anxieties upon encountering another race more than self-affirmation (158). Herbert also isolates a few cases (the treatments of missionaries, for example) where Melville does not follow the radical implications of his criticism of colonization (177).

23. Edward S. Grejda, *The Common Continent of Men: Racial Equality in the Writings of Herman Melville* (New York: Kennikat, 1974), 8.

24. Newton Arvin, *Herman Melville* (New York: William Sloane, 1950), 12; Milton R. Stern, "Typee," in Milton R. Stern, ed., *Critical Essays on Herman Melville's "Typee"* (Boston: G. K. Hall, 1982), 137; H. Bruce Franklin, "Melville in a World of Pagan Gods," in Milton R. Stern, ed., *Critical Essays on Herman Melville's "Typee,"* 166; Toni H. Oliviero, "Ambiguous Utopia: Savagery and Civilization in *Typee* and *Omoo*," *Modern Language Studies* 13 (1983): 42. See also Robert Abrams, "*Typee* and *Omoo*: Herman Melville and the Ungraspable Phantom of Identity," *Arizona Quarterly* 31 (1975): 33–50. Abrams sees the two texts as records of Melville's "growing awareness of the fundamental elasticity and mutability of his so-called 'identity'" (35).

25. The full title of the U.S. edition was *Typee: A Peep at Polynesian Life. During a Four Months' Residence in a Valley of the Marquesas with Notices of the French Occupation of Tahiti and the Provisional Cession of the Sandwich Islands to Lord Paulet.*

26. Herman Melville to John Murray, July 15, 1846, in *The Writings of Herman Melville: Correspondence*, 57.

27. Mitchell Breitwieser's study is the only one that reads *Typee* through the lens of colonialism. Breitwieser, however, maintains a definite separation between Melville and the narrator Tommo, suggesting that Melville was in fact exposing Tommo's ethnocentrism. I do not make the separation because I believe that the "real" author is a construct (revealed through letters, diaries, and so forth, which are simply different texts) and because I am dealing with the "author" or authorial voice as it emerges in the text. Further, my analysis of the aesthetic-ideological structure of the text makes it impossible to settle the question of intentionality versus irony. Who is responsible for the structure? The author or narrator? We cannot be sure. See Mitchell Breitwieser, "False Sympathy in Melville's *Typee*," *American Quarterly* 34 (1982): 396–417.

28. Herman Melville, *Moby Dick* (New York: Bantam, 1967), 72.

29. Dimock, *Empire for Liberty*, 115.

30. Melville, *Moby Dick*, 165.

31. Aijaz Ahmad points out that by "assembling a monstrous machinery of descriptions ... colonial discourse was able to classify and ideologically master the colonial subject, enabling itself to transform the descriptively verifiable multiplicity and difference into ideologically felt hierarchy of value"; see Aijaz Ahmad, "Jameson's Rhetoric of Otherness and 'National Allegory,'" *Social Text* 15 (Fall 1986): 6.

32. For specific analysis of the ways of maintaining cultural superiority and domination over the Marquesans, see Dening, *Islands and Beaches*, 125–28.

33. Slotkin, *The Fatal Environment*, 561.

34. Quoted in Carolyn Karcher, *Shadow over the Promised Land: Race and Violence in Herman Melville's America* (Baton Rouge: Louisiana State University Press, 1980), 25–26.

35. Ibid., 2.

36. Many writers used the plight of the almost-white woman to dramatize the cruelty of the slave system. Harriet Beecher Stowe took care to make her refined mulatto slave, Eliza, almost white. Post-reconstruction black writers such as Frances Harper used the almost-white figure to stress Southern slave cruelty and also to affirm black identity by showing the importance of choosing blackness.

37. Edward Said, *The World, the Text, and the Critic* (Cambridge, Mass.: Harvard University Press, 1983), 9.

38. Herman Melville, *Omoo*, in *Typee, Omoo, Mardi* (New York: Library of America, 1982), 353.

39. Walter Herbert notes that "Melville ... focuses his attack on targets that his readers would readily comprehend, on the moral failures of individual missionaries and on their mismanagement of an enterprise he asserts in principle to be glorious" (Herbert, *Marquesan Encounters*, 177).

40. Herman Melville, *Mardi*, in *Typee, Omoo, Mardi*, 728. Hereafter page references to *Mardi* will be cited parenthetically in the text.

41. See George L. Mosse, *Nationalism and Sexuality: Middle-Class Morality and Sexual Norms in Modern Europe* (Madison: University of Wisconsin Press, 1985), 1–3; and Edward Said, *Orientalism* (New York: Random House, 1978), 207.

42. Ralph Waldo Emerson, "Fate," in *The Conduct of Life* (Boston: Houghton Mifflin, 1904), 32.

43. Foucault, *The History of Sexuality*, 1:96.

44. Edward Said's criticism of Foucault hinges on the latter's apparent lack of distinction between power and resistance. Said writes, "If power oppresses and controls and manipulates, then everything that resists it is not morally equal to power. Resistance cannot equally be an adversarial alternative to power and a dependent function of it, except in some metaphysical, ultimately trivial sense" (*The World, the Text, and the Critic*, 246).

45. Ella Shohat, "Notes on the 'Post-Colonial,'" *Social Text* 31/32 (1992): 108–9.

Part II
A Language Poised against Death

5

Post-Foucauldian Criticism: Government, Death, Mimesis

Simon During

Foucault and literature. It seems an obvious enough conjunction. After all, nowhere in Foucault's writings do literary texts and examples completely fall out of sight, and for a short period they form its core. In broad terms, one can classify his remarks and essays on literature under four headings: first, the literary theory that underpins *Madness and Civilization*, the book on Roussel, and the essays on transgression; second, the literary history that lies embedded in those transgressive essays; third, his description of the uses to which literary realism was put in the production of the docile society; and, last, a not very fully developed description of literary criticism both as a particular manipulation of the author effect and as a mode of modern power. Yet Foucault rarely deals with literature itself as a category or an institution, for good reasons: in both his archaeological and genealogical work he is skeptical about the continuity, specificity, and abstraction implied by a topos like the "institution of literature." In this chapter, I want to comment on two post-Foucauldian books, both of which share—and elaborate on—Foucault's skepticism: Ian Hunter's *Culture and Government* and Stephen Greenblatt's *Shakespearean Negotiations*. Most of all, I want to use Hunter's and Greenblatt's works to begin to show what a genealogy of literature might look like. I also explore the possibilities, and limits, of a mode of analysis that does not presuppose concepts such as "representation" and "mimesis." For, as Foucault's career helps demonstrate, if it is becoming harder to accept the value and autonomy of

literature today, this is largely a result of its central strut—representation—
being so strongly contested not just analytically but politically. This is not to
say, however, that representation can be avoided as an analytic category.

Literature as Government

Of the compartments into which I have divided Foucault's contribution to
literary studies, the least explored has been the relation between literary criticism and modern power. But recently Ian Hunter, in his important if somewhat unrecognized book, has offered a radical revision of the whole academic literary critical project by arguing that it must be viewed as an arm of
modern power. *Culture and Government*, then, serves as a convenient starting
point for my analysis of the directions that literary studies after Foucault are
taking. Hunter's is a revisionist thesis: it is positioned against the cultural
studies movement inaugurated by Raymond Williams, which recorded the
story of criticism's "social mission." Hunter argues that the history of literary
criticism as taught in higher education ought not be regarded as a chain of
ideas and influences leading from Coleridge and Schiller, through Matthew
Arnold and I. A. Richards, to Leavis and the American New Critics.[1] He does
not tell the story of the emergence of "English" as a sustained bourgeois rejection of the alienations and divisions caused by industrialization and "mass
culture," a rejection whose actual effect, so Williams claimed, was to reproduce and legitimate depoliticized cultural values. For Hunter, expanding on
a Foucauldian line of analysis, literary education in England first appears in
the "governmental apparatus" whose object was the "moral and physical condition of the population," early in the nineteenth century. It does so at a specific
moment, one in which relations between various pedagogical institutions
were realigned. He argues that under the guidance of both the proto-welfarist
bureaucrats like James Kay-Shuttleworth, who administered the state's entry
into popular education from the 1830s on, and contemporary, professional
educationalists like David Stow, especially concerned with establishing the
spatial arrangement of schools, the rather progressive pedagogy previously
attached to some Sunday schools came to dominate the educational apparatus. In this move, state education replaced monitorial techniques by procedures that invited pupils to express themselves.

According to Hunter, it was only early in the twentieth century that tertiary literary education entered this history, in order to provide mass education with teachers and inspectors who could function as ethical exemplars and
invigilators. At that point so-called romantic criticism was called upon to

teach the teachers. For Hunter, Friedrich Schiller founds the critical tradition embodied in Britain by Arnold, and is a "romantic." Before the early twentieth century, Hunter believes, advanced critical discourse had not formed part of the transactions between culture and the state at all. That discourse's entry into pedagogy was made possible because of "romantic" criticism's claim that literary texts cannot be translated into propositions: romantic criticism produced an aesthetic, closely connected to Kant, for which literature was neither essentially rhetorical nor essentially representational. Reading literature becomes less a matter of acquiring or parroting certain beliefs, or of acquiring techniques of persuasion or expression, than of forming an "aesthetico-ethical" self, that is, a self that is harmonious and reconciled. Literary pedagogy controls by offering the promise of individual fulfillment or completion. Hunter also claims that, as criticism becomes firmly established in the academy, it is contested by literary theory, which, on the face of it, is neither humanist nor ethical. He argues that theory is the arm of the human sciences within advanced literary studies. For him, however, the differences between theory and criticism can be overvalued. The future-directedness of literary theory, the way that theory recovers a textual "unconscious," whether mythic, structural, or political, shares literary criticism's drive toward reconciliation. This is true even if theory aims at the fulfillment of a less tangible object—not, like criticism, individual selves grouped together as "man" but, instead, the mythic, structural, or political "subject" of writing.

What is refreshing and important about Hunter's account is that it begins to fulfill Foucault's advice to historians to work "from the bottom up" (from the layout of schools, for instance) so that the Marxian cultural studies approach now does indeed appear idealist. Hunter's work also allows us to see that recent literary theory is, at least in part, a moment in a more generalized intellectual framework—even if his appeal to the human sciences seems quite inadequate to deal with Derrida's deconstruction, arguably at the very center of current "literary theory." Yet his implicit claim to speak from outside history leads Hunter's account into difficulties, just as it undercuts Foucault's own archaeology. The story that he tells does not include his own project. Hunter cannot quite take account of his own double agenda, his writing simultaneously a disenchanted, truth-telling work and a polemical and corrective one. It is corrective in that, for Hunter, Schiller and Arnold were wrong because they thought that they were producing better selves while they were "really," far in the future, going to produce more administrable selves; the cultural studies movement is wrong in that it ignores the governmental genealogy of criticism; literary theorists are wrong insofar as they think that they are accounting for signification and its effects whereas they are in fact bringing to light "unsaid" conditions of possibility that can never be tightly enough connected to what these conditions are designed to explain. Yet a genealogy like Hunter's is truth-telling in that, for it, what there is is just what there is, and what has been said is just what has been said, so that *Culture and Government* supposes no foundational truth to place against Schiller, Leavis, Williams, and so on. Unlike Foucault, Hunter does not strategically ally himself with those who have little access to what power can offer. Hunter's desire to speak from a place at which the true story of institutionalized literary studies can be told (therefore, a place not inscribed by those studies or their objects) often seems to organize and bend the processes of historical narration, as well as to permit the discounting of crucial theoretical/methodological categories. Of these last the most telling are exchange, resistance, and inscription itself—terms around which much current criticism move. So it is worth enumerating certain historical and theoretical problems and difficulties that follow from Hunter's approach in more detail: here the two sides of the Foucauldian aftermath become clearest.

As far as history is concerned, Hunter's account finds a point of origin in the Sunday schools. Like most historians of education, he regards them as precursors of popular education, though, unlike the Marxists, he does not believe that they simply imposed an ideology on their students. Rather, they provided the framework for certain disciplinary practices, not at all against the will of the parents and pupils who were their clients. Nonetheless, many early connections between schooling and the state escape Hunter's attention. To begin with, the Sunday schools were, of course, not secular—they taught the Bible (which also legitimated their stress on literacy, "respectability," "cleanliness," and so on)—and they stood against both the older "charity schools" and the monitorial schools. Charity schools were regarded as contaminated by archaic values of patronage and servitude—most notoriously by William Cobbett, but ever since Bernard Mandeville in the early eighteenth century. In their turn, monitorial schools were widely criticized by liberals for their rigidity and lack of individual attention. These divisions within primary education were partly caused by the scarcity of money and teachers. Monitors were the cheapest way to educate pupils en masse (Andrew Bell's famous system was developed in India); Sunday schools, relying on volunteers, were somewhat less exposed to economic constraint. Most important, the divisions in primary education were organized around debates about class and religion. The Sunday school movement was primarily a dissenting movement, unlike the older charity schools that were under Anglican control and in which places were limited and relatively expensive. As Sunday schools became increasingly popular, they were subject to the complaint that they would educate their pupils "above their station." Such complaints, in fact, helped orchestrate arguments against the state's playing any part at all in the population's education. It is generally agreed that the British state intervened in education in the late 1840s quite reluctantly, by establishing pupil-teacher training schemes and by setting minimum standards for staff, equipment, and discipline in schools that wanted to receive funds. It did so mainly to prevent crippling struggles between the various religious denominations as to who was to control education at a time when satisfying proletarian demand for education made good political and administrative sense. This sense, of course, belongs to Foucault's biopower. An educated work force was thought to be more productive than an illiterate one. It was also less likely to be riotous or revolutionary.[2]

Thus, as the state began increasingly to encroach upon primary education it confronted the questions of how to move education from under the wing of religion, and how to avoid imposing class identities on pupils. The main strategy was to minimize the objectives that each student was to attain. Kay-Shuttleworth spelled these out as the ability to read a newspaper, to write a correctly spelled letter, to add up a bill, and to follow a sermon.[3] But during the 1850s and 1860s, lobby groups were formed that aimed to provide *every* child with education, and the restricted nature of elementary education became increasingly apparent. At this point an older discursive formation was revitalized—one that gradually filtered into the training manuals for teachers. This older discourse was that of the late-eighteenth-century so-called followers of Rousseau, in particular Thomas Day (author of *Sandford and Merton*, which appeared throughout the 1780s) and Richard and Maria Edgeworth, who, around the same time, had begun to promulgate for a "Rousseauistic" elementary education in their *Practical Education*.[4] The latter book is worth dwelling on, because it clearly indicates the terms in which the expansion of education was to be articulated. It begins with a chapter on toys that emphasizes the importance of "play" for learning. The Edgeworths attack those frivolous toys that do not instruct on the grounds that toys that both please and instruct could provide a bridge across which progressive pedagogy could move from domestic space to the schoolroom. (The vogue for "useful" toys had a decisive effect on the young Percy Shelley, for instance.) *Practical Education* also contains a careful account of how language and literature ought to be taught—asserting that reading and literature are central to modern self-formation because they develop sympathy and allow moral ideas to be associated with pleasure. For the Edgeworths, literature is important because it manages ideas and actions almost invisibly, consisting as it does of ordered—not "mad"— ideas and imitable representations of acts. It provided the means for a "true" or "natural" self to be expressed—one that appeared to be uncontaminated by doctrinal or class prejudices.

So reading was privileged over rhetoric, criticism, or grammar, and the management of children's reading becomes of acute importance. This emphasis will culminate in the value given to "close reading" in the twentieth century. The Edgeworths insist that children should not be exposed to gothic horror stories, only to moral texts like *The Robbers*, a preromantic and humanist play by the same Schiller whom Hunter regards as irrelevant to the history of infant pedagogy. They go so far as to include instances of children's written response to poetry—not directly (as in I. A. Richards's *Practical Criticism*, to take the most famous later example) but via the pupils' descriptions of nature after having read a poem. Like Richards and like Arnold in his *Reports on Elementary Schools* more than half a century later, who both also print students' writing, they prefer those exercises in which the students have *not* been "habituated to the poetic trade."[5] To increase "understanding," careful written expositions of difficult texts may be offered to pupils, but in forming children's minds, the human, invigilating presence is to be preferred. Writing itself is not a central element of "practical education" because that education aims at forming a way of being rather than a set of techniques of which literacy is merely one. When pupils *do* write, it is to express themselves, a practice that is permitted because, having read morally and psychologically correct books, their self-expression will be both original and imitative—where, of course, "imitative" no longer means the rote copying of the older "scholastic" or monitorial educational programs.

Ian Hunter neglects the impact of writings like the Edgeworths' on state pedagogy, especially as part of the resistance to the claim that mass education would lead to widespread unsatisfied wants. He also neglects the "cultural hygiene" movement.[6] Instead, he concentrates on David Stow's discussion of the school playground, seemingly because the state first took responsibility for infant pedagogy in England (in 1833) by providing grants for the building of schoolhouses. Were he directly to face the importance of both "Rousseauistic" education theory and the "cultural hygiene" movement, then the larger thrust of his work would falter, because the classical or "cultural critical" lineage from Schiller and Coleridge, through Arnold and Leavis, would *not* be wholly removed even from pioneers of state education like Stow. Indeed, Arnold's work on education is itself written in a very practical and immediate spirit against the economistic and laissez-faire values expressed in Robert Lowe's "Revised Code" legislation of 1862, which proposed minimal standards for mass education in the interests of the employers as against that of the population at large. Lowe's legislation prevented schools from receiving state grants except to teach the three Rs (reading, writing, and arithmetic), an act that Arnold considered to disadvantage both poor individuals and the national culture as a whole. In light of all this, we can say, against Hunter, that the "high" and the "low," the theoretical and the practical, become moments of a single historical, if fractured and contested, trajectory shared by the Edgeworths, Stow, Kay-Shuttleworth, Arnold, and, finally, Leavis. They do so within a larger formation articulated in broad terms by Rousseau, within which the administrative practices of popular education cannot easily be granted causal and narrative priority over the theorists or critics in the story of the unfolding of literary pedagogy.

There is a strong case to think about these matters in still larger terms. Since the Renaissance, figures such as Bacon, Hobbes, Locke, Mandeville, and Hume all write in explicit and tedious rejection of scholasticism and the *trivium* at the same time as, more or less implicitly, they write outside of religion. The paralogism of modern pedagogy from the seventeenth century is installed in this double gesture: how to teach (and assume secular authority) *against* scholastic and religious authority. How to provide pupils with individual autonomy while they are also being situated within received social norms? How to have them imitate spontaneously that which they are taught? The problem this large paralogism bequeaths to the sociological historian is, How to judge where continuities, discontinuities, grafts, and differences begin and end within it? For historians of the "discipline" of English studies, there can be no absolute choice between the analytic methods of Foucault and the post-Leavisite cultural studies that Foucault's work is positioned against by a writer like Hunter. It is more a matter of testing the ways in which each invoke the larger problematization of modern pedagogy and deal with the archival evidence of its detailed and material historical itinerary. What Hunter's work does show, however, is how difficult it is, today, simply to affirm the *progressivist* discourse of, say, Raymond Williams.

The second main difficulty with Ian Hunter's application of Foucault is that it discounts the fact that literature entered the pedagogical institutions precisely because it cannot be appropriated for the purposes of government. It is especially tempting to neglect the resistance that literature offers to government because, first, however much education leads to docility, by and large the proletariat desired it (which the Marxists tend to forget). Throughout the nineteenth century, literature in particular was widely studied by working-class, dissenting, and petit bourgeois adults who had no chance to go to university in noncertifying institutions such as the Mechanics Institutes, and in informal reading groups like the widespread "Literary Societies." The resistance that literature can offer government is also easy to ignore because, later, literary studies, and the "sympathy" and "imagination" that they were supposed to nurture, were deemed appropriate for (semi)professional careers in civil and imperial administration. Nevertheless, since the early nineteenth century much writing—including journalism—had allied itself with madness, death, drugs, crime, transgression, and the signifier, against the more or less officially sanctioned values embodied in literary pedagogy. This has led to the paradox around which teaching modernist writing has turned, a sharper, if more local, version of the larger problematic involved in teaching autonomy and spontaneity. How to maintain subversion within the academy? How to teach "life" in the classroom? Even today students who read, for instance, Shelley's "Julian and Maddalo," *Les Fleurs du mal*, "Howl," *Women in Love*, *The Trial*, *Good Morning Midnight*, *The Man Who Loved Children*, *Junky*, *Story of the Eye*, even *Madame Bovary* and *The Wings of the Dove*, may be shaped by these texts in ways that literary critical techniques of reading (including deconstruction) do not touch. To teach English at a tertiary level today, as the Arnoldian heritage declines, may be to manage the transformation of the desire to read literature into the ability to write (the shifting modes of) criticism/theory. Yet it is always too soon to concede that only the second involves a practice on the self. To put it this way is to gesture at a hidden essentialism that it is easy to take from Foucault's later work. For him, of course, selves, constituted by various "ethical substances" are formed, in the modern world, largely by "governmentalities." However useful it may be, such a formulation makes it too easy to assume that there *are* substances to be shaped into unified "selves." But an "ethical substance" simply consists of utterances, actions, thoughts, desires, modes of deportment, and so on: it is on *these* that education acts. Not only may thoughts, practices, and desires work against each other, but a single individual may be shaped by different discourses, different practices, different objects, each of which can exist in some tension to another internalized, and shaping, object. On occasions, Foucault himself was more than capable of recognizing this: let us emphasize again that for him history is to be written as much from the resistance out as from the bottom up.

Literature, then, is not able to be absorbed into the process of government as easily as Hunter supposes. Literary studies do not simply belong to the apparatuses that have produced the docile society, though they do not stand quite outside them either. This leaves literary studies with the question of how to account for their own relations to modern power. What are the internal properties that enable literature's complex interactions with both social order and individuals? I think that we must begin to consider this question by analyzing a category — representation — that is larger than literature itself. The first reason for this is that literature has long been considered a subspecies of representation. As Derrida puts it, "If, as we have been precisely tempted to think, literature is born/dead of a relatively recent break, it is nonetheless true that the whole history of the interpretation of the arts, of letters has moved and been transformed within the diverse logical possibilities opened up by the concept of *mimesis*."[7] Traditionally at least, the notion of "representation" legitimates and suffuses that of "literature"; it permits literature to be placed both inside and outside the "real world," to escape the logic of "true discourse."[8] Thus, it allows texts their glamour, which they cast back on the real world, and their ethical potential. Even the "romantic" claim that literature ultimately transcends representational categories like beliefs and ideas takes its force from the representational paradigm. Its energy is derived from its continual negation of representation. So we can ask, What might a writing look like that was thought of neither in terms of the paradigm of representation nor as its negation?

The use of literature for government rests on representation in another sense, too. Cultural pedagogy attempted to form individuals within a unified and coherent cultural tradition, a tradition for which each individual was a placeholder, though not quite in the same way as paternity was once a placeholder for sovereignty, for instance. It did so as administrations negotiated with wider social wants and collectivities. Writers such as Matthew Arnold and George Eliot argued that the stability of representative democracy rests on a belief that norms and traditions are shared, and that each individual represents them, and thus one another. Education was required to produce and reproduce those norms and traditions, so as to form individuals who, within a range of variations, represented a single entity: the culture and its values. Individuals invisibly embody and represent the culture; the political sphere represents (groups of) individuals. In these terms one can say that the complex system, within which education, culture (including literature), and politics are interlocked, rests on an acceptance of the efficacy and validity of the notion "representation." Where that system is being contested politically, as it is today, then, of course, that notion too must be interrogated, as Heidegger first realized. Furthermore, Foucault and other literary theorists have demonstrated that representation and mimesis are essentially unstable or "delirious"

categories, having been described as "madness" from the beginning of Western thought. It is partly this very madness that makes representation so powerful a concept, and so difficult to move beyond. Finally, representation is so
powerful a category because we use it in our attempts not to let the past
die—attempts in which modern governments play their part as they maintain the cultural tradition. To say that it may be difficult to abandon representation as a tool for analyzing culture, however, is not to push aside the
kind of nonrepresentational politics and work that Foucault pioneered. Nor
is it to return to the old mode of literary studies, aimed at producing sensitive
and representative—if not wholly vigilant—citizens.

The Delirium of Mimesis

To work toward a mode of thinking about literature that is not controlled by
the concept of mimesis we must ask how mimesis, writing, and madness in-
terlock. And to ask that is to return, however briefly, and before defining
mimesis in more detail, to Plato's *Phaedrus*, where the Western delirium of
representation is established. *Phaedrus* posits two kinds of madness: worldly
and divine. Worldly madness is uninteresting, worthless; but, as Plato's Socrates
declares, divine madness was previously regarded, and should be regarded, as
a fine thing. (Plato is already telling Foucault's story of madness's secularization, its split between insanity and *la folie*.) Divine madness is the channel
through which the godly is communicated to human beings. Divinely mad
people love, express themselves in lyric poetry inspired by the Muses, foretell the future by reading signs, and perceive the world as symbolic of the
Platonic forms or essences. Against this, writing eradicates the difference between the reality with which divine madness is in closest contact, and mere
appearance. To learn from writing is to learn mechanically, to know at second hand. Readers are always passive; like paintings, writings cannot answer
questions. The shifts of the argument may seem obscure, but it seems that
Plato's fear of writing is to be understood in terms of his pedagogy, his personal and, as it were, institutional need to maintain the force of "protreptic"—the branch of rhetoric designed to persuade an audience that a teacher
was fit to teach virtue and truth. "Spoken truths," he has Socrates say, "are to
be reckoned a man's legitimate sons, primarily if they originate within himself, but to a secondary degree if what we may call their children and kindred
come to birth, as they should, in the minds of others."[9] Writing, by removing
language from the teacher's mouth, destroys the basis of protreptic, makes of

pupils bastards, whereas divine madness, solely the possession of individuals and the absolute warrant of authoritative insight, is unteachable. This leaves the teacher — the dialectician — a tiny margin in which to exercise skill: the teacher's prestige rests on a vanishing point. Of course, Plato's preference for the teacher's bodily presence over the textbook is repeated by the Edge-worths, among many others, just as the problem of "spontaneous imitation" or "taught autonomy" is foreshadowed in his attack on writing.

Nowhere in modern thought is the logic that orders these relations more clearly examined than in the first sections of Derrida's essay "Plato's Phar-macy." For Derrida, Platonic *mimesis* may be in question whenever an event is repeated, an object copied, a feeling expressed, or language is considered to hook onto the world. It is also in question whenever a cultural product is interpreted as representing a social formation, in however displaced a fashion: where, for instance, a text is read as a "symptom" of a particular sociopoliti-cal tension, or as the expression of a particular ideological contradiction.

In general, mimetic objects are either the same as, or different from, their originals. If they are the same, then the very distinction between copy and original disappears. This is to enter the dangerous world of *simulacra*: the negative version of the mimetic relation that Foucault calls "similitude" in *This Is Not a Pipe*, his own treatise on mimesis.[10] Yet the closer mimesis comes to representing the presence of an original, the more it reveals of that object's essence; thus truth as unveiling (Heidegger's *aletheia*) has already buried within it a mimetic moment. To unveil is to reveal, mimetically, the external aspect of an inner essence. Here the potential for a mimetic object not to differ from its original is inflected positively, and can found a whole aesthetic the-ory, as it does with Aristotle's *poesis*. In *This Is Not a Pipe* Foucault called this form of repetition "resemblance."[11] If the mimetic object differs from its orig-inal, then it is false, though here again a positive inflection is possible. For both neoclassicism and classic realism, art, itself untrue, can reveal the deeper truth of nature or society. In fact, the concept of "representation" is implic-itly aimed at controlling both the category of repetition (simulacra) and that of absolute singularity (and the proliferation of otherness), but it does so at the cost of falling into either basket as soon as it is analyzed and conceptual-ized — then the forms of "bad mimesis" come to light. And because under the paradigm of mimesis the world is experienced as double (split between re-ality and its representation), it also becomes harder to affirm the ontological superficiality that Foucault and the transgressive theorists find there.

Despite these complexities and difficulties, mimetic categories seem so "natural" partly because they implicitly appeal to a hierarchical view of representation. An original, standing at the apex of a little hierarchy, acts as a standard of comparison for the image that mirrors it. Yet, as Derrida points out, trust in an originality behind resemblance — trust, that is, in logos — can only occur once a threat to the origin has been articulated. Logos, the vehicle of what is "true" before or behind representation, is, paradoxically, not older than but coeval with mimesis, for the question of "truth" can only arise when there is something to be true about or toward, as well as a subject to be true for. Derrida, repeating Plato, thinks of this necessity in terms of a story about patriarchal reproduction. Logos is not simply the "father" — the secure ground of truth-in-discourse — but a "son," displaced from the origin, who has a father next to him and who speaks for the father. This logocentric structure is inhabited both by the possibility that the son *precedes* the father and by the possibility that the relation between son and father is already one of similitude. (So, as rumor has it, Charlie Chaplin can enter a Charlie Chaplin-look-alike competition — and come in third.) Again we return to the proposition that to regard a copy as more like the original than the original is to broach a nondivine madness that cannot be avoided at all times and in all places. The self-present, that to which truth corresponds, turns out, at best, to be an effect of a system of *good* mimesis in which the re-presentation (or mirror image) is simultaneously different from and the same as its presentation.

So neither self-presence nor a structure of good mimesis or of bad mimesis can be drawn out singly from the system of representation. Indeed, bad mimesis is found not just in simulacra or sheer repetition but also where the relations between the representation and its object themselves break — in the mirage of autonomy. Autonomy, the form of negative mimesis favored in modernity, can only itself be represented as the consequence of a *will* to avoid repetition as one form of bad mimesis. Here modern pedagogy itself is entrapped in the fractured logic of mimesis. Autonomy can be represented, ascribed, or imagined only by supposing that an original and its image become detached from one another, as if a mirror were to shatter just in reflecting, letting the image become an original in its own right. The force that shatters the mirror is often imaged as dangerous, allied to madness, especially as it pushes toward radical subjectivity. The young Hegel rebukes Fichte in these terms, for instance: "We have sometimes heard tell of people who went mad in their efforts to produce the pure act of will and the intellectual intuition."[12] This rush to autonomy is, of course, not always or necessarily directed toward subjectivity; it can also be traced in the doomed attempt to separate the materiality of language from its referential and reflective force — to disengage the "signifier" from the "signified." Such theory expresses the hope that if there were such a thing as a signifier apart from a signified, then language would be freed from its mimetic dependence on the world yet still, somehow, remain *language*.

Though representation as a concept is *necessarily* unstable, the forms of that instability empty out any transcendental possibilities. To put a complex matter very simply: conditions of possibility for mimesis are indescribable because such conditions are always already in a mimetic relation to that which they ground. Reflections on, or theories of, mimesis are, for that reason, flat, trivial. There is no possibility of explaining how effects of representation are produced by a signifying system — though that was the aim of certain earlier movements, most notably structuralism, which attempted to escape the mimetic paradigm. Rather, the challenge is to analyze a history of writing (in particular) *outside* that paradigm, without trying to account for "meanings" nonmimetically.

To recapitulate a little, what does Foucault, the theorist of practices of the self, of discursive formations, of truth games and power relations, have to say to students of mimesis? He attempts to drag Western thought out of the logic of mimesis as far as possible: first, by presenting discourse and other domains of representation as ordered by immanent rules, that is, as not reflecting the world; second, by insisting on their "rarity" — by insisting on the material specificity of particular *énoncés* and their channels of distribution; third, by rigorously refusing to find a given and fixed human essence reflected in cultural products; and fourth, by accepting that "representations" are also events, if events of a particular kind. More "metaphysically," he also argues that discourse enters the paradigm of representation when it attempts to organize what cannot be organized — madness, for instance; or to replace what cannot be replaced — death. By questioning the notion that history consists of large progressive movements that sweep through time and leave the past behind (such as rationalization or liberation or, even, the anxiety of influence ...), Foucault encourages us to work at the level of local relations between events.

To think of Foucault like this certainly leads to projects different from those taken up by literary critics and historians who first turned to his work. They accepted and elaborated his specific accounts of sovereign and modern power and demonstrated how that power was reflected by, or structurally enacted in, particular texts or oeuvres. For instance, the narrative voice of the Victorian realist novel, together with its impossibly neat ending, becomes an agency of panoptical vision; the carnivalesque aspect of an Elizabethan play is shown not to subvert but to prop up the power and glory of the monarch.[13] Useful and perceptive as such work may be, the approach itself knows where it is going from the very beginning and passes too confidently from history to writing. It is especially difficult to account for the specificity not just of texts and genres but of sociocultural interactions when one starts from a theory of a historical epoch and moves mimetically to examine its products, though some of the strongest new historicist criticism (such as D. A. Miller's *The Novel and the Police* or Catherine Gallagher's essay on *Our Mutual Friend*) focuses on the strategies by which literary texts distance themselves from social power flows and circuits of exchange, and by those very strategies both belong to and resist modern power.[14] Analyses that begin with a theory of society and work outward, reading the text as an expression, an allegory, or a symptom — in a word, a representation — of the society in which they were written, also leave open the question of why this should matter now. Perhaps more important, most Foucauldian accounts fail to explore fully what is at stake when analysis, buffeted between mimetic and nonmimetic paradigms, tries to work in terms of the latter with all possible rigor and force. At this point in particular Foucault's long career of historical revisionism begins to involve a reformulation of the methods by which literature has been studied.

Such a project, then, would examine the technologies in which images and writings (as rare *énoncés*) are produced; the circuits through which they are transmitted; their relation to suffering, pleasure, power, seduction, and order; the cultural, social, and legal uses of and constraints on their circulation; the ever-present possibilities and effects of misfirings and loop mechanisms; and their complex effects on individual lives, which are not simply ethical or imitative. It would do so with some sensitivity to the systems by which populations have been administered and which fall outside the old divisions between the orders of politics, culture, and civil society. It would do so with a strong sense of its own social and institutional place and function, and a disposition not to take the side of those whom history has most advantaged and normalized. All this, if at all possible, without falling back on simple distinctions between the other and the same, especially where that other is the past and the same is the present; without assuming, at least too quickly, that "we" share a set of dispositions with "them" — the producers and consumers of past cultures. It seems to me that this kind of genealogy of the literary has been most carefully and subtly embarked upon by Stephen Greenblatt, especially in the essays on Shakespeare published under the title *Shakespearean*

Negotiations.[15] In his work the difficulties of such a project are most openly exposed.

Representations in History

Greenblatt's methodology is presented in the first chapter of *Shakespearean Negotiations*, which remains his most sustained exposition of his aims, presuppositions, and procedures. The essay begins by claiming that literature works most powerfully "in the formal, self-conscious miming of life" (1). In such "simulations," death's finality may be, to some degree at least, avoided in advance, and "traces" of the past transmitted into the future. Unlike most poststructuralist thought, including Foucault's account of Roussel, here representation is thought of less as death's emissary in life, or absence's structuration of presence, than as life's transcendence of death, presence's incorporation of absence. Unlike poststructuralism (but like an anthropological/sociological tradition that begins with Émile Durkheim and Marcel Mauss), these simulations are the product of a general "social will" (4). In Durkheim's famous phrase, they belong to a "conscience collective." Greenblatt remains in tune with Foucault and poststructuralism, however, in aiming to analyze representations through nonmimetic categories. He wishes to avoid falling back on the concept "reflection." Instead, he calls on transactional notions, in particular exchange and appropriation: "Mimesis is always accompanied by—and indeed is always produced by—negotiation and exchange" (13).[16] Leaving aside exchange for a moment, Greenblatt requires a concept like "negotiation" because for him the circulation of representations may be driven by tensions, differences, conflicts, and these, in turn, are not always to be separated from pleasure and seductions. Let us take two connected examples from the body of *Shakespearean Negotiations.* The anxiety that Elizabethan authority produces, and which invokes neither sheer fear of tyranny nor anticipation of mercy, is not so much sublimated as molded into a moment of pleasure and irony through Shakespeare's theatricalization of it. In return, a certain deferral of resistance and obedience proper to theatrical response may itself enter the apparatus of government. Second, a Shakespearean prince who is, like real monarchs, already a "collective invention" and a source of awe may talk to his subjects with a certain empathy and casualness, to the delight of the spectator. This unbending—in the play, half feigned, half not—repeats and consolidates occasions in the larger world where authorities, partly theatrically, partly out of necessity, relax their aura. On these occasions of

relatively free exchange they can, however, "record alien voices," and therefore rule all the more effectively and fearsomely. Within a model that can
shelter such nuances, social divisions and hierarchies are much less than absolute differences. After all, to take another connected example, where the
colonial conquerors' sympathy for the cultures they invade, their willingness
to learn new practices, and, indeed, the flow of puzzlement and wonder between the two sides, all help the colonialists turn the colonizer to their will,
then barriers between different social sectors do not merely shut out or repress, they transform and create.

We confront an immediate and difficult problem in this transactional model:
in Greenblatt's essay notions like exchange and negotiation have a function
analogous to that of the "regularities" or rules of Foucault's archaeological
work. Both avoid the kind of thought for which events, texts, or social formations represent larger, more "real" formations. That, as I have suggested,
is their strength. Yet, once Foucault's work is invoked, it is difficult not to
ask, To what degree are Greenblatt's cultural transactions themselves ordered?
Do they form patterns, that is, are certain kinds of exchanges and negotiations systematically connected to certain times, places, and institutions within,
say, a more or less well defined strategy? These are questions that Greenblatt
engages in several ways: by describing, in formal terms, the transactions favored by Shakespeare's theater, by insisting that theater's effects and functions
are not quite localizable and predictable, by analyzing the relation between
the theater and quite large social formations — atheism and colonialism, for
instance. Nonetheless, his work remains focused on specific cases. He forestalls our asking, why *this* instance? is it typical of, that is, representative of,
some larger social force? by invoking the quasi-aesthetic fascination of, even
the weirdness of, his skillfully chosen instances. Perhaps it does not matter
that this tactic forestalls rather than answers tendentious questions about
the representativeness of a particular example, for those questions merely
draw us back into the delirium of mimesis and interpretation. But his appeal
to the wonder or fascination of the individual case and his responsiveness to
the political use of such fascination can interrupt another, less easily deferred,
set of connections and continuities — those by which old divisive social forces
and formations reproduce themselves, religion and colonialism being good
examples of such forces. Does his fascinating, noninterpretative academic
work have, in the present, something like the relation to these divisive formations that Shakespeare's theater had in the past — in however minor a
key? This is an important and disquieting question, which once again relies

on mimesis—and can only be answered by breaking the spell both of the theater and of the wonderful story.

Let us turn to Greenblatt's typology of transactional modes. He figures the barriers, hierarchies, and distances across which transactions move, spatially. For him, cultural differentiation can be understood in terms of various "zones" so that exchange is defined as the shift from one zone to another. In these terms he offers a classification of those kinds of cultural transposition used by the Elizabethan theater. The first mode he distinguishes is "appropriation," in which shifts from one zone to another involve no cost, and of which language is the most important instance. Language, after all, costs nothing and circulates quite easily. The second example of cultural exchange is "purchase," in which objects are exchanged for money. The third he calls "symbolic acquisition." Here the theater takes possession of a thing from another zone by signifying or "representing" it. Representation may seem to reenter Greenblatt's methodology at this point, but he attempts to avoid it by drawing upon classical rhetorical/structuralist distinctions, that is, by returning to nonmimetic categories. He argues that symbolic acquisition takes both a metonymical form (as when the theater signifies the world by presenting part of a larger whole) and a metaphorical form (as when names of pagan gods are substituted for Christian ones to avoid censorship). But the theater may also "acquire" happenings from other zones by "simulation"—as when "the actor simulates what is already understood to be a theatrical representation" (10). As the staged repetition of an already staged event, this too is less than a reflection of the world.

What drives these transactions? To answer this, Greenblatt sets out what we might call an "ontology of culture." For him culture moves from, has its being as, "energy." This permits him to define his task as "the analysis of the cultural circulation of social energy" (13). Although Greenblatt insists that this "energy" is closer to the rhetorician's *energia* than to any physicist's notion, it is impossible to dissociate it from Carlyle's earlier "force" or Foucault's "power." Happy power, power voided of irredeemable suffering or metaphysical anxiety. Though, for Greenblatt, "everything produced by [Elizabethan] society can circulate," social energy then existed in particular as "power, charisma, sexual excitement, collective dreams, wonder, desire, anxiety, religious awe, free-floating intensities of experience" (19). Of course it can also take the form of money: Greenblatt, unlike Foucault, does not neglect the market. The dynamism of circulatory flow, the sheer currency of things, belongs to protocapitalism; Shakespeare is an entrepreneur, partner in a joint stock company, able, indeed required, to turn social conflict, anxiety, hierarchies, and negotiations into fun, wonder, pleasure, cash, and so on. Strangely enough this echoes and inverts the later puritan attacks on the theater, which saw it not just encouraging licentiousness but making use of the reputation of authorities for show business profits and salaries, as well as encouraging role-playing and maintaining the "pagan" in the Christian — or Protestant — world. Thus social energy, itself the expression of an expansionist, mercantile society, circulates into the theater simultaneously through social (especially economic) and rhetorical channels, which continually displace the intensities through which energy is experienced. There is another potential difficulty in this line of thought, however; it can easily slip into supposing that the characteristics like "wonder," "awe," and "anxiety," for instance, are basic human responses, rather than products of the interactions between the analytic method with its desire to modulate into a celebratory and life-affirming tone, and the drives and the objects or moments being described.

Still, it is important to remember that in *Shakespearean Negotiations*, Greenblatt's method, his "cultural poetics," as he calls it, is directed toward a specific historical moment, a specific institution, and even, often, specific texts or groups of texts. Thus it is not absolutely clear to what degree he is setting out a general method at all. Just as Foucault's work on power is positioned ambiguously — is it a theory of power in general or an account of modern power in particular? — so Greenblatt's schema for the "social circulation of energy" makes some claim to be both a general frame for a historical sociology of culture and a specific description of the relations between Shakespearean society and Shakespearean theater. Such ambivalence is probably unavoidable. After all, any method of sociocultural inquiry must borrow its features and its appeal from the context that it is designed to analyze. But the persuasiveness of Greenblatt's project today owes much to its focus on *this* historical era in particular, posed as it is at a threshold of modernity. To speak in large generalizations, we can say that in Greenblatt's work the era of the rise of modernity speaks as directly as is possible to the era of its decline. And without pushing this any further, it is important to the persuasiveness of Greenblatt's method that Shakespeare's theater was an urban phenomenon, not completely complicit with classical or absolutist power, and based on economic institutions like the joint stock company that were to provide a motor for later industrial capitalism. Yet Shakespeare belonged to a society in which a fully fledged capitalist mode of production had yet to emerge. There were, in particular, no "classes" as Marx understood the word. Shakespearean society knew no industrial proletariat, defined as having nothing to sell except a labor power available to be transformed into exchange value and profit by capital. Nor had literature and criticism, "culture" in one modern sense, been put to the kind of governmental use that Hunter describes. In fact, the universalist narratives of secular enlightenment had yet to be articulated. So, as a hybrid of absolutist and modern formations, Greenblatt's Elizabethan theater resists the kind of analysis that classical Marxism and Foucauldianism provide. The ambiguity between the general and its local applicability of Greenblatt's project is all the less visible because we can mirror our "postmodernity" in Shakespeare's theater. Here again Greenblatt's work takes its power from a mimetic claim that, on the face of it, it is designed to avoid.

It is possible to draw Greenblatt's work more closely into connection with Foucault's work on literature by examining it rather more philosophically. We can begin by noting that while his model does rely on a concept of cultural differentiation, Greenblatt makes it clear that, for him, the theater belongs simultaneously to a particular site (in the case of the Globe an immovable one) and to forms of acting that spread through society at large. For Greenblatt, theater was "nonexclusive" in three senses in Shakespeare's society: a wide variety of situations could be presented on stage; most, if not all, of the population had access to it; and theatrical performance was not limited to a narrow range of places and times — it was not simply institutionalized. Theater's nonexclusivity, especially in the first and second sense, was connected to its being construed as "nonuseful" — that is, formally disconnected from religious rites, productive work, or political institutions. And its nonexclusivity also meant that the division between what is theatrical and what is not theatrical becomes blurred: the distinction was "improvised," as Greenblatt puts it.

Nonetheless the failure of formal markers or barriers to divide the world from the stage did — and does — not quite grant the theater a mobility, or rather a pattern of mobility and immobility, like that available to language. Greenblatt's typology of cultural exchange recognizes this. For him, the theater freely "appropriates," rather than "purchases" or "symbolically acquires," language. That language costs nothing, that its mobility is relatively unpoliceable, means that literature is not as easily analyzed in terms of "zones," "exchanges," and "negotiations" as is theater, for all theater's constant evacuation and re-creation of its borders. This is not to say that language does not have internal divisions: idiolects mark geographical and class differences, as Gadamer notes against Habermas; professions have their own discourses; and print can be censored. Indeed, the significance and mobility of particular natural languages depends, in part, on their relation to other so-called natural languages in hierarchies of cultural value. English was not, in Shakespeare's time, the language of official knowledge, nor were relations between literary or written English and spoken English as well defined as they were to become—factors that would seem to have offered Shakespeare more liberty than they caused him anxiety. Further, as Foucault's work makes clear, statements are removed from everyday speech to form discursive unities as a result of techniques of exclusion like ordination, academic examinations, and other acts of certification. As Foucault fails to note, statements may also be separated from the *doxa* within a system set in place by inherited, filiative identities and differences. In Shakespeare's time, state power protected many of these filiations and rites of certification: to feign being a nobleman or a cleric, to say or write the words they can say or write, could be a crime. It was part of theater's nonexclusivity that such prohibitions did not apply there.

The vernacular, then, which moves across the social body so easily, constitutes a background across which exchanges and negotiations move. But once everyday discourse is repeated on the stage, it changes its status. It is no longer casual, free utterance, but chosen, scripted utterance—an effect to which Greenblatt himself is very sensitive. It follows that certain constitutive properties of the vernacular cannot be staged or, indeed, written. Even improvisation on stage is not everyday language, just because, from the point of view of the spectator, there can never be absolute certainty as to what is, and what is not, improvised. The spontaneity of everyday language can only be represented—as we so easily say. It is the way that everyday language eludes appropriation that we find one limit to Greenblatt's desire to avoid representation as an analytic category. For the transactional terms that he privileges do not quite account for the way in which theatrical language structurally differs from ordinary language. For that, we need concepts like "representation" that point to a more profound break between the theater and its social setting. These concepts lead us into the delirium of mimesis. They lead us to believe that it might not just be on stage, or in writing, that events—and words—are scripted. The most "spontaneous" discourse in the everyday world may be, in some sense, determined in advance, organized in what psychoanalysts might call an "other scene."

From the opposite side, to the degree that something is unique, cannot be bought, repeated, transported, or gestured to through metaphor or metonymy, then it too, by definition, is unavailable to social circulation as Greenblatt describes it. Do such things exist? It seems that they do, and, furthermore, it is from them too that the paradigm of representation gains its prestige. We can begin making this rather obscure claim clearer by noting the difference between, for instance, kissing, philosophizing, falling in love, undergoing a marriage ceremony, and dying on stage. One can kiss on or off stage: a kiss and, sometimes, its sensations, including pleasure, are merely repeated when theatricalized. When one philosophizes on stage, this too may be — to use the language of mimesis — simultaneously feigned and unfeigned: its truth value is not affected by its staging. One can also fall in love on stage: indeed, acting out love in a space separated from the "real" world may cause real love. Suspicion of the way this muddies the distinction between the authentic and the inauthentic motivates Jane Austen's animus against theatrical representation in Mansfield Park, for example. But to repeat the marriage ceremony on stage is merely to feign it: one can be married only as oneself — not as a fictional character, just as one can be a priest, lawyer, or nobleman only as oneself. The division between fiction and nonfiction derives some of its force from legal sanctions against pretending to be another in circumstances like the marriage ceremony. Death on stage is something else, however. Were an actor to die on stage, interactions between the proper and improper, the feigned and the unfeigned, the theater and the world would take another direction. At the moment of death, the actor stops acting, as in so-called snuff movies.

There are other events (such as having an orgasm) that to repeat on stage is never simply to feign, events in which the body takes over and which do not simply belong to what Foucault would call the "ethical substance" — that aspect of the self under sociocultural direction. Such examples remind us that what can, and what cannot, be repeated or feigned on stage is under the control of authorities who have used their power to restrict moments when the body takes over (like death or orgasm) being shown on stage, and to enforce the reality of the real and fictionality of fiction. Yet the sharpness of the division between repeating and feigning in a case like that of staged death is not simply under social or cultural control, because what dies, in the final instance, is a body rather than a mind. Thus one cannot repeat one's own death: when a person dies, then dialogue, exchange, and negotiation with that person ceases forever — in this world at least. Because bodies only die once and death is not fungible, death can enter the institution of theater only as feigned or as an accident. Not even performance artists who try as hard as possible to work outside the paradigm of representation script their death into their performances. If they did, in what would be simultaneously their last performance and their last action, the always problematic split between the performing self and the organizing self, that is, the self "behind" the performance who can move from one performance to the next, would at last disappear. It would be the organizing self, the self continuous across performances, whose loss would be mourned, whose corpse would be buried. In the "real" self's absence, she is finally separable from her performance — and, at the same stroke, mimetic categories reassert themselves.

As we have seen, Greenblatt declares his interest in the power of "simulations" to escape death's finality; indeed he begins his book by confessing his "desire to speak with the dead" (1). In his introductory essay, Shakespearean theater finally matters to him because it has some power to satisfy that desire. We can now note further that his analytics of the social circulation of energy avoids death in another sense. It fails to allow for those social breakdowns in exchange and negotiation of which death is the sharpest instance. This is particularly noticeable because the Elizabethan/Jacobean public theater — like most other institutions that disseminate what we now call "fictions" — almost obsessively dealt in acts of violence, murder, death as well as madness, all instances in which social negotiations falter or collapse. It is as if that theater wanted to draw such instances into representation — to keep their finality, or their failure to enter into social interactions, at bay. Two points follow: one formal, the other ethicopolitical. First, this relentless staging of death and violence does not simply rely on the modes of social exchange that Greenblatt calls symbolic acquisition because staged death, staged violence even, repeats the external face, the public side, of a recognizable event rather than signifying that event metonymically or metaphorically. After all, what tropes can we persuasively provide for the moment of death, which can never be experienced? Paradoxically, it is because death is not, finally, an experience, although it is a radically personal event, that staged death, even more than staged violence, can reenact or "appropriate" (to use Greenblatt's phrase) every last gasp of the death throe — a fact of which theater in Shakespeare's time took full advantage. Because a staged death may be simultaneously so real (repeating its outer aspect) and so unreal (not a bodily death at all), it is easier to describe it in mimetic categories — as feigned, simulated. This is the other side of Greenblatt's sense that "simulations" have the capacity to keep the dead alive. Second, it is partly through practices defined through mimetic categories, given value as "fictions," "representations," and so on, that individual lives are ethically formed in modern society, as Foucault reminds us. The way that the realm of fiction represents violence and death with such vigor helps us see that ethically formed individuals are formed against death, in modes of power that conceal and replace state-sanctioned violence, and the state's right to send people out of exchange or negotiation, to destroy the life in their bodies. When a culture is at home with death, directed toward life-after-death like Christian cultures confident of the possibility of individual salvation, then exchange and negotiation never cease, and the power of fictional representations to structure individuals' lives will be of less account.

When Greenblatt classifies the sources of Shakespeare's social energy he does not single out the force that motivates his own work: the desire to speak with the dead. Shakespeare's contemporaries could speak with the dead, at least in a manner. In particular, for them, ghosts still, just, existed. As a secular "shaman," as he engagingly calls himself, Greenblatt has to find more professional and "rational" means to keep in touch with the dead. Yet his desire to construe simulations as the ghosts of our culture, his desire to downgrade mimetic categories, even his emphasis on fascination and wonder can be understood in terms of his wish to avoid confirming representation's power to discipline lives. It is not a power that is easy to escape. If we ask the questions, why is the theater so fascinating? why do fictions circulate so widely? the answers are not just to be found in terms, so important to capitalist cultural production, like pleasure, wonder, sexual excitement, intensities of experience, or even in the will to keep the dead alive. The theater, or better, the theater-effect, is fascinating because its representations produce what Foucault called a "labyrinth" in which selves are no longer fixed but are "free" to change and be changed, by governments among others. And the delirium of mimesis is especially virulent when the living represent the dead. Then, the difference between the true and the false, the real and the feigned may be especially rigorously policed; as Greenblatt reminds us, there were good reasons why, for example, in Shakespeare's time it was always someone else who was an atheist. To think that life after death might be a fiction was a serious transgression. But let us remember that, in the West, representations of death and violence were, for centuries, most widely circulated in passion plays and other images of Christ on the cross. In these sacred and "true" images, violence, pain, death, the avoidance of death, and the promise of conversion, of a new self, merge — as well as, interminably, the possibility of their fictionality. One of the rewards of juxtaposing the kind of post-Foucauldian criticism represented by Hunter with that represented by Greenblatt is to be able to see that the most auratic representations in Western society belong to the genealogy of modern government. They do so because, despite their "truth" and sacredness, or rather, because of the very insecurity of that truth and sacredness, they exist at the heart of the labyrinth in which the identities of individuals are not fixed but are open to change. Yet — to make a final point — it is in the living's pain, sickness, poverty, and hunger that they are closest to the dead who, in this world, can only be represented. In Greenblatt's "desire to speak to the dead," and in his championing of what we might call the transactional paradigm, he too quickly passes over these marks of oppression, the ways that the life, health, and happiness of some can be expropriated, irredeemably, by others. He does so, I suppose, because, like most of us who read and write books like his (and this one too), he finds it hard to speak *as himself* from the position of those whom life offers least, to whom death is, in fact, closest. To represent such a position has, for some very good reasons, become almost impossible.

Notes

1. The kind of historiography that Hunter's work is directed against is represented at its best by Chris Baldick in *The Social Mission of English* (Cambridge: Cambridge University Press, 1983) and Francis Mulhern in *The Moment of Scrutiny* (London: New Left Books, 1979).

2. See, for instance, the chapter on education in Derek Fraser, *The Evolution of the British Welfare State* (London: Macmillan, 1984).

3. Ibid., 265.

4. We should note that the Edgeworths' personal opinion of Rousseau as an individual is ambivalent, and that Rousseau himself believed pedagogy ought to be based in the home.

5. Maria Edgeworth and Richard Lovell Edgeworth, *Practical Education* (New York: Garland, 1974), 2:618.

6. The debates on "liberal" versus "professional" (including teacher training) education in Oxbridge from about the 1860s until about the First World War are also absent from Hunter's account. Consideration of this material would make much more difficult his claim that English as it enters Oxbridge before Richards is a dead end, as well as his belief that "romantic criticism" is grafted onto the governmental apparatus in modern criticism. See Ian Hunter, *Culture and Government: The Emergence of Literary Education* (London: Macmillan, 1988).

7. Jacques Derrida, *Dissemination*, trans. Barbara Johnson (Chicago: University of Chicago Press, 1982), 187; emphasis in the original. Paul de Man repeats this remark with a slightly different stress: "It is impossible to conceive of a phenomenal experience that would not be mimetic, as it is impossible to conceive of an aesthetic judgment that would not be dependent on imitation as a constitutive category, also and especially when the judgment, as is the case in Kant, is interiorized as the consciousness of a subject"; see Paul de Man, *The Resistance to Theory* (Minneapolis: University of Minnesota Press), 67.

8. This is to pass over the extraordinarily virulent history of attacks on nonrepresentational or "nonreflective" modes of thoughts in Western thought—attacks that from about the seventeenth century begin to demonize, in particular, women and non-Europeans as being incapable of representational thought.

9. Plato, *Phaedrus and the Seventh and Eighth Letters*, trans. and intro. Walter Hamilton (Harmondsworth: Penguin, 1973), 101.

10. Michel Foucault, *This Is Not a Pipe*, trans. and ed. James Harkness, with illustrations and letters by René Magritte (Berkeley: University of California Press, 1982), 44.

11. Ibid.

12. G. W. F. Hegel, *Faith and Knowledge*, trans. W. Cerf and H. S. Harris (Albany: State University of New York Press, 1977), 157.

13. Among the very best of such works I would mention Jonathan Arac, *Commissioned Spir-*

its: The Shaping of Social Motion in Dickens, Carlyle, Melville, and Hawthorne (New Brunswick: Rutgers University Press, 1979); Jonathan Goldberg, *James I and the Politics of Literature: Jonson, Shakespeare, Donne and Their Contemporaries* (Baltimore: Johns Hopkins University Press, 1983); and John Bender, *Imagining the Penitentiary: Fiction and the Architecture of Mind in Eighteenth-Century England* (Chicago: University of Chicago Press, 1987).

14. See D. A. Miller, *The Novel and the Police* (Berkeley: University of California Press, 1988), and Catherine Gallagher, "The Bio-Economics of *Our Mutual Friend*," in Michel Feher, ed., *Fragments for the History of the Human Body*, 3 vols. (Cambridge, Mass.: MIT Press, 1989).

15. This is not to say that Foucault alone lies behind Greenblatt's work, which is also marked by a reading of modern ethnography and ethnographical theory. See Stephen Greenblatt, *Shakespearean Negotiations: The Circulation of Social Energy in Renaissance England* (Berkeley and Los Angeles: University of California Press, 1987). Page references to this volume are noted parenthetically in the text.

16. "Exchange" becomes a crucial analytic notion in the work of Marcel Mauss especially.

6

Cannibalizing the Humanist Subject: A Genealogy of Prospero

Tom Hayes

I am heartily sorry that, judging their faults rightly, we should be so blind to our own. I think there is more barbarity in eating a man alive than in eating him dead.

Michel de Montaigne, "Of Cannibals"

Representing the Subject

The Tempest is the last play Shakespeare wrote for the London stage before he retired to Stratford-upon-Avon in 1611. As an exercise in self-reflection, self-representation, and self-criticism, I am going to trace a genealogy of the hero of that play. That is, in the following pages I am going to conduct a (partial) history of representations of Prospero as part of what Foucault termed "an historical ontology" of the sense of self, the subjectivity, that originated in Europe at the end of the Middle Ages.[1] I choose Prospero as a *representative* humanist subject because he so glaringly illustrates the chief paradox of that sense of self. Namely, he is afraid to admit, to himself and to others, that he is not perfectly autonomous, that in order to *be* a person, a humanist subject, he must interact with others. But I also choose Prospero because he shows that it is possible for a humanist subject to change, to transform himself and acknowledge his dependence on others. At the end of Shakespeare's play, Prospero is, finally, a subject in process, one who is capable of consuming — of "cannibalizing" — himself.

Prospero's constitutive desire for dominance is illustrated throughout the play. He has so developed his control of nature that he is able to direct the tempest in order to make the ship on which his brother, Antonio, together with the king of Naples, his brother Sebastian and his son Ferdinand, the old councillor Gonzalo, and others founder on an island where Prospero has been living in exile. Twelve years previous to the opening of the play, Prospero, the duke of Milan, decided to allow his brother Antonio to govern his dukedom so that, like the good humanist that he was and is, he could devote more time to studying his books. Having grown accustomed to power, Antonio staged a coup d'état, at which time Gonzalo helped Prospero escape with his two-year-old daughter Miranda and several books from his personal library.

A Cautionary Tale

Men's concerns over the question of women's sexual fidelity, and hence of their own and their children's legitimacy, are replete throughout the play — even from the opening scene, when Antonio calls the boatswain a "whoreson" and Gonzalo suggests that the boatswain would not drown even if the ship were "as leaky as an unstanched wench" (1.1.44, 48–49).[2] Such bantering references to women's uncontrolled sexuality prepare us for Prospero's more serious interest in the same topic. When we first see him, Prospero is intent on ensuring that Miranda will produce a legitimate heir to what will be his restored dukedom. He is also very much concerned about Miranda's own legitimacy, as, for example, when he tells Miranda, "Thy mother was a piece of virtue, and / She said thou wast my daughter" (1.2.56–57). Prospero's anxiety over women's sexual fidelity becomes even more explicit one hundred lines later when he wonders aloud whether his brother and he had the same father; Miranda has to warn him that "Good wombs have borne bad sons" (1.2.119). Indeed, this concern over women's sexual fidelity is so pervasive that the first question Ferdinand asks Miranda is whether or not she is a virgin (1.2.428).

Not long afterward, we learn that anxiety over women's sexual fidelity, and thus over their allegiance to the kinship system, is coupled with a similar fear in regard to the sexual prowess of dark-skinned men, a fear that carries with it a fear that dark-skinned men are guilty of stealing white-skinned men's pleasure. After all, the *purpose* of the homeward-bound voyage that Prospero's tempest interrupts is to celebrate an interracial marriage between an African man (the king of Tunis) and a European woman (the daughter of the king of Naples). For as Sebastian tells Ferdinand's father, it is better to

have lost a son at sea than to "loose" one's daughter "to an African" (2.1.130).
And the only reason Prospero gives for enslaving the representative dark-
skinned man on the island, Caliban, is that he attempted to rape Miranda.
To which charge Caliban defiantly replies:

> O ho, O ho! Would't had been done!
> Thou didst prevent me; I had peopled else
> This isle with Calibans. (1.2.349–51)

For more than three hundred years these lines were cited in support of interpretations of *The Tempest* as a cautionary tale warning of the dangers of
not taking up the white man's burden of "civilizing" dark-skinned men. This
reading assumes that Prospero is simply fulfilling his fatherly duty when he
takes responsibility for his daughter's safety and guides her choice of a mari-
tal partner. Such is the case, for example, in the adaptation of *The Tempest*
written by John Dryden and William Davenant in 1669.[3] Recent academic
commentaries on *The Tempest* have questioned the patriarchal assumptions
of this canonical reading of the play, but virtually none of them questions
the sense of self that sustains—and is sustained by—the patriarchal assumptions they oppose. In other words, antipatriarchal (and anticolonialist) readings of *The Tempest* have not applied the critique of the humanist subject
that Foucault articulates in *The Order Of Things* (1966) the way Edward W.
Said does in *Orientalism* (1978). Said's great achievement is his demonstration that unless and until the humanist subject is put into question, *any* attempt to challenge colonial discourse—and the racism and sexism it promotes—will remain tentative.

One of the key Orientalists cited by Said, the French philologist Ernest
Renan (1823–1892), wrote a "continuation" of *The Tempest* entitled *Caliban, suite de La Tempête* (1878), in which Prospero's Renaissance humanism
has been informed by the French Enlightenment. In Renan's play, which is
set in Milan, Caliban leads a revolt against Prospero and effectively suppresses
Ariel, whom, Renan says, should be played by a woman. Even though Renan's Caliban has learned the conventions of European society, he is still
seen as a barbaric, immoral lout, still a figure "on whose nature / Nurture
can never stick" (4.1.188–89). To Ariel's reminder that "Prospero taught
thee the Aryan language, and with that divine tongue the channel of reason
has become inseparable from thee," Caliban simply replies, "Ingratitude is
the stamp of humanity."[4] And to Ariel's charge that "Thou wouldst also
have violated Miranda," Caliban retorts: "Well, after all, we should have
peopled the island. Men place some value on themselves. Her father owed

me wages" (19). Caliban goes on to explain that, in his eyes, Prospero has reigned over both of them "by means of false ideas." He tells Ariel, "Those monsters on which Prospero's prestige rested, were all imaginary, but they tormented me as greatly as if they had been real." Ariel explains that Prospero "believes that God is reason," but Caliban says: "As for the God of the Christians, he is only the God of the feebleminded and of women" (20).

In Renan's continuation of *The Tempest* Prospero has become a philosophe whose primary goal is to master nature. To that end, he agrees to yield everything except the right to laugh, but his devotion to understanding nature's secrets is unacceptable to the leaders of the Inquisition, who find him guilty of defaming the church. Before Prospero can be imprisoned, however, Caliban nullifies the guilty verdict and claims Prospero is *his* protégé. The choir declares that all civilization is the work of aristocrats and argues that "the inferior races ... such as the emancipated negro, evidence at once a monstrous ingratitude toward their civilizers." The choir admits defeat but states unequivocally: "As for the tender and loyal hearted, whose extreme delicacy of sentiment and personal fidelity make them dumb and helpless, there is no longer any place for them" (65). Ariel vanishes and Prospero falls dead.

Renan's play ends on a lachrymose — and cynical — note. Those who identified themselves with the point of view from which he wrote — that of a universal middle-class, masculine, heterosexual subject — had little choice but to see Caliban, no matter how much he was romanticized, as a barbaric other. Unsurprisingly, the sense of self represented by Renan's Prospero, with which the play encourages us to identify, conforms to the concept of the *belle âme* or "beautiful soul," which, as Hegel explained, is the result of self-consciousness withdrawing into its innermost being — withdrawing into contemplation of itself.[5]

The key here is to see how Renan's portrayal of Prospero as a *belle âme* veils the political implications of the racism and sexism he projects onto Caliban. As Nietzsche pointed out, Renan's voluptuous style and his insistence on seeing himself — and on being seen — as a *belle âme*, a Byronic lover of despair, infused everything he wrote with an air of cloying self-pity.[6] This self-pitying *belle âme*, as Jacques Lacan saw, became "the *moi* of modern man."[7]

Uncanny Caliban

In his deft psychoanalytic reading of *The Tempest* Leslie Fiedler advanced a more sexually aware interpretation of Prospero than that which had prevailed in the first half of the twentieth century. He pointed out that Prospero's fear of

Caliban's sexuality is the result of his own barely suppressed incestuous desire. Prospero leaves off a life of political action in order to study his books, and he ends up "enisled with a nubile daughter in an ultimate travesty of the endogamous family, an incestuous *ménage à deux*." He awakens from this incestuous dream to find himself in a place where "rape and miscegenation threaten the daughter too dearly loved in an ultimate travesty of the exogamous family."[8]

Caliban challenges the conventions of European patriarchal society because he knows that Prospero's two great obsessions—his books and his daughter's reproductive capacity—are connected. He knows that Prospero's books and Miranda's body are instrumental in the production of what Foucault termed power/knowledge. He knows, in other words, that it is not *nature* that Prospero seeks to control; it is not *science* that he learns from his books but how to manipulate and control the discursive field of knowledge and a whole range of techniques and practices for the discipline, surveillance, administration, and formation of his own and other bodies. Caliban sees that Prospero's books contain the secret knowledge that will enable him—insofar as possible—to become a humanist subject, to control Miranda's reproductive body, and to ensure the *legitimacy* of those children who issue from her womb.

Prospero wants to preserve the purity of Miranda's body, to prevent it from coupling with—and, in Prospero's eyes, being contaminated by—Caliban's seed. To Prospero, Miranda and Caliban represent inverse aspects of the forbidden and abjected body of the (m)other. If we were to follow the psychoanalytic paradigm of explanation we could cite Freud's belief that such incestuous yearnings were characteristic of white heterosexual men, men whose sense of themselves was formed in societies where the patriarchal nuclear family was the norm. This sense of self tries to achieve a coherent, stable identity but inevitably feels an impending sense of instability. But while psychoanalytic discourse sees this instability (an implied lack) that lies at the heart of this subject formation, it is reluctant to follow the logic of its own assumptions and see that the way men try to make up for this lack is to project it onto those who are invested with the power to provide what is lacking in themselves.

From a Foucauldian point of view the déclassé "fools" Stephano and Trinculo may be seen to challenge the boundaries of this psychoanalytic explanation, for their knowledge that European men would willingly pay to see Caliban's naked body, a body that is referred to in the list of characters as "deformed," suggests that they are also aware that Caliban's uncanny body, both familiar and monstrous, will reassure European men that the "natural" body, the body of the Other, has a penis and is thus masculine. Stephano and Trinculo, who are a kind of parodic homosocial couple, appear to know, perhaps because of the way, as "fools," they speak from a position that is culturally marginalized, that European men *need* to believe they are right to repress the sight of the maternal body, to fetishize that body to prevent it from swallowing them up, from stultifying their ability to function as autonomous humanist subjects.[9]

In other words, Stephano and Trinculo help us understand how Prospero sees Caliban as a projection of his own insecure, unstable struggle to control woman-as-Other and recover his own lack of wholeness. The marginalized point of view of Stephano and Trinculo is a critique of the humanist subject, for, through them, we are able to see how sexism and racism emerge as products of the humanist subject's sense of incompleteness. The distancing effect of the marginalized perspective of Stephano and Trinculo also shows that until the humanist subject recognizes the complicated ways the Other is used to hide this lack, sexism and racism will continue to be integral parts of that subjectivity.

The Caliban Controversy

This marginalized view of Caliban also helps us understand the role Caliban has played — and continues to play — in Latin American culture. One of the first writers to apply images from *The Tempest* to the Western Hemisphere's international rivalries was the Nicaraguan poet, diplomat, and leader of the *modernista* movement Rubén Darío (1867–1916). Like Renan, Darío saw Caliban as representative of everything that was crude and insensitive. Struck by the crass greed and vice he saw during his visit to New York City in 1893, Darío wrote that he was in "the gory, the cyclopean, the monstrous capital of the banknote," where "Caliban soaks up whiskey as he soaked up wine in Shakespeare's play." Five years later, Darío elaborated this image of North Americans as Calibans in an essay entitled "El Triunfo de Calibán."[10]

Other Latin American intellectuals readily accepted this image of North Americans. In a speech in Buenos Aires on May 2, 1898, the influential French émigré Paul Groussac, whom Darío praised, called the United States "Calibanesque." In his long essay entitled *Ariel* (1900), the Uruguayan philosopher and ardent admirer of Renan, José Enrique Rodó, adopted the voice of a "venerable old teacher, who by allusion to the wise magician of Shakespeare's *Tempest* was often called Prospero." Rodó told his youthful audience that

> Ariel is the rule of reason and feeling over the low stimulus of irrationality; it is
> generous enthusiasm, the high disinterested motive in action, spirituality in cul-
> ture, vivacity and wit in intelligence—the ideal term to which human selec-
> tion ascends, rectifying in higher man the tenacious vestiges of Caliban, symbol
> of sensuality and lewdness, with the persevering chisel of life.[11]

Thus while Ariel and Caliban represent opposing aspects of a son's relationship to his father, and taken together may be said to represent a single figure,
the oxymoronic noble savage or, perhaps more apt, the merging of Frankenstein and his monster, in Shakespeare's play this opposition is destabilized by
its juxtaposition with the opposition between Prospero as the "good" father
and his brother Antonio as the "bad" father. As Octave Mannoni pointed
out in his application of Hegel's analysis of the master/slave dialectic to the
relationship between Prospero and Caliban, such oppositions are *always* unstable. In his description of the "Prospero complex," Mannoni explained that
"the sum of those unconscious neurotic tendencies that delineate at the same
time the 'picture' of the paternalist colonial [also delineate] the portrait of
'the racist whose daughter has been the object of an attempted rape at the
hands of an inferior being.' "[12]

According to Mannoni, just as Prospero suffers from an authority complex
Caliban suffers from a paternalistic complex, which leads him to accept Prospero as his master. In the fourth chapter of *Black Skin, White Masks* (1952),
Frantz Fanon strongly objected to this characterization of black men as patho-
logical Calibans who sought to subject themselves to powerful white father
figures. He explained that black men are overdetermined as phobic objects;
that is, they are always already seen as, and expected to be, sexual threats.
Using Lacan's alternative to Freud's Oedipal theory of subject formation,
Fanon explained how colonialized black men's subjectivities were constructed
by miming the language, customs, and habits of the colonizers.

The Barbadian novelist George Lamming expanded on Fanon's interpretation in his postcolonialist reading of *The Tempest* in *The Pleasures of Exile*
(1960). Characterizing his own subject position as that of "a colonial and
exiled descendent of Caliban," Lamming said that Prospero is afraid of Caliban "because he knows that his encounter with Caliban is, largely, his encounter with himself."[13] As Lamming saw it, Caliban plots the murder of
Prospero "out of a deep sense of betrayal." To him, Miranda, not Ariel, "is
the innocent half of Caliban; Caliban is the possible deformity which Miranda, at the age of experiment, might become" (15). Prospero is afraid of
the possible sexual union of Caliban and Miranda because it represents "a
fusion which, within himself, Prospero needs and dreads!" (102).

Prospero projects his own repressed desires onto Caliban, but Caliban is not a humanist subject; he suffers no repression. His relationship to the symbolic order, to language, is thoroughly ambivalent. He is never "at home" in the language Prospero has taught him, and this is neither Prospero's fault nor his own. In his loneliness, Prospero refuses to face his hatred, his fear, and his need of Caliban. As father to Miranda, he must pay some attention to her, but the fact that he has waited thirteen years to explain to her how they got to the island, along with the fact that he sees her primarily as a potential bearer of *male* children, suggests that he does not recognize her as a person.

Lamming hypothesized that Caliban may be Prospero's own son begotten upon the witch Sycorax and that therefore when Prospero says, "This thing of darkness I / Acknowledge mine" (5.1.275–76), he is, for the first time, owning up to his paternity.[14] Prospero cannot dismiss Caliban's ingratitude because, to him, such ingratitude masks "a shattering kind of self-knowledge, the knowledge that he really desires such ingratitude" (116). When Prospero acknowledges Caliban as his own, he shatters his former sense of self and sees that "the real sin is not hatred, which implies an involvement, but the calculated and habitual annihilation of the person whose presence you can ignore but never exclude" (117).

Questioning Representation

In the novella *The Invention of Morel* (1940), on which Alain Robbe-Grillet based his filmscript for director Alain Resnais's *Last Year at Marienbad* (1962), the Argentinean writer whom Jorge Luis Borges called "really and secretly the master," Adolfo Bioy Casares, uses the stylistic techniques of magical realism (a marvelous blending or juxtaposition of natural and supernatural elements) to question the humanist idea that everyone has — or *should* have — a stable core self accessible through representation.

The Invention of Morel is based on H. G. Wells's chilling story of the oppressive use of scientific knowledge, *The Island of Dr. Moreau* (1896), and purports to be the diary of a Venezuelan fugitive who escapes to an island where he finds his "unconscious enemies" living in a museum.[15] He becomes obsessed with a woman named Faustine, for whom he makes a garden using flowers to form a likeness of her as he first saw her: "He felt like a magician because the finished work had no connection with the precise moment that produced it" (29). He sees a man named Morel who looks much like himself whose relationship with Faustine makes him intensely jealous. He learns that the people on the island cannot see him and that their conversations and behaviors are repeated.

The narrator gets ahold of a copy of a speech by Morel that explains that he has invented a machine that can reproduce the sensory impressions of a person or an animal or a thing so exactly that there is no way to tell the difference between these images and reality: "When all the senses are synchronized," Morel explained, "the soul emerges" (63). The narrator gradually overcomes the nervous repulsion he feels toward Morel's invention, especially after he discovers that he is able to view Faustine "dispassionately, as a simple object" (69). He sees that "when minds of greater refinement than Morel's begin to work on the invention, man will select a lonely, pleasant place, will go there with the persons he loves most, and will endure in an intimate paradise. A single garden ... will contain innumerable paradises" (72–73). Yet he is still ambivalent about Morel's invention and tries to destroy the machines that Morel has built, only to discover that the machines know how to reproduce themselves: "I was overcome by the horror of being in an enchanted place and by the confused realization that its vengeful magic was effective in spite of my disbelief" (78).

In his final attempt to account for Morel's behavior, the narrator sees that "perhaps the hell I ascribe to Morel is really my own. I am the one who is in love with Faustine, who is capable of murder and suicide; I am the monster" (87). He sees that Morel had no interest in any of the people on the island. "He loved the inaccessible Faustine. That is why he killed her, killed himself and all his friends, and invented immortality! Faustine's beauty deserves that madness, that tribute, that crime. When I denied that, I was too jealous or too stubborn to admit that I loved her. And now I see Morel's act as something sublime" (87). The narrator is drawn to identify himself with Morel and, in so doing, to acknowledge the egomaniacal quality of that self. The invention of Morel, i.e., humanist representation, associates the murder of a woman with the sublime. The story thus unmasks the ruthlessness of the humanist conception of self, which strives for godlike power. With this realization, the narrator pays such representation an ironic tribute: "My soul has not yet passed to the image," he observes; "if it had, I would have died, I (perhaps) would no longer see Faustine, and would be with her in a vision that no one can ever destroy" (90). Here the humanist subject acknowledges that it is not possible to ever fully represent itself.

A more overtly political, but ultimately less devastating, view of Prospero as a representative humanist subject is advanced in Aimé Césaire's *Une tempête: d'apress 'La Tempête' de Shakespeare, adaptation pour une théâtre nègre*

(1969). Here Caliban is a rebellious black slave and Ariel is a docile mulatto. Miranda is simply an object of Ferdinand's desire. Misogyny and masculine bravado become explicit in the character of Eshu, "a black devil-god," who intrudes on the masque celebrating "the spectacle of tomorrow's world" with the threat that he will whip the goddesses "with his dick."[16] As exemplified by this scene, Césaire's play is primarily concerned with the colonized *man's* struggle to assert himself in opposition to the white colonizer's attempts to castrate him. Césaire's play encourages Latin American *men* to become stable, confident selves much in accordance with the ideal celebrated by Renaissance humanism and the Enlightenment. But A *Tempest* does not put in question the ways in which that subject formation depends on and reinforces the subordination of women. In other words, Césaire's play leaves little room to question the attitudes and behaviors known as *machismo* as a way for Latin American men to assert themselves in opposition to colonialism.[17]

Cannibalism and Racism

Roberto Fernández Retamar's influential 1971 essay on the role of Caliban in Latin American culture is similarly flawed. Fernández Retamar tried to invert attempts by those such as Rodó to privilege Ariel over Caliban as a role model for Latin American men. However, as Gayatri Chakravorty Spivak has pointed out, although Fernández Retamar's location of the Caliban/Ariel binary *within* the postcolonial intellectual is "moving," if "Third World" intellectuals continue to see themselves as Ariels and yet privilege Caliban they run the risk of being "driven by a nostalgia for lost origins" and consequently "run the risk of effacing the 'native' and stepping forth as 'the real Caliban,' of forgetting that he is a name in a play, an inaccessible blankness circumscribed by an interpretable text." Instead of seeing Caliban as a "real" person, Spivak suggests that we should try to see how "the stagings of Caliban work alongside the narrativization of history: claiming to *be* Caliban legitimizes the very individualism that we must persistently attempt to undermine from within."[18] Inverting the Ariel/Caliban binary — privileging Caliban over Ariel — does not challenge assumptions regarding the sense of self that the Enlightenment inherited from Renaissance humanism.

Significantly, Fernández Retamar singled out Rodó's fellow countryman and editor of his complete works, Emir Rodríguez Monegal, as "a servant of imperialism" who tried "so coarsely to emasculate Rodó's work."[19] In a response to this attack, Rodríguez Monegal agreed that Rodó was influenced by Renan's view of Caliban as a crass utilitarian, but in reference to the issue of

castration — of who has or does not have the phallus — he said that cannibalism had been, and could be, used as a metaphor of cultural potency. Rodríguez Monegal pointed out that "more than twenty years before Mannoni
began the rehabilitation of Caliban, the Brazilian poet and novelist, [Os-
wald] de Andrade [1890–1954] ... postulated cannibalism as a legitimate
form of culture.... In his funny and outrageous *Manifesto Antropófago* [1928],
he combined Freud's and Nietzsche's views on culture to produce a concept
that was genuinely revolutionary." Basing his argument on the notion of ritual cannibalism that Freud articulated in *Totem and Taboo*, de Andrade "maintained that ... the only true revolution is the one which produces a transformation of the world at all levels, not just the social or political. To liberate
man it is necessary to free his eroticism as well as his view of science, his religion as well as his mind."[20]

Rodríguez Monegal called attention to the ways in which, in colonialist
discourse, alleged cannibalism on the part of Native Americans was seen as
a threat to the sexual potency of white men. David Bergman has explained
how, in Shakespeare's time, the alleged cannibalism of Native Americans
was "directly linked with sodomy."[21] This link confirms Georges Bataille's
argument that "cannibalism is the elementary example of the taboo as creating desire,"[22] and Julia Kristeva's observation that Oedipalized humanist subjects eschew cannibalism because fear of the uncontrollable generative capacity of the mother is repellent and leads to "respect for the body of the other,
my fellow man, my brother."[23] The long-standing identification of Caliban
with cannibalism is, as Lamming notes, certainly connected to Caliban's
sexuality. The charge of cannibalism is made because Caliban is thought to
be "incapable of differentiating between one kind of reality and another....
Hence the charge of rape. Caliban would think no more of raping Miranda
than he might of eating her if she were alone." Through Miranda, the product of Prospero's teaching, "we may glimpse the origin and perpetuation of
myth coming slowly but surely into its right as fact, history, absolute truth"
(111). That fact, that history, that absolute truth, is dependent on the white
racist's fear of dark-skinned men's desire for white women.

Cultural Cannibalism

Rodríguez Monegal believed that "in daring to face the problem of cannibalism (and implicitly the image of Caliban) not with shame but with defiance,
de Andrade succeeded in transposing the discussion of the true nature of

Latin American culture from the rather solemn and Frenchified atmosphere of Rodó's *Ariel* (and Fernández Retamar's *Caliban*, hélas), to the lively context of a truly iconoclastic Latin American culture" (82). Rodríguez Monegal held that this Latin American culture should acknowledge its cultural cannibalism and use it as a weapon. "By defending cannibalism and dating some of his texts from the day the Brazilian cannibals ate their first bishop (an effective if rash way of assimilating his religious virtue), [and] by introducing the fruitful notion of carnival as a key to the transformation of society," de Andrade anticipated Mikhail Bakhtin's theories of the carnivalization of literature that signified the symbolic destruction of authority and official culture (Rodríguez Monegal, 82).

Though he did not spell out the ways in which de Andrade's parodic humor constituted a challenge to the humanist subject, Rodríguez Monegal's observation that "to liberate man it is necessary to free his eroticism as well as his view of science," indicates that he was in agreement with the views expressed in Herbert Marcuse's *Eros and Civilization* (1955) and in Norman O. Brown's *Life against Death* (1959). Both of these books critiqued Freud's acceptance of — some would say, his failure to *understand* — Hegel's master/slave dialectic. Like Marcuse and Brown, Rodríguez Monegal did not question the ways in which the liberated eroticism he and the writers he admired (Oswald and Mário de Andrade, Bioy Casares, Gabriel García Márquez, Carlos Fuentes, Severo Sarduy, Guillermo Cabrera Infante, Manuel Puig) preserved humanist assumptions about gender that subordinated women, but by challenging the positive role of sublimation he facilitated challenges to the hegemonic representation of the humanist subject. That is, not just *despite* but *because of* their ambivalent position in regard to colonialist discourse Latin American writers such as Borges, Bioy Casares, and Rodríguez Monegal *problematize* the humanist subject in ways that less politically ambivalent writers do not. By promoting the proliferation of meanings, they undermined the nostalgic recuperation of the humanist notion of a core self — a Caucasian, masculine, heterosexual self — as the locus of all human experience.

Prospero in Popular Culture

Recent popular treatments of *The Tempest* also carnivalize humanist subjectivity. For example, both the sci-fi cult film *Forbidden Planet* (MGM, 1956), directed by Fred McLeod Wilcox, and the rock musical *Return to the Forbidden Planet* (1991), written by Bob Carlton, make fun of the humanist subject's attempts to see himself as autonomous and whole. The MGM film introduced Robby the Robot as an Ariel figure, thus demonstrating how technology may serve the needs of the Prospero figure, a philologist whose name, Dr. Morbius (Walter Pidgeon), points to his morbid self-absorption. Morbius has internalized what Caliban stands for as the power of repressed desire, called "the monster of the Id," which gradually undermines his autonomy and his patriarchal authority. In the rock musical Morbius's wife, Gloria, successfully challenges his patriarchal authority and, at the end, she delivers a version of Ariel's "men of sin" speech from *The Tempest* (3.3.53–82) to a group of men that includes Morbius and Miranda's lover as well as those who attempted to usurp Morbius's authority.

The hero of Paul Mazursky's film*Tempest* (Columbia Pictures, 1982) also has a truculent wife, but her challenge to his patriarchal authority is unsuccessful. This cynical interpretation of Shakespeare's play, which stars John Cassavetes as Phillip, an embittered New York architect, Gena Rowlands as his long-suffering wife Antonia, Molly Ringwald as Miranda, and Susan Sarandon as his docile lover Aretha (Ariel), is set on a Greek island inhabited by a lecherous buffoon named Kalibanos (Raul Julia). The film tries to recuperate stereotypical assumptions about the autonomy of the humanist subject, but Phillip is so self-absorbed and insensitive that the sympathy solicited for him is grudgingly given, if it is given at all. Evidently we, like his wife, his daughter, and his lover, are supposed to find Phillip so charismatic and attractive that we don't mind his misogynistic arrogance — or, indeed, love him all the more precisely *because he cannot help being such a childish and narcissistic boor.*

Parodic Orientalism

Peter Greenaway's recent film *Prospero's Books* (1991) puts the humanist subject in question in ways that Mazursky's film does not. Like other films directed by Greenaway — *The Belly of the Architect* (1987) and *The Cook, the Thief, His Wife, and Her Lover* (1990) — by exaggerating especially virulent and self-destructive aspects of one particular humanist subject, *Prospero's Books* demystifies and desacralizes that subjectivity as a universal norm. By portraying Prospero as *both* the duke of Milan and a master Renaissance playwright, Greenaway's film, like Bioy Casares's novella, foregrounds the humanist subject's relationship to representation itself.

The consequences of this concentration on representation can be demonstrated by applying to Greenaway's film an observation Said has made about

Renan. In his essay "The World, the Text, and the Critic," Said notes that one of Renan's major tasks as an Orientalist was to *divest* Semitic religious texts (the Torah, the Koran, and the derivative Gospels) of their sacredness.[24] Greenaway's film attempts to *reinvest* the twenty-four classic humanist texts Prospero took with him into exile with *something like* sacredness, but this effort comes off as parodic; that is, the hyperbolic ways in which the film fetishizes the books that Prospero took into exile as objects of holy adoration undercuts rather than encourages acceptance of them as sacred texts.

This parodic effect is heightened by having Prospero (John Gielgud) speak all of the lines of all the characters. Such a literalization of the way Shakespeare himself supposedly went about writing a play constantly reminds us of the control that a Renaissance humanist artist exercised—or *attempted* to exercise—over himself and over his world, as well as over a work of art. This representation of the writing of *The Tempest* dramatizes what Said has called "the text's insufficient authority to make a representation or performance of itself work 'properly'" (*The World, the Text, and the Critic*, 198). Like Dickens's treatment of *Hamlet* in *Great Expectations*, what Greenaway gives us in *Prospero's Books* is "a double scene or ... a theme and variation in which one text or theme and a confused new version of it take place simultaneously" (198). Thus what Said says of Dickens's narrative concerning the production of *Hamlet* can even more aptly be applied to Greenaway's film:

> It somehow manages to portray [*The Tempest*] and [*The Tempest*] travestied, together, not so much only as montage but as criticism, opening the venerated masterpiece to its own vulnerability, letting a monument of literature accept and actually accommodate the fact of its written, and hence unprotected, consequence, which is that each time it is performed the performance is a substitute for the original, and so on to infinity, with the original becoming a more and more hypothetical "original." (*The World, the Text, and the Critic*, 198)

Moreover, Greenaway's emphasis on the relationship between Prospero and Ariel draws attention to the underlying arrogance of the assumption that the world is most properly seen from the perspective of a white, heterosexual male. We first see Ariel, played by four different actors in the film, in the bathhouse. As Prospero begins to create his magical tempest, he looks up at Ariel. Greenaway describes how "the child smiles and stands and, holding his small penis like an ornamental waterspout—he sends an arc of crystal clear, backlit water into the shallow bath." The next scenes are interrupted with cuts to Ariel in the act of urination, which is, in Greenaway's words, "an image of exhibitionistic impudence."[25] This parodic image of the master (phallic) signifier, whose function Prospero refused to perform when he retreated to his study and let his brother assume his duties as duke of Milan, diminishes its potency, trivializes it, and divests it of its sacredness.

The Parodic Body

The lush exoticism of the sets in Greenaway's film exemplifies Said's concept of Orientalism. In their exuberant baroque excess these sets parody high Renaissance paintings. The variety of naked bodies presented to view also undermines idealized humanist depictions of the body. There are fat bodies and thin bodies, young bodies and old bodies, beautiful bodies and grotesque bodies, male bodies and female bodies of all shapes and sizes. At one point our gaze at a woman's body is suddenly disrupted as her flesh falls away and we see her inner organs. The scene in which we see the birth of a monster (Caliban) is a parodic commentary on the humanist subject's desire to see, to witness, the primal scene of its own origin.[26]

We see drawings, representations, of naked Native American bodies in Renaissance humanist texts. But there is no dominant or privileged size, shape, or gender, nor are any of these bodies presented (posed) in the conventional postures, inherited from the Renaissance, that assert phallic mastery and male dominance. Unlike paintings and drawings created from the perspective of Renaissance humanism, where the point of view remains fixed, Greenaway's camera and the myriad bodies are constantly in motion. Our eyes — our gaze — are never allowed to rest or dwell on any one scene or body.

Caliban's sexuality is problematized through the representation of his naked body. Instead of portraying him in the conventional manner as a rough-hewn, crass, heavyset, oafish and loutish brute, i.e., as a barbarian, Greenaway sees him as a beautifully muscled, and hairless, ballet dancer (Michael Clark). Like Robert Mapplethorpe's photographs of nude black men, Greenaway's Caliban embodies both hostile, aggressive masculinity and receptive, passive femininity. In other words, he represents the kind of split in the humanist subject that is both produced and repressed by the demands of compulsive heterosexuality.

In the final scene of the part of the film called "The Past" (section 43), Prospero and Miranda approach Caliban's pit. Here we see Caliban reflected in Prospero's mirror, at first curled fetuslike and protecting his genitals; later, as he surfaces, fully revealed, he sits straddle-legged, "showing with brazen exhibitionism his mandrill-coloured genitals — bright-blue scrotum, orange penis, pink groin and vermilion anus … a travesty of a mortal — somewhat like a young Silenus" (*Prospero's Books*, 94–95). As he calmly masturbates while reading classical stories of bestiality from one of Prospero's books, *The Ninety-Two Conceits of the Minotaur*, he reflects the paradoxical and contradictory quality of Prospero's unconscious (repressed) desire. That is, he not only represents Prospero's desire to control everyone and everything around him, he also illustrates the narcissistic quality of that desire, Prospero's unwillingness to understand that his frustration stems from his denial of existential equality — of otherness — to those who could recognize him for what he is.

Greenaway's Prospero finally does come to see that in order to reconcile his desire to control others with his need to be recognized by others he has to let go of his (humanist) notion of selfhood, which is the basis of his claims to autonomy and wholeness. Prospero learns that there is no inherent personal quality he can point to that makes him *deserve* to be duke of Milan. While he is in exile on the small island Prospero discovers that as long as he refuses to acknowledge that he is not whole, that there will always be a difference between his needs and his desires, that there will always be a lack in his being for which he cannot compensate, and that he needs other people to affirm his identity, he will be caught in self-loathing cynicism.

The point is not that Prospero should give up his dreams and complacently accept his fate. He should, rather, cease bemoaning his fate, cease being a *belle âme*. Like Richard II and King Lear, Prospero undergoes a hystericization whereby he loses the second, sublime body that makes him a noble patriarch. On the island he confronts the void of his subjectivity outside the title he inherited from his father. *After* Prospero achieves his ends, *after* he chastises his brother and wreaks his revenge, *after* he has everyone in the palm of his hand, what he comes to accept is that he *is* the duke of Milan, and he must live up to that responsibility not by controlling nature or manipulating others, but by acknowledging that he is not free to dictate the Law to everyone, to order everyone's moral universe.

The Law does not reside in him to change as he pleases; it resides in the fact that he inherited the title of duke of Milan from his father. Thus, what Prospero finally sees when he abjures his power is that the role of the duke of Milan — as well as that of father and patriarch — is a purely formal one. Its framework is determined by patrimony and by precedent (tradition). The concrete content of his decisions is directed by councillors such as Gonzalo, so that he has only to sign his name — the Name of the Father — in order to perform his function, but that function is of the utmost significance. It is the operative, legitimizing word.

A Postscript

Some recent commentators have questioned the sincerity of Prospero's renunciation of his desire to control everyone and everything around him. According to Stephen Greenblatt, Prospero's pardon of his enemies "is not a release from the power in which Prospero holds everyone around him but, as with Latimer and James I, its ultimate expression."[27] The point is well taken, but to put it this way is to make the same categorical error that Spivak saw Fernández Retamar making. That is, when he questions the significance of Prospero's pardon — and thus of his renunciation — Greenblatt is reading Prospero as if he were an actual historical person instead of a character in a play.

I do not disagree with Greenblatt, but his reading makes it harder to see Prospero as a representative humanist subject who is able to have an insight about himself and is able to act on that insight. In other words, if I join Greenblatt in seeing Prospero as an actual historical person, I distance myself from him and thus avoid calling into question my own position as a humanist subject. By distancing myself from Prospero I make it more difficult to see his renunciation as a renunciation of the virilizing violence that has happened to him and therefore makes it more difficult for me to renounce such violence that has also happened to me. But if I allow myself to see Prospero as a representation of a particular white, masculine, heterosexual subjectivity, I can then see his renunciation as part of a transformation of who he was, even of who he is, a renunciation of the subject position that has been imposed on him and on those of us who are identified with that subject position.

Prospero's renunciation of the *desire for* hegemonic (phallic) power — he breaks his magic staff and buries it "certain fathoms in the earth" (5.1.54–55) — does not lead him to ascend to another world, a utopian philosophic republic, but it does lead him to experience something not yet done or thought in the world of humanist subjectivity. Such a supplement to Joel Fineman's invaluable work affirms the central assumption of his postpsychoanalytical project: that "modernist — and, for that matter, postmodernist — theories of the self are not so much a theoretical account or explanation of subjectivity as they are the conclusion of the literary subjectivity initially invented in the Renaissance," a subjectivity epitomized in the figure of Prospero/Shakespeare.[28]

The single, virtuoso, bravura take with which Greenaway's film ends supports that assumption. Prospero picks up Ariel, and embraces and kisses him before he turns and looks straight at us. As he speaks the famous final lines, the camera draws near, and, according to Greenaway, we see that Prospero is neither a god nor a magician. Just as he has set everyone else in the play free from their false selves, he asks us to set him free from the sense of self that has sustained him but which he now sees as no less false than others. Prospero thus cannibalizes himself as a humanist subject and invites all of us to join in the banquet.

Notes

1. See "On the Genealogy of Ethics: An Overview of Work in Progress," in Herbert L. Dreyfus and Paul Rabinow, *Michel Foucault: Beyond Structuralism and Hermeneutics*, 2d ed. (Chicago: University of Chicago Press, 1983), 237. I am using the word genealogy in its Nietzschean sense to suggest that, in Foucault's words, "The purpose of history, guided by genealogy, is not to discover the roots of our identity but to commit itself to its dissipation"; see Michel Foucault, "Nietzsche, Genealogy, History," in *Language, Counter-Memory, Practice*, ed. Donald F. Bouchard (Ithaca: Cornell University Press, 1977), 162.

2. All quotations from *The Tempest* are from the Signet Classics edition, ed. Robert Langbaum (New York: New American Library, 1987).

3. The editors of the modern scholarly edition point out that although "Prospero's internal conflict, and his external conflict with his enemies, are diminished" in the Dryden-Davenant collaboration, and Prospero is "puzzled by the operation of fate" and has "about as much control over the lives and loves of his daughters and his ward as have most of the exasperated fathers of Restoration comedy," his control over Caliban is kept intact; see *The Works of John Dryden*, ed. Maximillian E. Novak (Berkeley: University of California Press, 1970), 10:340–41.

4. I am quoting Ernest Renan, *Caliban, suite de la Tempête* from the translation by Eleanor Grant Vickery (New York: New York Shakespeare Society Press, 1896), 18. Subsequent page references to this work will be given parenthetically in the text.

5. See G. W. F. Hegel, *Phenomenology of Spirit*, trans. A. V. Miller (Oxford: Oxford University Press, 1977), para. 658.

6. See Friedrich Nietzsche, *The Genealogy of Morals*, trans. Walter Kaufmann and R. J. Hollingdale (New York: Vintage Books, 1989), 157. In his survey of the use of Caliban in "Third World" texts, Alden T. Vaughan remarks, "The French intellectual community was not wholly sympathetic to Renan's formulation; some critics found it too cynical, too anti-democratic. [Alfred] Fouillée, especially, expressed philosophical dissatisfaction.... Renan responded with another play, *L'eau de jouvence: suite de Caliban* (1881), but ... again the theme is cynical and elitist"; see Alden T. Vaughan, "Caliban in the 'Third World': Shakespeare's Savage as Sociopolitical Symbol," *The Massachusetts Review* 29 (Summer 1988): 293.

7. See Jacques Lacan, *The Function of Language in Psychoanalysis*, trans. Anthony Wilden, in *Speech and Language in Psychoanalysis* (Baltimore: Johns Hopkins University Press, 1968), 44.

8. According to Fiedler, Caliban's alleged attempted rape of Miranda makes him "the first nonwhite rapist in white man's literature, ancestor of innumerable Indian warriors and sulking niggers who have threatened ever since in print, as well as on stage and screen, the fragile honor of their oppressors' daughters"; see Leslie Fiedler, *The Stranger in Shakespeare* (New York:

Stein and Day, 1972), 232, 234. On this point see also Alden T. Vaughan, "Shakespeare's Indian: The Americanization of Caliban," *SQ* 39 (1988): 137–53.

9. We can only speculate about what Trinculo is doing to Caliban after he creeps under his garment and Caliban repeatedly cries out, "Do not torment me! O!" (2.2.57), but the lines suggest that some form of sexual activity is going on.

10. Quotations from Darío are from Alden T. Vaughan and Virginia Mason Vaughan, *Shakespeare's Caliban: A Cultural History* (New York: Cambridge University Press, 1991), 147, which cites John T. Reid, *Spanish American Images of the United States, 1790–1960* (Gainesville: University Presses of Florida, 1977), 195. Darío's 1898 essay is reprinted in *Escritos inéditos de Rubén Darío*, ed. E. K. Mapes (New York: Instituto de las Españas en los Estados Unidos, 1938), 160–62.

11. I am quoting from the translation of José Enrique Rodó's *Ariel* in Jean Franco, *An Introduction to Spanish-American Literature* (London: Cambridge University Press, 1969), 159.

12. Octave Mannoni, *Prospero and Caliban: The Psychology of Colonialism*, trans. Pamela Powesland (1956; rpt., New York: Praeger, 1964), 70. Mannoni wrote this book in Madagascar in 1948 during a bloody anticolonialist revolt.

13. George Lamming, *The Pleasures of Exile* (Ann Arbor: University of Michigan Press, 1992), 13, 15. Subsequent references to this work will be given parenthetically in the text.

14. At the end of his summary of the Caliban controversy Alfred J. MacAdam observes that "Latin Americans have come increasingly to see themselves as Caliban, the cannibal, the exploited native of the island Prospero (the United States) conquers. The idea that Caliban is the first mestizo in literature, possibly the product of the union between Prospero and the witch Sycorax ... heightens this identification"; see Alfred J. MacAdam, *Textual Confrontations: Comparative Readings in Latin American Literature* (Chicago: University of Chicago Press, 1987), 19.

15. Adolfo Bioy Casares, *The Invention of Morel and Other Stories*, trans. Ruth L. C. Simms (Austin: University of Texas Press, 1964), 11. Subsequent page references to this work will be given parenthetically in the text.

16. Aimé Césaire, *A Tempest: Based on Shakespeare's "The Tempest"—Adaptation for a Black Theatre*, trans. Richard Miller (New York: Ubu Repertory Theater Publications, 1986). Cf. Eve Kosofsky Sedgwick's observation that "the concept of homosexual identity per se tends not to make sense readily in [Latin American] cultural contexts, or tends to make sense to self-identified *jotos* or *pasivos* but not *machos* or *activos*"; see Eve Kosofsky Sedgwick, *Epistemology of the Closet* (Berkeley: University of California Press, 1990), 159 (note 32). For more on this point, see Ana Maria Alonso and Maria Teresa Koreck, "Silences: 'Hispanics,' AIDS, and Sexual Practices," *Differences* 1 (Winter 1989): 101–24.

17. Citing Wole Soyinka's withering critique written in 1976, Edward W. Said has pointed out how Césaire's concept of *negritude* incorporates essentialist—and inherently masculinist—assumptions about bourgeois subjectivity; see Edward W. Said, *Culture and Imperialism* (New York: Knopf, 1993), 228–33, 263. In *Orientalism* (New York: Vintage Books, 1979), Said observed that "Renan's is a peculiarly ravaged, ragingly masculine world of history and learning; it is indeed the world, not of fathers, mothers, and children, but of men like his ... Caliban" (147).

18. Gayatri Chakravorty Spivak, "Three Women's Texts and a Critique of Imperialism," in Henry Louis Gates Jr., ed., *"Race," Writing, and Difference* (Chicago: University of Chicago Press, 1986), 264.

19. Roberto Fernández Retamar, "Caliban: Notes toward a Discussion of Culture in Our America," trans. Edward Baker, in *Caliban and Other Essays* (Minneapolis: University of Minnesota Press, 1989), 15.

20. Emir Rodríguez Monegal, "The Metamorphoses of Caliban," *Diacritics* 7 (Fall 1977): 82. Rodríguez Monegal also mentions Oswald de Andrade's friend and namesake Mário de Andrade (1893–1945), whose Rabelasian novel *Macunaíma: The Hero without a Character* (1928) uses

cannibalism to parody Brazilian men's claims to a bravura masculine identity. An English translation of the latter work by E. A. Goodland was published by Quartet Books in 1984.

21. See David Bergman, *Gaiety Transfigured Gay Self-Representation in American Literature* (Madison: University of Wisconsin Press, 1991), 142. As Bergman observes, "the correlation of homosexuality and cannibalism is quite old."

22. Georges Bataille, *Erotism: Death and Sensuality,* trans. Mary Dalwood (1962; rpt., New York: City Lights, 1986), 72.

23. Julia Kristeva, *Powers of Horror: An Essay on Abjection,* trans. Leon S. Roudiez (New York: Columbia University Press, 1982), 78–79.

24. Edward W. Said, *The World, the Text, and the Critic* (Cambridge: Harvard University Press, 1983), 46–47.

25. Peter Greenaway, *Prospero's Books* (New York: Four Walls Eight Windows Press, 1991), 45, 49. I regret that I have not been able to see the film of *The Tempest* directed by Derek Jarman that was released in 1979.

26. Cf. Freud's comments on children's theories of birth (394–95) and his later comment on scopophilia in Sigmund Freud, *Introductory Lectures on Psycho-Analysis,* trans. James Strachey (New York: Norton, 1966): "The extreme achievement on these lines is a phantasy of observing parental intercourse while one is still an unborn baby in the womb" (460).

27. Stephen Greenblatt, "Martial Law in the Land of Cockaigne," in *Shakespearean Negotiations: The Circulation of Social Energy in Renaissance England* (Berkeley: University of California Press, 1988), 146.

28. Joel Fineman, *Shakespeare's Perjured Eye: The Invention of Poetic Subjectivity in the Sonnets* (Berkeley: University of California Press, 1986), 43, 47.

7

Grounds for Decolonization: Arguedas's *Foxes*

Claudette Kemper Columbus

> And now the highland fox has himself begun to make us sing and dance.
> He has begun to make the world dance, as, in the old time, the drum and
> voice of Huatyacuri, the hero deity who seemed a beggar, made the world
> sing and dance.
>
> José María Arguedas, *El zorro de arriba y el zorro de abajo*

An assumption underlying this essay is that colonization is as inescapable as cultural conditioning. The effort of this essay is nonetheless to discover distinctions among types of colonization, distinctions in colonizing processes, and options for decolonization. These options may be found cast not in terms of colonizer and colonized, but in terms of sufficiency or insufficiency of choice in decolonizing oneself.

José María Arguedas, the Peruvian novelist and anthropologist, intercalates the diary of his suicide with the chapters of his unfinished novel, *El zorro de arriba y el zorro de abajo* (hereafter referred to as *The Foxes*).[1] Although Arguedas failed to find viable, decolonizing options for himself, he is among those who grasp what is necessary to intimate some grounds for decolonization. Sublime space, nonlinear time, a self that acknowledges deep dependence on others, and nonanthropocentric contacts with other forms of life provide decolonizing options. Sublime space and nonlinear time help reveal an economy not based on self-interest, cash, and commodity accumulation. The ability to integrate outsiders, to hear other languages and idiolects, to maintain a sensitivity to silence, helps provide hard-won access to the heterogenous.

In *The Foxes*, Arguedas translates life situations into "fictive scenes." I put the phrase in quotation marks because Arguedas denies the "ficticity" of any of his work. Although he understands the arts of representation and understands that he is arranging material, he believes words have a compact with truth, and that his writing voices realities.[2] The novelistic chapters of *The Foxes* do not bear directly on Arguedas's life, and even the diaries are carefully edited, but both novel and diaries are intended to convey reality with immediacy, intimacy, and urgency.

Arguedas opens the first diary with a representation of obsessive, chronological time. Discussing several attempts to draw his life to a close, Arguedas "records,"

> Santiago, Chile, the 10th of May, 1968
> In April of 1966, a little over two years ago, I tried to kill myself. In May of 1944, a recurrence of the psychological crisis I first suffered in childhood ... Last night I decided to hang myself ... (7)

The Caribbean novelist Wilson Harris, addressing issues of colonization, speaks of obsessive time as a possession and "as comma and period, age and full-stop." He reads the source of obsessive time as springing "from a base idolatry, from a desire to conscript time itself into a material commodity."[3] Harris attributes obsessive time to attempts to "stockpile" time and defines colonization in part as time's despotic capture by materialism.[4] By beginning his novel with despotic capture by colonized, "material" time, Arguedas shows the calendared days of the diary as obsessive.

Given that *The Foxes* addresses issues of colonization in a culturally plural context, it is significant that Arguedas begins with material, obsessive, colonized time and, in Fabian's words, with a "*geopolitics* [that] has its ideological foundations in a *chronopolitics*."[5] But no sooner has Arguedas introduced a chronology calculated by the calendar than he shows chronological time to be colonized time. In contrast to disempowering, colonized time, the diary moves directly to a representation of Arguedas's life expanded into other lives and other social "times," in Peru and elsewhere. However little chronological, material time is left to him, he also represents his life as outlasting his death. The scene of his suicide thus paradoxically posits surplus. This surplus functions as resistance by renewing expectations for social change and requiring heterogeneity in the reader; both contribute to decolonization. In dramatizing social conscience through his suicide, Arguedas incorporates death as a plea on behalf of multiethnic life. This dramatic act may be read as having done more to attract the conscience of the world than his remaining alive might have done.

One avenue to noncolonized time is to draw on myths that stretch time. Arguedas draws on two archaic Andean myths as forces in the present. Both the myth of Huatyacuri and the myth of Tutaykire depict colonized time and colonized space. Both show an economy based on private accumulation that colonizes space, time, sexuality, physical contact, and the Other, and this before the Conquest and the appearance of the so-called plunder economies of the West. Both pre- and post-Conquest representations address economies of self-interest at variance with social welfare. But the *huarochirí* myth of Huatyacuri and his father, Pariaqaqa, also shows how time and space may be decolonized. It offers a sufficiency of choice.

Huatyacuri, a "culture" hero, mountain and shaman and weather deity from the deep past, a newcomer to Huarochirí, overhears two foxes talking about a rich man. The rich man, who controls the town, has showily covered his house in feathers and owns llamas of every color, even blue ("unnatural" capital accumulation). This man also pretends to be rich in wisdom, although a mysterious illness (a venereal disease?) would to an Andean indicate the contrary. Huatyacuri offers to cure the false wise man, with the proviso that Huatyacuri, principle of fecundity, may then marry the false wise man's daughter. And because Huatyacuri listens to foxes and is attuned to the rhythms in nature, he knows what is wrong with the false wise man: the false wise man's wife has sinned by feeding a stranger a colored corncob kernel that jumped from the hearth into her vagina. After curing the man by making the wife confess and ridding the household of harmful elements, Huatyacuri marries the daughter but afterward must win seven contests proposed by his envious, greedy, and inhospitable brother-in-law.

The myth of Huatyacuri shows surplus time (enough for everybody—for a nonanthropocentric while) associated with openness. His receptivity to instruction from environmental elements, his generosity to strangers, and his accepting a challenge seven times show Huatyacuri succeeding at surplus: bounty, creativity, new rituals, and new music. He redresses a sick socioeconomic situation with a different geocosmic vision that has the potential to generate fruitful totemic relationships and to generate sufficiencies of choice. But the myth of Huatyacuri also shows time as possession (the self-defensive circles of egoism and materialism, symbolized by the false wisdom and sexual "sickness" of a rich man and of his wife and first son-in-law).

The second and apposite mythic temporality is of Tutaykire, Wound of Night (50), shaman healer and water cult deity, whose time remains "present." His paralysis is the bondage of possession. First seen sweeping triumphantly from the sierra to the coast, Tutaykire is captivated by a seductress who holds him in dalliance for the centuries intervening between then and now. Yet like Huatyacuri, and like Arguedas, this imprisoned shaman healer Tutaykire could have brought and might still bring the surplus of released consciousness and a new era to the corrupted coast.

Tutaykire's name encodes the Quechua word for darkness, *tuta*. This rare and great compilation of the Huarochirí myths and rites from which Arguedas draws begins with the origin myth of Dark Night Yanañamca Tutañamca (as in Wound of Night, as in Generative Hole, *namca*, perhaps referring to the Llama, a dark constellation). "Tutayayacpacha" is the lightless epoch of origin. Yet although *tutay* means the coming of dark night, Tutaykire's name also suggests night's ending, the end of one epoch and the birth of another.[6] Rouillón argues that Tutaykire represents a vertical axis from the sierra to the coast that might healingly connect the most high to the lowest.[7] Of the originary names evocative of first generative darkness and a belated but regenerative darkness, Tutaykire seems to represent fallow time "between." His name may also mean, fittingly enough in the context of the fishing port of the novel, "deep sea."[8] Tutaykire was extending his domain from the heights to the ocean, the mythic reach of where he "should have" been, when he was entrapped. Hence Tutaykire is "between two lights": the promise of his beginning that his realm would expand to the sea is the first light, and the possibility of his release from captivity the second.

In the diary, the voice of the third-person narrator describes the myth of Tutaykire as twenty-five hundred years old: "For two thousand five hundred years, Tutaykire has been braiding a net of gold and silver" (29; the myth could date back to the Tiwanaku-Wari civilization). Yet this ancient myth depicts colonization by materialism, noise, sexual contamination, and sexual obsession.

Arguedas's personal crisis refracted onto that of mythic Tutaykire in arrest, and into the characters in the novel who all endure capture by despotic (materialist) historical time, transcends temporal and personal boundaries. Multitudes are under a death sentence in time colonized and encoded by socially irresponsible capitalism, expansionist technology, and a state that supports them: the subject matter of Arguedas's novel and of Peru's history. The overcoding of the state is "a system of *machinic enslavement*: the first 'megamachine.'"[9] Arguedas pits the subject matter of his novel against machinic

enslavement in a mafia-ridden city during those years the world was enduring the war in Vietnam (another indication in the novel of material, obsessive
time). It is as if Arguedas's life, drawing to a close, is simultaneously entering
that mythic realm of existence that chronological, calendric time interrupts.
Yet in that mythic realm, time as surplus struggles against the despotic capture of obsessive time. The capture component of colonialism represented in
the myths of Huatyacuri and Tutaykire was present in the realm of myth and
long predated "the" Conquest.

Peoples conquered other peoples more or less routinely in Andean prehis-
tory. The mistrust and denigration of one another by different groups, preju-
dice, and xenophobia are nothing new. *Huarochirí* tells how the Checas ver-
bally abused the Quintis, for instance. But adaptive structures were in place
in the Andes that made decolonization not only possible but not infrequent.
Some conquests turned out to be forms of affiliation and integration. Although acts of colonization, they also offered decolonizing options, for when
colonization integrates groups and finds forms for mutual adaptation, decolonization occurs, the One and the Other reconciled through mediation and
through filiation. No small part was played in decolonization by sharing material wealth, such as the stockpiling of goods as a communal resource and
the establishment of new patterns of trade on principles of reciprocity.

As for the present, one may only hope that, with resources diminishing
worldwide, the outcome for interethnic encounters will be as capable of ab-
sorbing changes as the adaptive procedures reflected in the *huarochirí* myths
of Huatyacuri and his father. These myths show forms of conquest that, although introducing modifications, also preserve heritages and forms of gov-
ernance already in place. These are myths of fecundity that dispose of self-
interested accumulators of property.

Arguedas juxtaposes the "moment of writing a diary"—linear, conscripted
time—to myth's expressions of limitless and unframable time. Together, they
generate a simultaneity of conflicting modes of duration. While introducing
his death, Arguedas also introduces a duration that does not pass away; no
personal moment is isolated from mythic time. The timescape of Arguedas's
life as it draws to its obsessive close dichotomously suggests a timescape of
surplus (life abounding). The tension between the past represented not as
past but as depth in the present and the past represented as imprisoning the
present is not resolved either in the diaries or in the novel or in the Andes.

The invocation of optative and mythic times subverts time as datebound,
as period, comma, full stop. Optative time and some representations of mythic
time offer a surplus that enfolds historical periodization. Historical events

become period, comma, and full stop, and colonize and paralyze time when represented as anthropocentrically possessed, when represented as a human commodity. But when an optative myth enfolds an event, enfolds chronological and historical times, it decenters the authority of history, and, in so doing, decolonizes.

Features of the deep past of ancient civilizations remain alive in Peru in actuality. Not yet inconsiderable Quechuaymara and other native cultures are coeval with the contemporary cultural hash of manufacturing cities. With no gap between the temporality of the deep past and the various temporalities of the ongoing present, the ancient Andean mythology of obsession and the ancient Andean mythology of regenerative surplus influence not only Arguedas's and his characters' lives, but also depict the hopes and fears of Andeans catapulted into the age of modern technology. The long darkness of the mythic Tutaykire, captive to sexuality and loss of vitality, is an unbroken excess of night that is being lived.

The timescapes of these myths draw attention to one disempowering aspect of an ongoing "politics of time." Those anthropologists who study the Other as not inhabiting the same time as themselves provide an example when they look on the Other as remnants from earlier, less advanced times. Arguedas deploys the myths of Huatyacuri and Tutaykire to counteract such distancing of other times. Hence, when Arguedas plants all times as an ongoing present in the diary, he commits a political act that occludes separation and distance both from himself and from his characters. A chronopolitics of immediacy causes the alienation of distance to vanish — that is, for the reader who, in seeking the Other, has the patience to absorb meaning from the myths of the Other.

In the diaries, Arguedas resists the construction of himself as a distanced, "provincial" object. The representation of the conflictual plurality of his cultural heritage is as much at war within him as it was in the fishing port of Chimbote, Peru, in 1968, the setting for most of the action of the novel. In all temporalities, Arguedas attempts to delete distance by showing distance as disempowering: in the politics of colonizing relationships in his personal life, in sociopolitical public life, in historical time, in mythical time. Oxymoronically, distance deprives people of space. Arguedas's death sent him on his way as a messenger to and from what only seems to be the past, his present, and this, his future, one that has acquired mythic dimension for many of the peoples of Peru who look on him as the culture hero who heals with his words and with music. Arguedas's death sent him dichotomously to the realms of a myth of surplus and a myth of stasis.

Arguedas depicts time and sexuality past and present, and agrarian and capitalist exchange, both as possession (forms of violation and exploitation) and as surplus (revivification and regeneration) through the mythic beings of the foxes; through the mythic deities, the hyperreal shaman healer artists Huatyacuri and Tutaykire; through personal memories; and through characters "taken" from life. "Mythic" does not mean "fictive" except in degraded usage; it means hyperreal.

Durkheim describes one of the dualities of suicide as a tension between social commitment and social detachment: "When man has become detached from society he encounters less resistance to suicide in himself, and he does so likewise when social integration is too strong."[10] Arguedas exhibits relations of detachment from and also strong integration with the social world in the diaries and elsewhere. For instance, Arguedas writes of the *condenado* suicide folktale: "The condemned [who must wander the night] is beneficent, a tender, poetic personage who expiates the sin of suicide.... He has supernatural powers, is deeply loving and deeply sorrowful."[11]

Arguedas represents suicide in the diaries as trebly motivated. First, suicide is a desire to be detached from society. Second, suicide is a desire for social integration. Arguedas attributes his desire to die in part to the degradation of peoples and culture. These first two forms of suicide protest incessant violation; the "length and degree of exposure" to threateningly impersonal social forces have become too great (Durkheim, 147–48). Life has become "possessed" — colonized by demonic forces such as the woman who holds Tutaykire sexually captive in an Andean counterpart to Venusberg. But thirdly, this desire to die can also be read as a protest against the impersonal element of suicide: a protest against the anonymity of the forces out there overwhelming the vulnerable members of the social world. The desire to die is an assault against those who cannot become "Other" wise.

Arguedas executes his suicide when social and aesthetic prostitution seem all but invincible. Arguedas desires to die as a demonstration of his strong respect for the people's cultures (the surplus of wonderful storytellers, preachers, musicians, and populist political activists). He expects the expressive strength of his death will call attention to the critical condition of the people's cultures, for a "strong" suicide is potentially a magical act.[12]

The polyvalence of Arguedas's suicide becomes apparent if one thinks of it as "Death suggested by the Collectivity," death that altruistically impedes the death of the collectivity by staging the death of its defender. And because "strong" suicide seems a component of a desire to kill the otherwise invulnerable, very "often the part of himself that the suicide tries to kill is *precisely the social superego which is causing him to die*."[13] As an act of aggression, Arguedas's suicide gestures against the world of transnational businesses that break down national and social loyalties; gestures against the world of the petite bourgeoisie defending the smaller comforts; gestures against commodity capitalism divorced from social and environmental loyalties and scarred by extreme individuation, by cultural conflicts, by the disintegration of social solidarity, by the disappearance of values that may be thought of as healthily social and concerned with the Other.

Máximo Damián Huamani, the violinist who played at Arguedas's funeral, read Arguedas's suicide as surplus when he mourned Arguedas by declaring that Arguedas's life was not his to take: the life of Arguedas belonged to the people (surplus, in that his life extended beyond him). Huamani did not see the resistance of this surplus when he asked, What right had Arguedas to take that bounty that belonged to others, to the Andean peoples, and to that land?[14]

Lingis and Levinas might reply: Arguedas's suicide does not represent a capitulation to death.[15] The immanence of Arguedas's absence establishes a bond of tenderness and of poetry with the condemned Others. In the absence of an equitably multiethnic world, he dies "totemically" in hopes of reifying solidarity among peoples as well as in support of understanding differences. The sense of alterity itself

> maintains open every kind of openness, even that to distant terms or immediately oncoming elements. The "deepest" level of life—that of vulnerability and susceptibility to pleasure and pain—is taken to be constituted not by a relationship with death, a relationship of being with nothingness, but by a relationship with alterity. (Lingis, xvi)

Arguedas's suicide affiliates with the passion and agony of Maxwell from the States, of Hilario the Aymara, of Esteban the Quechua, of Moncada, the black man, of Orfa, the prostitute, and so on.

By dying, Arguedas sought a way to the others, others who cannot be defined merely by being indigenous. His suicide is a negation of all those who oppress through self-interested, material concerns. It is a publicized declaration of his vulnerability, of openness to the Other. Committing suicide maintains that openness, in the way that the Other also is willing to commit suicide in defense of the integrity in and of the frail.

This suicide of surplus on the part of the poet Arguedas is in contrast to the suicide of Orfa in the "Last Diary?" Victimized by poverty, violated by the brutalized, she commits a suicide of the potential, of the could have been. The female Orpheus represents women lost to the future. Orfa as artist who has borne the child of rape is analogous and obverse and converse to Arguedas's suicide. It is as if all possible outcomes to suicide, ranging from the magical—a mythic and musical, healing and tender suicide—to a hopeless and degraded death are being played out before the pueblo and the world. Orfa's suicide from colonization in the "Last Diary?" darkens the potential for surplus in the author-poet's suicide of potential. When Orfa commits suicide, the weight of sterile exploitation seems insuperable even in a multiethnic city such as Chimbote, a port that could be a cauldron of change and social integration but instead suffers a near absolute social collapse, in part attributable to the brutalizing acts of criminal transnational corporate managers, in part attributable to the continuing destruction by homogenization of indigenous cultures. In light of Orfa's suicide, the efforts of Arguedas would seem negligible were it not for the interrogative, weak as it is, of "Last Diary?" Is this actually the last diary for those who not only read but revere this book?

Arguedas's suicide has not hastened the awakening of conscience. As the socioeconomic plight continues unresolved in Peru, one need not ask who died when Arguedas committed suicide. Of the estimated twenty thousand lives lost to terrorism in the 1980s, the question arises: who is committing suicide? People whose conscience does not awaken? Who are colonized by material concerns and captured in conscienceless history? Who mark time off on the obsessed time of calendars? How many have caught the spark of surplus Arguedas attempted to light with his suicide (247)?

Arguedas remains rare in representing in fiction native Andean voices with authenticity, "from within," so credibly that his native "characters" speak idiolectically.[16] A culture hero himself, an "anthropologist of urgent circumstances" ("de urgencia": "Notas"), Arguedas dedicates the residue of his lifespan to the future, in hope that time may become collective, plural, mythic.

Having represented his preparations for suicide—a representation of despotic capture in period and comma calendar time that reduces his suicide to historical event—the diary moves into duration differently conceived, and space measured not by place. Arguedas translates space into an extraindividual dimension, into a geography punctuated differently from the blocks of mapped cities.

Charles Long points to a major component in the definition of colonization when he describes it as a "market economy [that] interposes itself between persons, mediating direct awareness of social relations by the abstract law of relationships between commodities."[17] Arguedas connects the semantic field that is chronological time to "commercial" time, time bought and sold. But Arguedas juxtaposes this also to another semantic field: socionatural relations.

Arguedas scratches a mountain pig until its contented grunts rise to cascades that fall from unclimbable heights. The shift in scale from the earthbound to the sublime, the shift in tone from funereal to ludic hymn translate the time of Arguedas's private torment in obsessional time into the vastness of space, where trees clinging to precipices defy the abyss. The beyond oneself and a consolation of grunting animal pleasure offer surplus and open a vista of sublime space that frees him from despotic capture by time.

In light of the abyss, people (including Arguedas) are represented as "beautiful and powerful worms, misprized by the crafty assassins governing Peru" (9). These minuscule people are powerful because vulnerability has opened them to the Other Wise of Being. Expanse and helplessness make them receptive, and receptiveness leads to depth, space, surplus, poetry, myth.

The powerful, narrative violations of time that mark the writing of history wittingly or not pimp for anthropocentrism and the economics of possession. But Chimbote, the horrible urban sprawl, its sardine factories representing despotic capture by a market economy, shrinks when embedded in sublime space. Chimbote's commercial world is "denominated" by exposure to sublime space. History itself becomes puny when embedded in myth, in a sublime geography, in the vast reaches of biological life.

As with time, no sooner does Arguedas set up the boundaries of space than he shatters them by breaking open space and event, and by dilating the tiny and "insignificant." Small worms, he writes, are powerful. Small, powerful, beautiful worms subvert the assassins, subvert (ostensibly) Peruvian history and mafia manufacturers interposing international corporate graft between managers and workers.

Worm and pig are carried over as motifs in the novel. As does the worm, the pig offers a denominating alterity to anthropocentrism and commercial materialism. In another context, Stallybrass and White read the pig as the image of displaced abjection. They see the pig as revealing the process whereby "'low' social groups turn their figurative and actual power, not against those in authority, but against those who are even 'lower'"[18] In contrast, Arguedas values disprized forms of life: pigs, worms, lice, foxes, himself, and other people who show themselves vulnerable.

Arguedas's transvaluation of values is completely un-Carlylian, completely un-Nietzschean, in that the pig matters as pig, *before* it counts as symbol. Surplus of meaning is grounded in the sense of this animal's pleasure in life, and *not* in what the symbol of pig may mean or in how rich the symbol is in leaping over oppositions and ambivalences in the cultural grid.[19] What is most important about the pig is that it reconnects Arguedas to unrefereed feelings (surplus of emotion, sensuality), even though symbolic surplus is also inherent in the scene. The pig, like all "creatures of the threshold," creatures of ambivalent and degraded status (pig, worm, fox), is semantically saturate. These creatures suggest in their physicality modes of resilience and alternative modes of making meaning. Their semiotic surplus indicates the fertility of heterocompetency, signaled in this case not by an understanding of the language and sensibility of the Other as a person but of the Other as a companion beast. Heterocompetency evades purely human systematization, totalitarian control, colonization.

Often in *The Foxes* and in *huarochirí*, time is "told" in terms of space and sexuality is told in terms of time. Sexual experiences form consonances or dissonances that are essentially temporal and economic (having to do with household management and environmental affect).[20] Both the pre-sixteenth-century myths and the twentieth-century city manifest colonized time (possession by) with a counterpart in sexual abuse.

The passage that follows shows strands of temporalities, mythologies, economies, and sexual experience inseparable from one another and from issues of colonization. A pregnant and probably mentally handicapped Indian pauper passes through the household of the adolescent Arguedas. In doing so, the visitor from outside crosses his life, divided between the warmth of the Indian kitchen and the stiffly mannered and frequently cruel parlor, divided between the warmth of Indian elders and the brutal rape of Indian women. Her transit marks the indigent Fidela as a permanent present on Arguedas's memory and also as an unresolvable fracture in his conscience. She also becomes a divinatory wound on his sexuality (as noted in reference to her spider fingers; spiders in various Andean contexts are used for divination). Her disappearance into the unknown contributes to the permanence of her effect on him. Through her, Arguedas represents the Other by showing his own personal vulnerability and exposure to pain, a vulnerability that, in his search for the heterogenous, he pushes past the breaking point. Recounting the memory, he performs an extraordinarily empowering anthropology of surplus rather than an anthropology of possession (taking over the account of the objectified and distanced Other).

To refute Cortázar's charge that Arguedas is provincial, Arguedas writes:

> We are all provincial.... Fidela stroked my stomach with warm fingers like half-desperate spiders. What I felt then was suffocation. I thought death was coming to me in the form of hot air. My whole body yearned for it. She lifted the poncho that covered me. In that cold, the young people didn't bare themselves. Fidela lay down at my side. She lifted her skirt. I touched her body with my hands....
>
> With her bag on her back, Fidela climbed the long slope. We servants accompanied her to the field of farewells, which, back then, all Hispanic-Indian towns had. Weeping, she said good-bye there. She always had a few damp strands of hair in her mouth and lacing one side of her face. That line of spittle summarized the skies. The highest clouds, there in the saliva. The small movement of the qopayso, acrobatic on that line. And even more so when Fidela really wept.... We watched her for a long time as she made her way behind the wall of thorns.... The cook said, "She goes to give birth to an orphan, an outsider; who knows where she goes." (21–22)

Two salient factors in the "passing through" of the socially victimized Fidela are the enduring, "provincial" immediacy of her absolute helplessness combined with her fertile, warming and wounding sexuality.

> This closeness without distance, this immediacy of an approach ... [not] circumscribable ... Levinas calls proximity. The other ... afflicts me with a closeness ... closer than the closeness of entities.... The relationship with alterity, which is what escapes apprehension, exceeds all comprehension, is infinitely remote, is, paradoxically enough, the most extreme immediacy, proximity closer than presence, obsessive contact. (Lingis, xix)

But this obsessive contact is surplus. Fidela afflicts Arguedas with closeness, that expansive immediacy and unconfinability of alterity.

Arguedas creates a similar proximity that exceeds as "surplus," not as "possession": the proximity between himself and his reader, an implosive closeness and intimacy that opens the reader to Arguedas's pain and the pain of his characters. The Arguedean critic Saguier calls this phenomenon "adhesion," a not particularly pleasant term, but expressive of the closeness this text achieves, entering the sympathetic reader's world.[21] It comes as close to the reader as Arguedas's sense of the "Other" to him. The eclipse of distance among human beings may create space, for, paradoxically, the dissolution of boundaries between reader and character creates rather than reduces space.

> It is not the object of the story to convey a happening per se, which is the purpose of information; rather, it embeds it in the life of the storyteller in order to pass it on as experience to those listening.[22]

Fidela's unknowable future stretches the comprehension of the young writer-to-be, on whom her spider hands leave a wound that exceeds him. "Alterity comes to me from without, and comes by exceeding my capacities" (Lingis, xvii). Sensitive and vulnerable young Arguedas accepts the consequences of remaining vulnerable, accepts sentience that lies "otherwise" than in his being. Being sentient lies in being Other wise. The wisdom of alterity lies in vulnerability to the vulnerable. It also lies in sensual alertness: "skin caressed contrasted with face addressed" (Lingis, citing Levinas, xv). "The other is not experienced as an empty pure place and means for the world to exhibit another perspective, but as a contestation of my appropriation of the world, as a disturbance in the play of the world, a break in its cohesion" (Lingis, xxiii).

To experience alterity makes demands beyond the practical and the pleasurable. Sociation and alterity demand dissociation, disorientation at "home," contestation if not disinheritance of oneself, a willingness to accept pain. (You reading this have interest in issues of colonization. So your ghost guesses why decolonization is often spoken about, but rarely enacted.) Fidela's physical "surplus" is far more than sexual contact between herself and an Other, and far more significant than crossing class and ethnic barriers. Her face crossed by damp hair and spittle summarizes a world of hurt. She comes close to the reader as a disturbance that makes its demands. She provides a "strange filiation," to use Merleau-Ponty's phrase. She is a necessary stranger in another "dwelling."[23] In this context, she has nowhere to call home; "dwelling" is wholly metaphorical, figurative, spiritual.

Fidela crosses Arguedas's life but does not pass from it. Perhaps the absence of mediation contributes to the lasting and depth of her impact on him. The immediacy of need is not curable, and may perhaps constitute a wound of night, without which we remain monsters.

> The appeal and contestation of alterity ... is the very experience of immediacy. Alterity is closer still to me than the present ... neither the subject's own materiality nor intervening objects form a screen.... (Lingis, xix)

And yet, unexpectedly, Levinas claims that alterity lacks presence. As Lingis observes, presence involves and maintains distance, indeed, establishes distance (Lingis, xix).

> Alterity is irreducible in not being interchangeable with me, even if finally my whole subjective reality consists in substituting myself for him. The dimension of irreversibility in the relationship, that by which alterity, unendingly withdrawing, infinitely withdrawing, remains other.... The irreversibility is essential to the whole analysis. (Lingis, xxxiii)

Photographs of beggars may depict Fidela's otherness, but photographs "distance." However poignant, photographs remain "dissociated" entities, obsessed objects even when they are adhesive. A photograph would place Fidela in another place and posit a relationship with an insufficiently physical Other, an Other not so much lacking in spittle that summarizes the skies, but lacking acoustic resonance. The moment is already over when the photograph is seen; the impresssion of immediacy is ersatz. The viewer experiences time vicariously and the viewer does not hear the voices, smell the smell, touch the body. Of the much that is lost, the quality of a silence is lost, too, when the image "tells the tale."

In Arguedas's diaries, the biographical springs into the collective historical, springs into the creature world, into space, and springs into the mythic world. Yet, as noted, Arguedas represents the mythic world as itself under the despotic capture of possessive overcontrol.

When colonization is totalitarian, the violence it engenders divides the subject person inwardly. Colonization includes the imposition of nonintegratable, alien systems: an alien economy, an alien agriculture, an alien religion, "hard" time, commercialized, mechanized sexuality, the detritus of a language that uglifies. Such violence produces a "double consciousness" (as W. E. B. DuBois observed), with little access to surplus, for the inwardly divided subject person has internalized the oppressor. In the double consciousness of the self engendered by colonization, ongoingly violent conquest wages war on the self from within.

Arguedas experienced "from within" why a deeply rooted culture such as the Quechuaymara was difficult to colonize[24] — much more so, let us suppose in a very broad brush generalization, than the Indians in India under British rule. (Butler is quite correct when she insists on the need to discriminate among imperial attitudes and regulatory systems.[25]) The British (as a hypothetical instance) were relatively monolithic in their colonialist enterprise. For an extended period, the British maintained themselves apart as members of a superior civilization of a different color. Their subjects were "foreign" beyond the possibility of altering appearances, with the result that, in British colonies, interethnic marriage and crossbreeding were rarely officially sanctioned. The conquest of Peru followed a different model. After the still-inexplicable elimination of the Inka armies and the subsequent mass rape of the native women, the conquerors "extirpated" native religions and rituals and reorganized Andean space, drawing populations into grid-shaped villages around plazas dominated by churches. "Marriages" and crossbreeding between native and "white" were at first far from rare, although the appearance of Spanish women on the scene "dissolved" many of these marriages.

Tutaykire has time to escape despotic capture, being immortal. But Tutaykire can also remain captive forever. Mythic time itself can remain frozen, as when Tutaykire in the novel's "Last Diary?" is seen nailed to the dead bone of the cross.

> The Fox from Above, spinning like a top, has been calling ... from the summit ...
>
> I was going to ... I tried to ... I tried to show a Calgary, stirring in facts and symbols, but he who gazed through the eyes of the Foxes from the summit of the Cross of Bone has been reached as yet by no human being nor did I reach that summit and I did not reach those eyes. (244–45)

The diaries and the chapters contract and expand in a pulse between sierra heights and coastal depths and back up to the heights. The expansion/contraction is temporal as well. It is as if several hydraulics are in motion (surplus: Huatyacuri, Paula Melchora, Crispin, Maxwell, all associated with music). It is as if several other characters have been arrested by extremes (Orfa, Braschi). A few balance motion and arrest, surplus and possession (Arguedas, the foxes, Tutaykire, Gustavo Gutiérrez).[26]

Having placed the phenomenon of colonization as preexisting the conquest, Arguedas uses these expansions and contractions of scale and of time to place the nonimperial author in Tutaykire's space. Tutaykire is thus also trapped among contemporary systems of value—the beautiful and powerful worms that are Andean natives and the strength of their helplessness: Catholic and Protestant evangelism, Peace Corps intercession, political movements, international commercialism, and so on. These nonsyncopated, surplus/possession expansions and contractions of scale, of space, of time in the ancient myths precipitate into the mafioso economics and religious turmoil of the obsessed "present."

Perhaps the conjunction of different mythologies shows what it means to have heterogenous frames of reference. To have a sense of the heterohistorical, to have a sense of how multiculturalism is balked by sterile sexuality and lethal materialism, is to know that if there is no time for scratching a pig, if there is no time for languages other than our own, then we will have no time.

In the first diary, flux and pulse and deanthropocentralization decolonize time. The confluence of pine and pig and worm open "protagonist" roles in areas usually dismissed as—well, the word "marginal" too much dignifies the dismissal of such creatures as pigs and worms from contemporary life and art. But Arguedas's diary dehierarchizes and deidolatrizes. The grunting of the pig is as curative as psychoanalysis too frequently is not. It is curative even as writing is too frequently not for Arguedas. In these diaries, as in the "boiler" chapters of the novel, the multitude of voices raised could bring "the conditions of possibility of intersubjective knowledge. *Somehow we must be able to share each other's past in order to be knowingly in each other's present*" (Fabian, 92; emphasis in the original). If epochal changes do not offer decolonizing options today, our world will either be liquidated by homogenization or we will always be at war: class war, gender battle, struggle among "ethnic" groups unable to be Other wise, to be open to difference, unable to risk vulnerability, unable to accept, if need be, that death in defense of difference. In offering this possibility of intersubjective knowledge and interactive myths, *The Foxes* offers surplus, the possibility of sharing different pasts, and doing so in part through sharing different languages, different idiolects.

In search of that "somehow we must be able," Arguedas subsumes himself in this first diary in geography and incorporates himself into the collective of other lives and other forms of life. Symbiosis both affirms his singularity and absorbs it. He passes into the agglutinative, where persons pigs worms place and space interconnect with infinition. The writer ticks off the days remaining in obsessive time and slips free of linear time, "digresses" through heterogenous, time-space worlds. Such digression resists normalization, colonization, deculturation, emplotment, capture. Therefore, although Arguedas sets up time lines, spaces, narratives of proximity porous as the Quechua language, scenes vigilantly and sensitively responsive to context, he incorporates durations, accumulates times and spaces otherwise than being, times other than ourselves; spaces other than our "own"; languages other than our own as well as other languages in our own; narratives other than our own.

To make use of the polylinguism of one's own language, to make a minor or intensive use of it, to oppose the oppressed quality of this language to its oppressive quality, to find points of nonculture or underdevelopment, linguistic Third World zones by which a language can escape, an animal enters into things, an assemblage comes into play.... know how to create a becoming-minor.[27]

The deep sense of suicide: to become at the same time *oneself* and *the other*, male and female, subject and object, killer and killed — our only chance of communion with ourselves.[28]

Notes

1. The page numbers cited throughout the chapter refer to the critical edition *El zorro de arriba y el zorro de abajo*, coordinated by Eve-Marie Fell (Madrid: CEP, 1990). All translations into English are mine; Frances Barraclough is translating the novel into English. The myth of the foxes that Huatyacuri overhears is to be found in the priceless Quechua manuscript of the

rites and myths of Huarochirí compiled by Francisco de Avila circa 1608. José María Arguedas translated these myths into Spanish as *Dioses y hombres de Huarochirí* (Lima: Siglo XXI, 1966). Gerald Taylor transcribed the Quechua and translated the text as *Ritos y tradiciones de Huarochirí del siglo XVII* (Lima: IEP, 1987). Urioste brought out a translation into Spanish, *Hijos de Pariya Qaqa: La tradición oral de Waru Chiri* (Syracuse: Syracuse University Press, 1983). Frank Salomon and George L. Urioste translated the text into English as *The Huarochirí Manuscript*, transcription of the Quechua by George L. Urioste (Austin: The University of Texas Press, 1991).

2. José María Arguedas, *Primer encuentro de narradores peruanos* (Arequipa, Peru: Casa de la Cultura del Peru, 1965 [1969]), 140.

3. Wilson Harris, *Tradition, the Writer and Society: Critical Essays* (London: New Beacon Books, 1967), 84.

4. The phrase "despotic capture" as of time comes from Gilles Deleuze and Félix Guattari, *A Thousand Plateaus: Capitalism and Schizophrenia*, trans. Brian Massumi (Minneapolis: University of Minnesota Press, 1987): "A State apparatus is erected upon the primitive or agricultural communities, which already have lineal-territorial codes; *but it overcodes them*, submitting to the power of a despotic emperor, the sole and transcendent public-property owner, the master of the surplus or the stock, the organizer of large-scale works (surplus labor), the source of public functions and bureaucracy" (427–28; emphasis in the original). Theodor W. Adorno addresses the static and immutable effect of time captured and "mechanical" experience as static in *Introduction to the Sociology of Music*, trans. E. B. Ashton (New York: Seabury Press, 1976), 47.

5. Johannes Fabian, *Time and the Other: How Anthropology Makes Its Object* (New York: Columbia University Press, 1983), x, 144; emphasis in the original.

6. Thérèse Bouysse-Cassagne and Olivia Harris, "I. Pacha: en torno al pensamiento Aymara," *Tres reflexiones sobre el pensamiento Andino* (La Paz: HISBOL, 1987), translate *tutayan* as "become dark": "La palabra *tutayan* antes citado es precisamente 'anochecer'" (22).

7. José Luis Rouillón's excellent essay "La luz que nadie apagará" is included in the Fell edition of *The Foxes*, 341–59; see 344–45 for the discussion relevant here.

8. "Este tiempo 'entre dos luces'—*tutayan pacha o chamaca pacha*—no sólo se refiere a la ya mencionada región de los cerros. El contenido léxico y la carga metafórica de estas palabras evocan otras regiones. Según Bertonio *cchamaca* significa también 'lago sin suelo' y *tuta* 'mar profunda'" (Bouysse-Cassagne and Harris, 26).

9. Arthur C. Danto, *Analytic Philosophy of History* (New York: Cambridge University Press, 1965), 428; emphasis in the original.

10. See the chapter entitled "Altruistic Suicide," book 2 of Emile Durkheim, *Suicide: A Study in Sociology*, trans. John A. Spaulding and George Simpson (New York: Free Press, 1951), 217.

11. See José Maríd Arguedas, *Folklore Americano*, Año 1, no. 1, ed. Luis E. Valcárcel (Lima: Editora Médica Peruana, 1953): 128.

12. In "Suicide as a Magical Act," Charles William Wahl argues that suicide is an attempt to solve an "identification conflict"; see Edwin S. Schneidman and Norman L. Farberow, eds., *Clues to Suicide*, (New York: McGraw-Hill, 1957), 24. When Wahl writes about suicide as a "phenomenon of infantile cosmic identification" (28), however, he subverts the magical action that he detects and grants little to magic's ontological possibilities.

13. Daniel Lawrence O'Keefe, *Stolen Lightning: The Social Theory of Magic* (New York: Continuum, 1982), 306; emphasis in the original.

14. This comes from a radio address Máximo Damián Huamani taped (Lima, Circa 1970), and also from "Con lágrimas, no con fingimiento," *Recopilación de textos sobre José María Arguedas* (Havana: Casa de las Américas, 1976), 341–43. The latter was published in English as "With Tears, Not Words," trans. Luis Harss, *Review: Latin American Literature & Arts* 25/26 (n.d.): 49–50.

15. Emmanuel Levinas, *Otherwise than Being or Beyond Essence*, trans. with an introduction by Alphonso Lingis (Dordrecht, Boston, and London: Kluwer Academic Publishers, [1974] 1991).

16. Marcín Mróz, "José María Arguedas como representante de la cultura Quechua. Análisis de la novela *El zorro de arriba y el zorro de abajo*," *Allpanchis* 15, nos. 17–18 (Cuzco, 1981): 133–60.

17. Charles Long, *Significations: Signs, Symbols, and Images in the Interpretation of Religion* (Philadelphia: Fortress Press, 1986), 110.

18. Peter Stallybrass and Allon White, *The Politics and Poetics of Transgression* (Ithaca: Cornell University Press, 1986), 53; emphasis in the original.

19. Edmund Leach, "Anthropological Aspects of Language: Animal Categories and Verbal Abuse," in E. H. Lenneberg, ed., *New Directions in the Study of Language* (Cambridge: Harvard University Press, 1964), 23–63.

20. Martin Lienhard has done excellent work on this material; see especially his *Cultura popular andina y forma novelesca: zorros y danzantes en la última novela de Arguedas* (Lima: Tarea, Latino-americana editores, 1981).

21. Rubén Bareiro Saguier, "José María Arguedas o la palabra herida," in the Fell edition of *The Foxes*, xv.

22. Walter Benjamin, *Illuminations*, trans. Harry Zohn (New York: Schocken, 1969), 159.

23. Maurice Merleau-Ponty, *The Prose of the World*, trans. John O'Neill (Evanston: Northwestern University Press, 1973), 135. Merleau-Ponty also uses another haunting phrase, "there is a myself which is other" (135).

24. José María Arguedas, Francisco Miró Quesada Contuarias, and Fernando de Szyszlo, *Notas sobre la cultura latinoamericana y su destino* (Lima, 1966), 21–26.

25. Judith Butler notes, "It has become increasingly important to resist the colonizing epistemological strategy that would subordinate different configurations of domination"; see Judith Butler, *Gender Trouble: Feminism and the Subversion of Identity* (New York and London: Routledge, 1990), 35. A superb article on differences among groups and influences globally shared is Aijaz Ahmad, "Jameson's Rhetoric of Otherness," *Social Text* 17 (1987): 3–25.

26. Gustavo Gutiérrez is a liberation theologian of note, and a friend of and writer on Arguedas.

27. Gilles Deleuze and Félix Guattari, *Kafka: Toward a Minor Literature*, trans. Dana Polan (Minneapolis: University of Minnesota Press, 1986), 26–27.

28. Michel Leiris, *L'âge d'homme*, cited in Edmond Jabes, "Dedication," *The Book of Questions: Yaël, Elya, Aely*, vols. 4–6, trans. Rosmarie Waldrop (Middletown, Conn.: Wesleyan University Press, 1983).

8

Genealogical Determinism in Achebe's *Things Fall Apart*

Imafedia Okhamafe

Things indeed fall apart in Umuofia. The center can no longer hold. But things begin to fall apart in this nine-village Umuofia clan long before a European colonialist missionary culture inserts itself there. The tragedy of Umuofia, therefore, lies not so much in white missionary arrival as in Umuofia's hierarchical failure to fruitfully engage certain internal cultural differences that were already simmering in the general economy of Umuofia long before and even after the presence of any formidable Christian difference in Umuofia. The hierarchical failure derives from an *egwugwu* genealogy that forms and informs the general economy of Umuofia. By general economy I mean the arch network of power relations that structures the thinking and life practices and thus the destiny of Umuofia. The greatest inheritor, defender, promoter, and spokesman of this *egwugwu* culture in Umuofia is Okonkwo.

Read from a genealogical perspective, Chinua Achebe's seminal novel *Things Fall Apart* becomes more about the powers and limits of one dominant interpretation and practice of a certain polygynous and misogynic tradition in Umuofia.[1] This *egwugwu* genealogy defines strength only in martial terms or only in terms of the will to physical power. Furthermore, manhood and this strength are synonymous. The clan recognizes this strength through four titles, the fourth and highest one being lord of the clan. Each title marks the degree of strength and thus of manhood. Okonkwo's monomaniacal task in life becomes making himself, his sons, and Umuofia males into this kind of man. Manliness so defined is Okonkwo's existential litmus test for himself, his family, and his clan. A male without any title is often called an *agbala* (a woman). Where a male stands in the general economy of Umuofia more or less depends on whether the male is a man or a woman. This *egwugwu* genealogy rests on Umuofia's agricultural economy of yams (men's crops) and non-yams (women's crops, such as cassava). Umuofia's dominant tradition makes Umuofia culture into Umuofia nature, a nature that demands and insists on its subjects' following the line of manliness and womanness as strength and weakness. In Umuofia all females are women and all women are weak. No woman can be strong. Only males can be men and only men are strong. A male who fails to be a man is a woman. Umuofia culture calls on its women to be women and on its males to be men. All women are women. All men are males, but not all males are men. Patriarchy, however, requires the partnership or cooperation of both biological males and biological females. Not even nature itself privileges males or females in the reproductive process. Umuofia does not explain why that which is supposedly potentially strong (the male) would need that which is allegedly inherently weak (the female) to produce those who can become strong (males): that which can be strong needs that which cannot be strong to produce those who can be strong. A woman's proper role is to help Umuofia *reproduce* males who will become men and women who will remain women. There is no room in Umuofia for womanly males or unwomanly women. A man's proper task is to help his women *reproduce* patriarchy (Umuofia style). A man has to fight constantly not to become a woman. But how does this multiplication process (of strength and weakness so defined) produce a creative (healthy) strength that can indefinitely sustain (on its own terms) Umuofia's patriarchal reality and ideal? This question, which roots itself in the beginning of the novel, is what finally does in both Okonkwo and his Umuofia culture. Umuofia falls because it leaves no space for creative utopian speculation or for the imagination of other ways (from within and without) of being in Umuofia culture. Internal disturbers of the *egwugwu*, tradition are dismissed as *agbala*, *efulefu* (effeminate men), or *osu* (outcasts) of some sort and are treated accordingly.

Okonkwo's father (Unoka), we are told, was a woman or a weak male because he never earned any title. He was always in debt and was more interested in being a musician than in being a man. Okonkwo inherited no wealth from his father; in fact, his father was buried in a place reserved for shamed males, female males, and other outcasts. Determined to not be like his father, Okonkwo assumed his manly or economic responsibility very early in life. His goal: to be a man, to be one of the greatest men ever in Umuofia, to obtain all four honorifics Umuofia has to offer to men. His greatest fear: to be a woman or to father a male who becomes a woman. For Okonkwo, to be an Umuofia man means to use physical power in defense or promotion of Umuofia manhood. Anything short of this expectation means cowardice, womanliness, betrayal. When Okonkwo can no longer be an Umuofia man, he takes his own life rather than risk the stigma of being a woman. Umuofia's origin stories and all Okonkwo's ends for his Umuofia culture involve the de-womanizing of men or the de-manizing of women. Okonkwo disowns or disregards the legacy of Unoka because his father allegedly lived like a woman; Okonkwo's father's womanness shames Okonkwo, and he therefore wants a new beginning. He decides to resituate his personal genealogy and thus reclaim a line more in tune with his village and clan's ancestry.

Okonkwo begins and maintains his manhood through the agricultural genealogy/hierarchy already in place in his Umuofia general economy. Umuofia's political economy parallels its yam-centered agricultural economy. Okonkwo's "mother and sisters worked hard enough, but they grew women's crops, like coco-yams, beans and cassava. Yam, the king of crops, was a man's crop" (25). If the most valued crop is the yam, if the yam is the king, then the more yams one has the greater one's kingdom and the greater one's manhood and authority. Yam is man and man is king and all other crops (including women) are subjects. Okonkwo starts sowing seeds of his own kingdom with sixteen hundred seed yams, eight hundred of which he borrows from Nwakibie, a manhood veteran with "three huge barns [of yams], nine wives and thirty children," a man already with three clan titles (21). Unoka is no longer his father. The new seeds come not from Unoka but Nwakibie, his new father. The narrator has pointed out earlier that Okonkwo's "whole life was dominated by fear, the fear of failure and of weakness" (16). His fear here is deeper than a fear of evil or a fear of an awesome being (human or superhuman). This fear "was not external but lay deep within himself. It was the fear of himself, lest he should be found to resemble his father. Even as a little boy he had resented his father's failure and weakness, and even now he still remembered how he had suffered when a playmate had told him that his father was *agbala*. That was how Okonkwo first came to know that *agbala* was not only another name for a woman, it could also mean a man who had taken no title. And so Okonkwo was ruled by one passion: to hate everything that his father Unoka had loved" (17). His father Unoka died without any title. Yet Umuofia does not judge a man's worth by his father's worth, and Okonkwo wastes no time in establishing his own worth. At eighteen, he was the champion wrestler in all of Umuofia clan and beyond. At a relatively young age he is already a revered veteran of two intertribal wars, a wealthy farmer with many yams, three wives, many children, and two clan titles. He is indeed an example of the Igbo saying of the elders that "if a child washed his hands he could eat with kings" and his elders (12).

But Okonkwo does not just want to eat with kings — he also wants to be a king. A king tries to ensure that his subjects follow the values that sustain and perpetuate the kingdom. A king has a fatherly role to beget sons who will be the men to carry on the tradition to the succeeding generations. Because "yam stood for manliness," it is appropriate to initiate boys early into "the difficult art of preparing yams" (34). Manhood and yamhood somewhat create each other. Okonkwo tries to initiate into manhood through yam education his son (Nwoye) and Ikemefuna (the Mbaino boy in Okonkwo's temporary care). Umuofia holds Ikemefuna as ransom for an Umuofia woman who was killed by a Mbaino man in Mbaino market. As Okonkwo prepares his seed yams for sowing, he makes Nwoye and Ikemefuna assist him. Education in yam-raising is an essential part of Umuofia education in manhood. Okonkwo wants to start this manly education of his son early because he is determined to "stamp out the disquieting signs of laziness which he thought he already saw" in Nwoye. He adds, "I will not have a son who cannot hold up his head in the gathering of the clan. I would sooner strangle him with my own hands" (34). Okonkwo's memory of his father is not of a man but a woman; hence Okonkwo the father wants to make sure that he does not fail his son as a manly father. Okonkwo disaffiliates from his womanly father and would not only disaffiliate but even kill any womanly son of his own. He somehow does both: he kills his sonlike Ikemefuna and he manhandles and ultimately disowns his son Nwoye, who likewise disowns Okonkwo the father. The manly thing to do to a male who fails to be a man is to eliminate him. A man who cannot kill a womanly son has to do the manly thing by killing himself. Okonkwo will not have a son who is not a man. Similarly, Okonkwo cannot have a womanly Umuofia, an Umuofia of only women. When Umuofia becomes a woman, Okonkwo also becomes a woman. Okonkwo can no longer live when he ceases to be a man. He would rather die than live as a woman, so he commits suicide.

Planting yams and raising men become synonymous as women become only a means for raising or meeting the ends of Umuofia culture: women as a means for bringing great humans (men) into being. We are told that "the women planted [women's crops] maize, melons and beans between the yam mounds.... The women weeded the farm three times at definite periods in the life of the yams" (35). The main task of Umuofia culture is the massive reproduction of male seed crops. Women are the caretakers of yams (and, of course, of men). The weak exist to cater to the needs of the strong. The women's crops were planted between the yam mounds to protect and nurture the yams. The female crops care for the male crops to ensure the stability and continuity of the kingdom of yams. Women exist to reproduce and reinforce patriarchy.

Three days before the New Yam Festival, an occasion for thanking Ani (Umuofia's earth goddess) and other ancestral spirits, Okonkwo shows Ekwefi (his second wife) and others what manhood means for women. When Ekwefi cuts off a few banana-tree leaves to wrap some food, Okonkwo assaults her. When Okonkwo decides to go hunting, Ekwefi, who had just been beaten, talks about a hunter who "had not killed a rat with his gun" and murmurs "something about guns that never shot" (39). This unwomanly remark invites another show of manhood. Okonkwo fires at her but misses. When Okonkwo hears a beat of drums that summons his household to the *ilo* (the village playground), fire fills him up and he trembles "with the desire to conquer and subdue. It was like the desire for women" (43). The desire to conquer whom? To subdue whom? *Woman. Women.* Women are the object of manhood. When strength triumphs, man prevails. When weakness results, women prevail. When Okonkwo's favorite daughter Ezinma brings her mother's dish to her father and sits down beside Obiageli (her younger half-sister), Okonkwo speaks manly to Ezinma, "Sit like a woman!" Ezinma then brings her two legs together and stretches them in front of her (45). When Ezinma unwittingly tries to function as a "male daughter" by asking to carry her father's chair to the playground for the wrestling contest, she experiences his biological determinism as he responds, "No, that is a boy's job" (45).

Okonkwo's manliness reaches a climax in the case of Ikemefuna, the boy who has lived for three years in Okonkwo's household. Ikemefuna grows "rapidly like a yam tendril" and acts "like an elder brother to Nwoye"; he appeared "to have kindled a new fire" in the younger Nwoye (51). Ikemefuna "made him feel grown-up; and they no longer spent the evenings in mother's hut while she cooked, but now sat with Okonkwo in his *obi*" (51). Nwoye delighted in being asked by his mother or his father's other wives to do "difficult and masculine tasks in the home," but he "would feign annoyance and grumble aloud about women and their troubles" (51). Nwoye's development "inwardly" pleases Okonkwo, who knows "it was due to Ikemefuna. He wanted Nwoye to grow into a tough young man capable of ruling his father's household when he was dead and gone to join the ancestors. He wanted him to be a prosperous man, having enough in his barn to feed the ancestors with regular sacrifices" (51–52). Okonkwo "was always happy when he heard" his son "grumbling about women. That showed that in time he would be able to control his women-folk" (52).

Ikemefuna and Nwoye are growing up like brothers, growing up like men, and growing up as the sons of the manly Okonkwo. Okonkwo is becoming confident that he is going to leave behind him a new line, a line of men, a non-Unoka line. Nwoye's signs of manliness please Okonkwo. The narrator states, "No matter how prosperous a man was, if he was unable to rule his women and his children (and especially his women) he was not really a man" (52). Such a man, for Okonkwo and his Umuofia, is an *agbala*, a woman, a failed man. In accordance with this view of men and women, Okonkwo "encouraged the boys to sit with him in his *obi*, and he told them stories of the land: masculine stories of violence and bloodshed" (52). At first Nwoye responds ambivalently to his father's manly economy. The narrator further tells us that "Nwoye knew that it was right to be masculine and to be violent, but somehow he still preferred the stories that his mother used to tell," stories about "the tortoise and his wily ways, and of the bird" (52). His mother's stories are "the kind of story that Nwoye loved. But he now knew that they were for foolish women and children and he knew his father wanted him to be a man. And so he feigned that he no longer cared for women's stories. And when he did this he saw that his father was pleased, and no longer rebuked or beat him" (53). As the women cook, "Nwoye and Ikemefuna would listen to Okonkwo's stories about tribal wars, or how ... he stalked his victim, overpowered him and obtained his first human head" (53).

The murder of Ikemefuna becomes Okonkwo's last chance to exhibit his definition of manhood, but it is not the last challenge to his manliness. Other challenges to his manhood come, but he would no longer be able to respond manly. Killing Ikemefuna ends Okonkwo's manliness and sets the stage for the beginning of his most feared and most despised weakness: being an *agbala*, being a woman. Ogbuefi Ezeudu, a titled old Umuofia man, one of the most learned and respected interpreters of Umuofia culture, tells Okonkwo that in accordance with the bidding of Agbala (the Oracle of the Hills and Cave), "Umuofia has decided to kill" Ikemefuna. He strongly warns Okonkwo not to participate in the killing, because the boy calls him father. A group of machete-carrying Umuofia men takes Ikemefuna away the following day. Okonkwo joins the party. Ikemefuna carries a black pot of wine on his head. As their journey begins, the men joke about the locusts, about Umuofia "women, and about some effeminate men who had refused to come with them." Ikemefuna feels "uneasy at first" but this uneasiness evaporates as Okonkwo walks behind him: "He could hardly imagine that Okonkwo was not his real father. He had never been fond of his real father, and at the end of three years he had become very distant indeed." As Ikemefuna silently reflects about what it would be like to rejoin his mother and younger sister after three years of separation, a man clears his throat. When Ikemefuna looks back, the man orders him to proceed and not look back. Okonkwo withdraws to the rear of the party. As the man who clears his throat strikes Ikemefuna with his machete, Okonkwo looks away. The pot falls and Ikemefuna runs toward Okonkwo for help, crying, "My father, they have killed me!" Okonkwo responds by killing him. He kills him because he "was afraid of being thought weak" (59). He is afraid of becoming a woman. A father figure kills a son figure, and Nwoye the son wonders about this kind of father.

This killing of Ikemefuna also marks the beginning of Nwoye's disaffiliation from his father. Nwoye's disavowal of his father stems from his father's warped sense of manhood and precedes the arrival of any foreign cultural difference in Umuofia or its neighboring clans; the white man or European culture or Christianity had nothing to do with this separation of son and father. Nwoye likens his feeling in the aftermath of his father's killing of Ikemefuna to a feeling he had the year before when he witnessed for the first time another kind of murder: Umuofia's disgusting tradition of discarding infant twins in the forest to die. The agonizing cries of these abandoned, innocent twins made him realize that something was rotten in the clan of Umuofia. This disposition readies Nwoye for an alignment with any bearer of cultural difference (whether from within or outside Umuofia) who speaks to the things that trouble him about his clan's *egwugwu*-dominated culture.

Nwoye's fears of his father arise from his father's concerns over his son's proper manhood. As Okonkwo tells his friend Obierika, "I am worried about Nwoye.... His two younger brothers are more promising. But ... my children do not resemble me.... If Ezinma had been a boy I would have been happier. She has the right spirit" (63). But right spirit without the natural proper gender is useless to Okonkwo. Okonkwo laments, "I have done my best to make Nwoye grow into a man, but there is too much of his mother in him" (64). Obierika adds, but only to himself, "Too much of his grandfather in him" (64). For Okonkwo, Nwoye's problem is that he has too much of Nwoye's mother (Okonkwo's first or most senior wife) and too much of Unoka (Okonkwo's womanly father) and little or none of Okonkwo himself (the embodiment of man par excellence). Men are made, but they first have to be born as males before they can be men. If all nature does is decide genetic maleness, culture then has to be held responsible for deciding manhood—and not culture in general but feminine culture. This kind of logic enables Okonkwo to refuse any responsibility for how Nwoye turns out; Okonkwo is indicting Nwoye's mother. She is an unwomanly woman. She fails his test of motherhood. One irony here is that Okonkwo says that he has done his best to make a man out of his son, but the power of weakness (woman) is so much that he the strong Okonkwo fails in his duty as a man, as a father, to make his son a man. Another telling point involves Obierika's linkage of Nwoye's effeminacy with the paternal (Okonkwo's father) rather than the maternal (Nwoye's mother). In his aside Obierika agrees with Okonkwo that Nwoye is womanly but he does not hold women or Nwoye's mother as solely or mainly responsible as Okonkwo does. Obierika speaks out but only to himself, presumably not to incur unnecessarily the wrath of Okonkwo, who is his guest on this occasion. Even though Obierika, accepts, lives, and contributes to the ongoing sexism of Umuofia, he seems to do so less or nonegregiously. His character serves more as a foil to Okonkwo's character. Almost every dialogue Obierika holds with Okonkwo tells us more about Okonkwo.

Okonkwo often grounds his *egwugwu* patriarchy in a specious biological determinism by linking patriarchy to tradition and tradition to nature or nonhuman powers. For example, Okonkwo insists that in killing Ikemefuna he is only fulfilling tradition. When Okonkwo asks Obierika why he did not join him and the other men who killed Ikemefuna, Obierika answers, "Because I did not want to. I had something better to do." Okonkwo says, "You sound as if you question the authority and the decision of the Oracle, who said he should die." Obierika replies, "I do not. Why should I? But the Oracle did not ask me to carry out its decision" (64). This reason appears to fall on its face given that Ogbuefi Ezeudu, a reputable interpreter of Umuofia culture and Okonkwo's mentor, from his own village (Iguedo), had already explicitly warned him not to participate in the killing of Ikemefuna. Ezeudu's voice here does not speak for the patriarchal culture of Umuofia. Okonkwo tends to read almost every sign only in terms of physical strength (men) and physical weakness (women and womanly men). As he tells Obierika, "But someone had to do it. If we were all afraid of blood, it would not be done. And what do you think the Oracle would do then?" (64). Obierika rejects Okonkwo's charge that he is afraid of blood, adding, "If I were you I would have stayed at home. What you have done will not please the Earth. It is the kind of action for which the goddess wipes out whole families" (64). The sign *Agbala* with a capital A names the Oracle that supposedly orders the sacrificing of Ikemefuna. Okonkwo is afraid of becoming the sign *agbala* with a lowercase *a*. Okonkwo kills Ikemefuna in the name of his beloved goddess *Agbala* so that he would not become an *agbala* or die with his most hated name *agbala*. Okonkwo does not want to live or die as a woman. Okonkwo would not want the epitaph or epithet *agbala*. He believes that "the Earth cannot punish me for obeying her messenger. A child's fingers are not scalded by a piece of hot yam which its mother puts into its palm" (64). For Obierika, however, "if the Oracle said that my son should be killed I would neither dispute it nor be the one to do it" (64–65).

Okonkwo never hesitates to disobey a divine messenger when the message would get in the way of his manhood. He disobeys the Earth (goddess) by violating the sacred week; of course, Okonkwo believes, a man can beat his woman anytime, even during the sacred week, in order to maintain his manhood. The call of manhood is a call to arms (power, physical power). Okonkwo's misogynic reading of his culture is captured succinctly by the incident when he wakes at midnight to scratch the spot where a mosquito has bitten him. As another mosquito wails by his ear, he slaps the ear. He wonders why mosquitoes (women) "always go for one's ears" (72). He then recollects the mosquito and ear story his mother had told him as a child. He dismisses the story "as silly as all women's stories" (72). Okonkwo has no ear for hearing women's stories; he has only mouth and arms for women.

At no time the does Umuofia *egwugwu* elite give a serious hearing or consideration to the causes of the *osu* (outcasts), the *efulefu* (womanly males), parents of twins, and so forth, that abound within Umuofia. Consequently, Umuofia lacks experience in dealing with such internal cultural differences fruitfully. This tradition of not transvaluing the *egwugwu* culture and of not listening to Umuofia's minority bearers of anti-*egwugwu* values makes Umuofia unprepared for or vulnerable to any formidable force (domestic or foreign) that may actively or forcefully challenge its hierarchy. On one occasion the issue of interclan cultural differences surfaces. When Machi (Obierika's brother) points out certain cultural differences between Umuofia and some other clans, Okonkwo says, "I have even heard that in some tribes a man's children belong to his wife and her family" (71). Machi doubts, "That cannot be. You might as well say that the woman lies on top of the man when they are making the children" (71). Obierika then links this question of cultural difference to "the story of white men who, they say, are white like this piece of chalk. And those white men, they say, have no toes." Machi says that one white man (Amadi) passes through the neighborhood frequently. Amadi is a leper, and the euphemism for leprosy is "the white skin" (71). This kind of offhanded discussion of cultural difference suggests the unreadiness of Umuofia leadership to engage with any cultural difference (from within or outside) that insists on inserting and asserting itself on the body politics of Umuofia.

Umuofia patriarchal culture never critically considers cultural differences within Umuofia, between Umuofia and other neighboring clans, between Umuofia's Igbo tribe and other tribes, and between African tribes and non-African tribes. Therein arguably lies the heart of Umuofia's tragedy. How can a culture know how to respond most creatively to an opposing cultural difference if the culture is unwilling to consider the rationality and nonrationality of the difference, be it domestic or foreign? I say nonrationality because irrationality is a rationality that another rationality is unable or unwilling to admit into its center. How can one scatter the center of what one offhandedly dismisses as irrational? If rationality is a relationality and if one's culture is unwilling to at least theoretically resituate its own center in order to work out how best to relate to the new or incoming cultural difference, such cultural unwillingness sooner or later congeals into a detrimental inability. What started as a cultural unwillingness begins to look like a natural inability of one culture to withstand a seemingly superior foreign culture. Such is the story of Okonkwo and his Umuofia. The story of the *egwugwu* domination of Umuofia culture is the story of its preeminent son and father: Okonkwo.

The leading most visible inheritor and reinforcer of this dominant androcentric tradition is Umuofia's present *egwugwu*. This body of nine supreme judges and interpreters constitutes the most secret and mystified cult in Umuofia. The *egwugwu* (all male) are nine masked spirits of the ancestors that together represent each of the nine villages of the Umuofia clan. The masking helps to mystify its nature and origins and give it some divine aura. To demystify the *egwugwu*, one first has to unmask the *egwugwu*, which would reveal them as mere mortals rather than spirits with some divine connection; hence it is an egregious offense to unmask an *egwugwu*. Okonkwo is an *egwugwu* representing his Iguedo village: "The nine villages of Umuofia had grown out of the nine sons of the first father of the clan" (85). The *egwugwu* leader (Evil Forest) represents Umueru village; Umueru means the children of Eru, the oldest of the patriarch's nine sons. The *egwugwu* are the fathers, forefathers, ancestors of Umuofia.

The *uri* (dowry-payment ceremony) of Ibe and Akueke (Obierika's daughter) points to the *egwugwu* (men) as the genealogical foundation of Okonkwo's Umuofia and to women as the purveyors of these foundations. In toasting his in-laws, Obierika's oldest brother says, "We are giving you our daughter today. She will be a good wife to you. She will bear you nine sons like the mother of our town" (110). Again women are the instruments for reproducing and perpetuating patriarchy. The oldest man among Ibe's camp looks in

Okonkwo's direction and responds: "Prosperous men and great warriors. Your daughter will bear us sons like you" (110). Some of the elders are praised as great farmers, some as clan orators. The young men celebrate Okonkwo as "the greatest wrestler and warrior alive" (111). Men's cultural function of productivity is continually stressed, but for women only their biological function of reproductivity is emphasized again and again.

Umuofia is repeatedly called the land of the brave. When the titled Og-buefi Ezeudu dies, he is eulogized as a man who met the clan's highest values: he lived as a wealthy, fearless warrior, and he died old. During his funeral, Okonkwo's gun accidentally explodes and kills Ezeudu's sixteen-year-old son. Killing a clansman is a female or male crime against the earth goddess, punishable by exile from one's clan. In Okonkwo's case, he commits a female *ochu* (manslaughter), which carries a seven-year exile. Obierika and others destroy his compound as demanded by Umuofia custom. Okonkwo and his family immediately go into exile in his motherland (Mbanta, just beyond Mbaino territory). Obierika wonders why a man should suffer so much for an offense he commits inadvertently. He arrives at no answer, but he remembers his wife's twins whom he himself threw away and also wonders what crime those abandoned twins committed. This reservation about the fate of twins in Umuofia echoes Okonkwo's son's earlier concern. Nature is evoked, however. Mother earth, we are told, regards twins as "an offense on the land [that] must be destroyed" (118).

With the death of Ezeudu begins the death of Okonkwo as a man, at least Okonkwo's kind of man. Even Okonkwo acknowledges the manliness (greatness) of Ezeudu. But the days and nights of the Ezeudus are over. An Ezeudu son, one of the young Umuofians expected to carry on the tradition of this patriarch, dies with his father through the hands of Okonkwo. Is this apparently accidental death some possibly unconscious desire on the part of Okonkwo to exhibit his manhood? Whatever the case, this triple death (of Ezeudu, Ezeudu's son, and in a sense Okonkwo) hammers a nail in Umuofia's coffin of business as usual. Umuofia's center (of manliness) has been wittingly struck by itself, and things can no longer be the same.

Okonkwo and family now live in exile in Mbanta, Okonkwo's mother's home. The father (Umuofia) has expelled his leading son (Okonkwo) to Mbanta (motherland). In other words, Okonkwo is to live with "women," his dreaded subject(s). Thirty years before, Uchendu (Okonkwo's maternal uncle) went to Umuofia to return the corpse of his younger sister (Okonkwo's mother) to Mbanta for burial. The help given to Okonkwo by his maternal relatives facilitates his transition into resettling in Mbanta. He wants to reroot his *egwugwu* genealogy while he is there, even though he is no longer an *egwugwu*. He builds one *obi* for himself and three huts for his three wives. He installs "the symbols of his departed fathers. Each of Uchendu's five sons contributed three hundred seed-yams to enable their cousin to plant a farm" (120). Okonkwo's life ambition to be a lord of Umuofia clan and thus stand at the top of manhood appears derailed; in Mbanta Okonkwo is a fish on dry land. The beginning of his exile in Mbanta is also the beginning of his effeminization. He tries to transform his family line in order to realign his manliness — which, he realizes, is now in crisis. Uchendu, concerned about his nephew's melancholy, delivers to Okonkwo his first lesson on the meaning of motherhood. He asks Okonkwo why Nneka ("mother is supreme") is one of the most common proper names for Mbanta females even though "a man is the head of the family and his wives do his bidding," even though a "child belongs to its father and his family and not to its mother and her family," and even though "a man belongs to his fatherland and not to his motherland" (123). Okonkwo admits that he does not know why. But here the why is irrelevant and unimportant to Okonkwo because he does not even accept the proposition in either theory or practice. The statement flies in the face of Okonkwo's Umuofia conventional wisdom. Uchendu follows up with another question: "Why is it that when a woman dies she is taken home to be buried with her husband's kinsmen? Why is that? Your mother was brought home to me and buried with my people. Why was that?" (123). Uchendu's declaration of motherhood as supreme is at best nominal or merely linguistic; such verbal reality does not correlate with nonverbal reality in Mbanta or Umuofia. Furthermore, when Okonkwo's mother died, she was not buried with the kinsmen of her husband (Unoka, who is from Umuofia rather than Mbanta, where Okonkwo's maternal grandfather comes from). Unoka was presumably not manly enough to deserve such funereal honor. Uchendu spells out the logic behind the name Nneka when says that "a child belongs to its father. But when a father beats his child, it seeks sympathy in its mother's hut. A man belongs to his fatherland when things are good and life is sweet. But when there is sorrow and bitterness he finds refuge in his motherland" (124). When a man is in good times he stays and enjoys them with his father(land), but when he falls into bad times he seeks comfort with his mother(land). In times of man's tragedy, tradition demands that mothers console the man. Fathers should not be bothered with such sorrows, which naturally belong to a mother's province.

Beliefs about women in Uchendu's Mbanta do not differ fundamentally from those of Umuofia. For both clans, mother(hood), not woman(hood), is supreme. To say that woman is supreme would of course be another reprehensible or unacceptable equivalent of the presently dominant reality: man(hood) is supreme. If motherhood is supreme, it is supreme only in a benign form. What is fatherhood in relation to this motherhood that is supreme? What is the relationship between fatherhood and manhood? Is fatherhood subordinate to motherhood if motherhood is indeed superior to fatherhood? Such questions point to one direction: in both Umuofia and Mbanta, woman's only basic function remains the same: to reproduce and cater to patriarchy. But Uchendu (unlike Okonkwo) at least tends to recognize (although in an apparently hyperbolic and perhaps patronizing way) the significance of motherhood. Uchendu's etymological explanation does not and perhaps cannot account for the gap between this linguistic adornment of womanhood and the non-*egwugwu* status of this same womanhood. At best the account is seductively condescending. Would a woman who is respected only nominally as a mother be loyal to that same culture that also undermines her motherhood or maternity?

The first Mbanta woman to convert to the white man's faith was Nneka, the pregnant wife of the prosperous farmer Amadi. Nneka experiences motherhood as nadirhood, not supremeness. Nneka the woman, rather than Nneka of language and fable, "had had four previous pregnancies and childbirths. But each time she had borne twins, and they had been immediately thrown away. Her husband and his family were already becoming highly critical of such a woman and were not unduly perturbed when they found she had fled to join the Christians. It was a good riddance" (140–41). When things are reproductively "bad," blame only the woman. Uchendu's logic works here. If Mbanta culture cannot fruitfully integrate the difference (the coming of twins) occasioned by nature from within the culture, then the ability of Mbanta to withstand an external and more potent cultural difference for which Mbanta is less prepared becomes highly questionable. Similarly, Nwoye's unaddressed questions (Ikemefuna, the twins, and the meaning of manhood) in Umuofia and later in Mbanta contribute heavily to his susceptibility in Mbanta to any new logic (from within or without) that responds creatively to such questions. In Nwoye's case the white Christian missionaries responded satisfactorily to his own difference and issues. For him, the "poetry of the new religion" appears to "answer a vague and persistent question that haunted" his "young soul: the question of the twins crying in the bush and the question of Ikeme-

funa who was killed" (137). Nneka and Nwoye are soul brother and sister waiting to embrace any force that responds healthily to their agonies and fundamental concerns.

I analyze the power relations in Mbanta and Umuofia before and after the
arrival of British Christians and officials against this background of certain
Okonkwonian meanings of man and woman. Obierika's first visit to his friend
Okonkwo in exile turns out to forebode ironically the end of Okonkwo's
life. During this visit to Mbanta, Obierika tells Okonkwo that Abame clan
no longer exists because the white man (who "was quite different") has
erased it. He tells how the first Abame people "who saw him ran away" and
how the white man "stood beckoning to them" and how eventually "the
fearless ones went near and even touched him. The elders consulted their
Oracle and it told them that the strange man would break their clan and
spread destruction among others. And so they killed the white man" (128).
Much later "three white men led by a band of ordinary men like us came" to
Abame, surrounded the market, and killed everybody "except the old and
the sick who were at home and a handful of men and women whose *chi* were
wide awake" (129). Okonkwo remarks that Abame people "had been
warned that danger was ahead. They should have armed themselves with
their guns and machetes even when they went to market" (130). When
Okonkwo says he doesn't know how to thank Obierika for continuing to
help him take care of his economic interests in Umuofia (tending his yams,
and so on), Obierika replies, "Kill one of your sons for me" (131).When
Okonkwo responds that "that will not be enough," Obierika tells him,
"Then kill yourself." Amid smiles, Okonkwo says, "Forgive me. I shall not
talk about thanking you any more" (132). Okonkwo is on a mission to kill
any male who becomes a man or who stands in his way to the pinnacle of
manhood. He has already killed Ikemefuna. He has already killed Ezeudu's
son. He has already virtually killed his own son (Nwoye). When Okonkwo is
unable to kill the foreign challenger of his manhood and the manhood of his
Umuofia, he kills himself. The white Christian presence brings him face to
face with the concrete reality of his worst fear (the fear of becoming an *agbala*, a woman, of becoming his son Nwoye, whom he has already written off
as a woman). His logic demands nothing short of suicide as he eventually
confronts a cultural difference that tragically confounds and paralyzes him.
He kills himself. Okonkwo would rather die than live as a woman, a womanly male. He unwittingly asks his friend Obierika to forgive him in advance
for killing himself.

Obierika's first visit announced the womanization of Abame by British white difference. His next crucial visit to Okonkwo announces the spread of this effeminization to Okonkwo's own fatherland (the land of brave men, the land where men are men and women are women). Most significantly for Obierika, this new presence directly implicates the son of Umuofia's symbol of indomitable strength (manhood): Okonkwo. Okonkwo was already aware of Nwoye's membership in the new white missionary church, but he was still un-aware (until Obierika's visit) of the British presence in Umuofia, of Umuofia's response to the presence, and of his own son's complicity with whites in the affair. Nwoye's effeminization begins in Mbanta (the motherland). When Okonkwo first learns of Nwoye's involvement with Mbanta Christians, he responds to the situation as a *man*. He grabs Nwoye and asks, "Where have you been?" As Nwoye tries to escape his father's grip, Okonkwo demands, "Answer me before I kill you" (141). He beats him until Uchendu orders him to "Leave the boy at once!" and then asks, "Are you mad?" (141). Nwoye walks away from Mbanta, never to return. Through the help of the local (Mbanta) Christian head and interpreter (Mr. Kiaga), Nwoye leaves moth-erland for fatherland. Nwoye changes his name to Isaac. Kiaga compliments Nwoye for disowning his father in order to follow the Christian church: "Blessed is he who forsakes his father and his mother for my sake. Those that hear my words are my father and my mother" (142). But according to Okon-kwo, "To abandon the gods of one's father and go about with a lot of effemi-nate men clucking like old hens was the very depth of abomination. Sup-pose when he died all his male children decided to follow Nwoye's steps and abandon their ancestors?" (142). Okonkwo's initial impulse was to invade "the church and wipe out the entire vile and miscreant gang" with his ma-chete, but he concludes later that "Nwoye was not worth fighting for." He believes that what has happened in Mbanta cannot happen in Umuofia. Okonkwo wonders how he, a flaming fire, could "have begotten a son like Nwoye, degenerate and effeminate.... Perhaps he was not his son. No! he could not be. His wife had played him false.... But Nwoye resembled his grandfather, Unoka, who was Okonkwo's father. He pushed the thought out of his mind" (143). Soon another explanation comes to Okonkwo: "Living fire begets cold, impotent ash" (143).

Mbanta clan continues to worry about the new faith, while also continu-ing to dismiss it as "a gang of *efulefu*" who decide to live in the Evil Forest. The Evil Forest appropriately fits the church, for it is traditionally the home of society's undesirable elements. In violation of Mbanta traditional laws, the church rescues abandoned twins. Mbanta villagers, however, do not think that "the earth goddess would . . . visit the sins of the missionaries on the innocent villagers" (144). Stories continue to spread that the white man has come not only with "a religion but also with a government" (144–45). It is also said that one man who killed a missionary was hanged, but many did not believe or take these stories seriously. The church has welcomed not only twins but also *osu*. This admission of outcasts into the growing Mbanta church (a move spearheaded by Mr. Kiaga) caused much controversy, because many of the other converts vigorously opposed it, at least initially. The first two outcasts converted became "the strongest adherents of the new faith" and "nearly all the *osu* in Mbanta followed their example" (147). One *osu* "in his zeal brought the church into serious conflict with the clan a year later by killing the sacred python" (147). Okonkwo, who now plays a role in Mbanta affairs, has only one response: a manly act. He says that "until the abominable gang was chased out of the village with whips there would be no peace" (148). Other Mbanta see the situation differently from Okonkwo, and their position of ostracizing the Christians by excluding them from the life and privileges of the clan eventually prevails. Okonkwo dismisses opponents of war as cowards and adds, "If a man comes into my hut and defecates on the floor, what do I do? Do I shut my eyes? No! I take a stick and break his head. That is what a man does" (148).

Okonkwo regards Mbanta as "a womanly clan" and thinks that "such a thing could never happen in his fatherland, Umuofia" (148). Obierika's news about the white presence in Umuofia and Nwoye's active cooperation with these white enemies thus demoralize him. Yet he still believes that he can make a difference when he returns to Umuofia, which is presently ruled mostly by women or womanly males. Okonkwo never learns a different sense of womanhood or manhood while in Mbanta. Uchendu's Mbanta has nothing to offer Okonkwo in terms of different conceptions of manhood or womanhood. The only superficial lesson Okonkwo learns from his days and nights in Mbanta is shown in his giving the name Nneka to the daughter he begets in exile, "out of politeness to his mother's kinsmen" (151). But he names the male child he begets in Mbanta Nwofia ("begotten in the wilderness"). These two names Nneka and Nwofia entrench Okonkwo's definitions of what it means to be a woman or a man in culture. The wilderness evokes manhood and wildness and strength. Nneka suggests motherhood and empty linguistic maternal honorifics. This kind of naming is fully in line with Okonkwo's way of looking at his world, the Umuofia world. He still grieves over the tragedy of the loss of his first son to Christianity, but he takes comfort in the fact that he had "five other sons and he would bring them up in the way of the clan" (158). Shortly before he leaves Mbanta, he assembles these five sons and announces to them his renunciation of Nwoye:

> You have all seen the great abomination of your brother. Now he is no longer my son or your brother. I will only have a son who is a man, who will hold his head up among my people. If any one of you prefers to be a woman, let him follow Nwoye now while I am alive so that I can curse him. If you turn against me when I am dead I will visit you and break your neck. (158)

Okonkwo constantly wishes Ezinma were a boy and never stops "regretting that Ezinma was a girl" (158). Because the Nwoye line has turned into a woman line, Okonkwo has to eliminate it from his genealogy and start working with the other sons on a new line, a men's line, a line that will continue the *egwugwu* tradition in Umuofia. Mbanta is hopeless for Okonkwo because he is unable to prevail there. Furthermore, Mbanta is not his fatherland, but only a place of sojourn while he is down as a man.

Umuofia responds to Christian invasion in the same way as Mbanta. The missionary development in Umuofia saddens the leaders of Umuofia, "but many of them believed that the strange faith and the white man's god would not last. None of his converts was a man whose word was heeded in the assembly of the people. None of them was a man of title. They were mostly the kind of people that were called *efulefu*, worthless, empty men.... Chielo, the priestess of Agbala, called the converts the excrement of the clan, and the new faith was a mad dog that had come to eat it up" (133). Just as in Mbanta, outcasts are among the very first to accept and be agents of this new Christian religion in Umuofia. Obierika recalls to Okonkwo that when he asked Nwoye what he was doing with the white missionaries, he said, "I am one of them" (133). When he asked Nwoye about his father (Okonkwo), Nwoye sadly replied, "I don't know. He is not my father" (134). But Okonkwo refuses to talk with Obierika about Nwoye.

Obierika then briefs him more on the state of the Christian church in Umuofia. Obierika says that Christianity has attracted not just "the low-born and the outcast" but worthy titled men such as Ogbuefi Ugonna (159). Okonkwo wonders why Umuofians lost the will to fight the Christian missionaries with their guns and machetes. Obierika reminds Okonkwo of the Abame case and lets him know that Umuofian firepower is no match for that of the Christians. Okonkwo insists that Umuofians "would be cowards to compare ourselves with the men of Abame. Their fathers had never dared to stand before our ancestors. We must fight these men and drive them from the land"

(161). Obierika tells him that his warrior message comes "too late" (161). Okonkwo's only way of dealing with any difference that threatens the *egwugwu* way of being is to eliminate it by force of arms; he knows no nonmartial approach. Obierika tells him that the white man "has won our brothers, and our clan can no longer act like one. He has put a knife on the things that held us together and we have fallen apart" (162). By paying attention only to the things that supposedly held them together and totally ignoring the other things that divided them, the *egwugwu* hierarchy was ill-equipped to handle the long-brewing internal differences that coalesced into the greatest weapon in the hands of the incoming British Christians.

Many Umuofia men and women do not dislike the new order as strongly as Okonkwo does. For them, the "white men had indeed brought a lunatic religion," but also commerce in palm oil and kernel that now makes much money flow in Umuofia (163). Even in the matter of religion a growing feeling among some Umuofians admits that there might be a method in the madness. Furthermore, Mr. Brown (the white missionary representative most responsible for this growing reception) warns his followers against excess. His pragmatic principle of "everything was possible, but everything was not expedient" prevails. After debating with Akunna (a theologian of Umuofia religion), he rules out any "frontal attack" on Umuofia religion. Right from the beginning he links his Christian religion with education and commerce and the colonial government and warns Umuofian leadership to take advantage of these seeming opportunities or risk being ruled by strangers from outside Umuofia. He builds churches and schools and hospitals and courthouses. His strategy works, and he takes pride in noting that "the Seed ... first sown among you" has begun to bear fruit in less than two years (149). Brown is grounding a new genealogy—also patriarchal and insidious, but differently so. The new church threatens to put an end to Okonkwo's kind of seeds. The days and nights of yams are over. A new crop is in the ground, and a new king is in the making.

Fundamentally unchanged Okonkwo returns to this changed Umuofia. Brown visits him and hopes that Okonkwo would be happy to learn that the Christian church has sent Nwoye (now called Isaac) to Umuru to attend a teacher-training college. Nwoye is to begin a new genealogy. Again, Okonkwo acts as a *man*. He drives Brown away and threatens to kill him should he ever return to his compound. Okonkwo "mourned for the clan, which he saw breaking up and falling apart, and he mourned for the warlike men of Umuofia, who had so unaccountably become soft like women" (168).

Ironically, Rev. James Smith, who succeeds Brown after his return to England, is very different from Brown and very much more like Okonkwo in his view of the world as a war ground. He rejects Brown's compromise and accommodation policy. He sees the world in black and white and associates evil with darkness. For him the world is a battleground between the children of light and the children of darkness, thus resembling Okonkwo, who sees the world only in terms of sheer physical strength (men) versus weakness (women).

Enoch, a fanatical Umuofian follower of Smith, thrives under such regime. He allegedly slays and eats the sacred python. This action sets the stage for the battle that finally does Okonkwo in. Enoch, a Christian, takes on the bastion of Umuofia authority and not only flauntingly commits the unheard-of sacrilege of killing and eating an ancestral spirit (the python), but also tauntingly and publicly unmasks the *egwugwu*. In Umuofia the *egwugwu* as the source and dispenser of justice is supreme. This unmasking of an *egwugwu* widens the tension between the Christian church and Umuofia clan. To "unmask an *egwugwu* in public, or to say or do anything which might reduce its immortal prestige in the eyes of the uninitiated," is regarded as one of the most serious human crimes (171). This double sacrilege prompts the *egwugwu* to incinerate Enoch's compound and move to the church to get him. Ajofia, the leading *egwugwu* and spokesman of the nine ancestors of justice in Umuofia, orders Smith, who is outside the church, to leave so that they can capture Enoch. Smith stood his ground, but to no avail. The *egwugwu* burn down the church that Brown built. This manly measure momentarily pacifies the spirit of Umuofia.

This manly destruction of the Christian church renews Okonkwo's faith in the manliness of Umuofia. Although his fellow clansmen did not agree to kill Smith or expel his Christians, "they had agreed to do something substantial," and they did it. But shortly after this leveling of the church into ashes, the district commissioner summons six Umuofia leaders (including Okonkwo) to his headquarters. Okonkwo warns his fellow leaders: "An Umuofia man does not refuse a call. He may refuse to do what he is asked; he does not refuse to be asked. But the times have changed, and we must be fully prepared" (177). The times have indeed changed, but Okonkwo has not. Okonkwo and the other leaders are handcuffed and imprisoned until they can pay the imposed fine. While they are in jail the prison officials taunt them and shave their heads. Okonkwo chokes with hate and humiliation. Umuofia men pay the fine, and the leaders are released.

The six prisoners return home in silence. With scars of prison torture, Okonkwo swears vengeance. For him, "If Umuofia decided on war, all would be well. But if they chose to be cowards he would go out and avenge himself"

(183). Umuofia men meet at the marketplace to decide what to do in light of these recent developments. Okika, an orator and one of the six prisoners, calls for war and laments that some of "our brothers have deserted us and joined a stranger to soil their fatherland" (187).

The sudden appearance of five court messengers interrupts Okika's speech. As soon as Okonkwo recognizes the head messenger, he hatefully and wordlessly confronts him. The head messenger stands his ground and the other four messengers stand behind him. The head court messenger commands Okonkwo, "Let me pass!" Okonkwo has already put himself in a situation where, by his own logic, he has no choice but to let the new order's representative pass. With relish the messenger tells Okonkwo: "The white man whose power you know too well has ordered this meeting to stop" (181). Okonkwo quickly draws his machete and kills the head messenger. Okonkwo now knows that "Umuofia would not go to war" because "they had let the other messengers escape. They had broken into tumult instead of action. He discerned fright in that tumult. He heard voices asking: 'Why did he do it?'" Okonkwo wipes his weapon and goes away (188). His ailing father's words to him at the beginning of his career as a man eventually come to haunt him. Said his father, "It is more difficult and more bitter when a man fails *alone*" (27; emphasis in the original).

Obierika leads the colonial and new leader of Umuofia to the corpse of the dead Umuofia leader. Obierika requests a favor of the new leader: "Perhaps your men can help us bring him down and bury him. We have sent for strangers from another village to do it for us, but they may be a long time coming." One of Obierika's men explains to the commissioner that suicide violates Umuofia tradition, for it offends the Earth, and a man who commits suicide "will not be buried by his kinsmen" (191). Only strangers can touch or bury such a body, which is now regarded as evil. Gazing painfully at his friend's dangling body, Obierika says to the commissioner, "That man was one of the greatest men in Umuofia. You drove him to kill himself; and now he will be buried like a dog" (191).

Okonkwo, the yam of Umuofia earth. Okonkwo, the king of Umuofia men. Okonkwo, the man who lived to be like a god, dies like a dog. His outcast body emblematizes the internal crisis in the *egwugwu* genealogy, an economy of power relations that can no longer maintain their own hierarchy or combat the hierarchy of Christian colonialism. Okonkwo would rather die than be a woman. He does not know how to live except as a man. For Okonkwo, there is no nonmartial way of engaging such enemy force as the Christian missionary. The only alternative to war is capitulation.

Steve Biko has aptly noted that the greatest weapon in the hands of the oppressor is the mind of the oppressed. Chinua Achebe's fiction (including his other four novels) powerfully demonstrates the need for a culture to utilize utopian speculative analytical power if it is to develop fruitfully. Umuofia's tragedy lies not in its fall per se. Things (especially the *egwugwu* tradition) needed to fall apart there. The tragedy of Umuofia lies in the fact that when the center eventually falls apart, it falls to another improperly constituted cultural structure or genealogy. Worse still, it falls without the *egwugwu* leaders ever realizing or recognizing that the *egwugwu* economy has very much to do with the fall and inauguration of a colonial regime in Umuofia.

Notes

1. Chinua Achebe, *Things Fall Apart* (Greenwich, Conn.: Fawcett, 1959). All subsequent page references are to this text and are cited parenthetically in my text.

Part III
Seeking the Limits of the Possible

9

Sex Matters: Genealogical Inquiries, Pedagogical Implications

Lee Quinby

Scene I: A Matter of Sex, December 6, 1993

CNN takes us live to a New Bedford, Massachusetts, courtroom where James Porter, former Roman Catholic priest, awaits sentencing. In October 1993, Porter, now married with four children, pleaded guilty to charges of sexual assault of twenty-eight children, both male and female, dating from the 1960s. Church authorities had long been aware of the abuse, requiring that Porter undergo treatment in facilities established and run by the church for priests who are sexual abusers. Porter's treatment was deemed unsuccessful; he continued the abuse even while undergoing treatment and was finally dismissed from the priesthood in 1974.

As the judge deliberates, the prosecuting attorney asks that some of those who were abused as children be allowed to speak. Twenty-one men and one woman come forward to describe the trauma Porter's actions wrought on their lives and their resentment about the hypocrisy and deception of church authorities who kept his case quiet while knowing that the abuse continued. They beseech the judge for just punishment. Porter is sentenced to eighteen to twenty years in prison; under Massachusetts law he is eligible for parole in six years. Porter's sentence also requires that he seek treatment for pedophilia upon his release from prison and that he spend no time with anyone under sixteen years of age, except for his own children.[1]

Scene II: A Matter of Sex, Of Plymouth Plantation, 1625

William Bradford retrospectively traces the fall of the Reverend John Lyford, who had come ashore the previous year, in 1624, "as if he had been made all of love" but in a short while had become "very perverse, and showed a spirit of great malignancy."[2] Lyford, it seems, had been writing letters to England in which he ridiculed the Pilgrims, accused them of unjust practices of food distribution, and, along with John Oldham, plotted doctrinal reforms in the church and colony. Confronted with the evidence, Lyford confessed publicly to slander and wrongdoing, with such fervor that some colonists began to reconsider his proposed exile. They retracted their mercy, however, when it was discovered that he had written yet another letter in which he claimed that all his accusations against the Pilgrims were in fact true.

This last letter proved too much for Lyford's wife, who was also to suffer his punishment of exile. Fearing that her silence about her husband's wrongdoings would justify God's wrath upon her, specifically that she would "fall into the Indian's [sic] hands and be defiled by them as he had defiled other women," she divulged his sinful sexual history, including his having had "a bastard by another before they were married." She had heard this rumor before their marriage, but had been persuaded then by his "solemn oath" that it was false. After they were married, when she gained more certain knowledge of this child, he begged for her pardon, admitting that he had initially lied for fear that she would not marry him. Here Lyford's pattern of wrongdoing, impassioned confession, and recurrent misdeed clearly emerges. Bradford records her further testimony that after they were married "she could keep no maids but [her husband] would be meddling with them; and some time she hath taken him in the manner, as they lay at their beds' feet, with such other circumstances as [he, Bradford, is] ashamed to relate" (185). Bradford alludes to "further intimations" from Sarah Lyford about her husband's sexual practices but refrains from detailing them. Instead, he cites an earlier instance of Lyford's sexual sinfulness, probably to establish that he had brought his waywardness with him from Ireland. During a private conference with a woman betrothed to a member of his congregation, he had "overcome her and defiled her body before marriage." Once again, Bradford forbears the circumstances, "for they would offend chaste ears to hear them related," but adds parenthetically that "though he satisfied his lust on her, yet he endeavored to hinder conception" (186–87). When found out, Lyford had been forced to leave Ireland.

Bradford explains that Lyford's letters were deemed sufficient to justify exile, but the sexual matters "made him unmeet forever to bear ministry anymore" (188). As it turns out, following his banishment from Plymouth, Lyford continued his preaching and eventually became an Anglican minister in Virginia, where he died. Sarah Lyford was not defiled by Indians; after her husband's death, she returned to Massachusetts and remarried.

Scene III: A Matter of Sex, The Scarlet Letter, 1850

Nathaniel Hawthorne takes us back to the Massachusetts Bay Colony of the 1640s. Richard Bellingham actually served as governor before the action of The Scarlet Letter begins; nevertheless, as in William Bradford's history, Bellingham plays a central role as governor in the novel's deliberations on matters of sin, crime, and just punishment. The sexual incident this time involves an adulterous act that has resulted in the birth of a child. Because of her pregnancy, the woman's sin has long been established, but the man in question remains unknown to the community. The governor urges the woman's minister to make her divulge the name of her sexual partner. Hawthorne's irony is exquisitely wrought: " 'Good Master Dimmesdale,... the responsibility of this woman's soul lies greatly with you. It behooves you, therefore, to exhort her to repentance, and to confession, as a proof and consequence thereof' " The Reverend Dimmesdale does indeed exhort her to "speak out the name of [her] fellow-sinner and fellow-sufferer" in words that, we are told, "affected [many] like the speech of an angel."[3]

Hester Prynne refuses to reveal the name of her partner in sin. She is sentenced to stand on the platform of the pillory for three hours and " 'to wear a mark of shame upon her bosom' " for the rest of her life. Arthur Dimmesdale endures seven years of silence and self-imposed suffering, but finally, assisted by Hester and Pearl, ascends the scaffold and makes public confession of his "sin and infamy." Her scarlet letter, he declares, is "but the shadow of what he bears on his own breast, and that even this, his own red stigma, is no more than the type of what has seared his inmost heart!" (240). After words of forgiveness to his tormentor Roger Chillingworth, a kiss from his daughter Pearl, and a final admonition to Hester that her expressed hope for an immortal reunion was in vain, he dies.

I better put away my remote control and stop switching scenes before you grow too restless to care whether there is any connection between these moments in time. These three scenes have some significant features in common.

First, of course, each scene involves matters of sex. Another shared element: Massachusetts. Perhaps less immediately obvious, these scenes are all portrayals of white men whose bodies are differentiated from the bodies of culturally defined others — children, women, and Native Americans. The opening of this chapter could have been titled "Pastoral Perversions," given that the three scenes focus on sexual wrongdoing committed by clergymen. All three focus on sexual acts construed by the larger community to be immoral or illicit. In each case, because the line of acceptability has been transgressed, questions of just punishment intersect with deliberations about whether or not the minister in question acknowledges the gravity of his crime. Confession is thus a recurrent motif, carrying with it the various possibilities of being required to speak, refusing to speak, fearing to speak, and desiring to speak.

All three scenes underscore the difficulties of maintaining the order of sexual things — to be more precise in regard to these three scenes, the order of heterosexual things. The vocation of all three men is relevant, for as clergy they are obligated to represent the ideal formation of male heterosexuality, which for married ministers mandates fidelity and for unmarried ministers includes celibacy understood as nonpracticing heterosexuality. The logic of sexual ordering is also where certain commonalities begin to drift into distinctions. Both are crucial: the commonalities indicate certain continuities in the history of white men's heterosexualized bodies, and the distinctions make visible the ways in which the materiality of sexuality and sexual differentiation in the modern era are fraught with contradictory compulsions, confusing requirements, and dangerous denials.

Before pursuing those distinctions I want to remark on my method, which is encapsulated here by juxtaposing a current event, a historical account, and a work of fiction. I invoke Michel Foucault's use of the term genealogy. In *Power/Knowledge*, Foucault writes: "Let us give the term *genealogy* to the union of erudite knowledge and local memories which allows us to establish a historical knowledge of struggles and to make use of this knowledge tactically today."[4] Genealogical inquiry is the approach I think most valuable for teaching and writing about American culture. Genealogy is thus my choice regarding the direction that American studies should take in the nineties: American studies as an academic program should undertake the making of genealogists.

The study of U.S. society within the academy carries with it an obligation to serve as specific intellectuals. Some reject this idea out of hand, insisting on a dissociation between knowledge, power, and personal ethical judgment. From such a perspective, a specific intellectual is an abuser of norms of objectivity. Other critics of genealogy see a specific intellectual as a diminished version of what it means to be an intellectual; they too uphold the notion of objectivity, recalling the days when *universal* intellectuals spoke the great truth that transcends circumstance. Although both camps are correct in noting genealogy's challenges to objectivity and transcendence, they are wrong in two respects. There is no diminishment of either the truth or the intellectual as a teller of truth; instead, there is an enhancement in understanding how truth is established. American studies has a unique role here. We are situated professionally to be questioners of hegemonic ideas about U.S. society. As part of our work, we can look for the lines of force linking such knowledge to popular culture, institutional practices, and official government actions. In doing so—if we do so—we have the potential to forge a "new politics of truth."[5]

Juxtaposing historical, literary, and contemporary events will not in and of itself bring about a new politics of truth, yet it is one way to loosen the hold that assumptions of causality and coherence have on the entrenched truth. As a tool of genealogical inquiry, constituting odd connections helps prize open the old stories that become naturalized by virtue of their recurrence. I could have begun this essay with the sexual scandals of televangelists Jim Bakker and Jimmy Swaggart, but (though useful for establishing a legacy of hypocrisy and exploitation) their similarity to John Lyford risked naturalizing the category of pastoral perversion through sheer redundancy. The element of the unpredictable helps denaturalize the familiar, and even then denaturalization can quickly become renaturalized. To be more specific: over the past decade the method of creating a "dialogue" between two texts has been favored as a way of emphasizing what is usually called "difference," a word that blithely skates across categories of gender, ethnicity, sexuality, class, and race. Many an MLA panel or sample set of syllabi for American studies courses employ this device, as have I. One sets up, for example, a dialogue between F. Scott Fitzgerald's *The Great Gatsby* and Anzia Yezierska's *Bread-Givers* to deconstruct the myth of the "American dream." I now think that a problem is structured into this approach, namely, the tendency to resolve the ostensible dialogue in favor of the moral superiority of the marginalized text, which then becomes a new sort of scripture.

One of the reasons for juxtaposing at least three somewhat discrepant texts or events in the service of genealogy is to prevent an easy resolution. No formula exists for choosing which items to study, but the exercise works best when it throws a wrench into the process of thought that leads too quickly toward platitudes about oppression and struggle. For example, to the now-customary pairing of Dr. S. Weir Mitchell, the "nerve specialist" who pre-scribed the rest cure for discontent married women, and Charlotte Perkins Gilman's "The Yellow Wallpaper," let's add Zora Neale Hurston's short story "Sweat," in which an abused woman chooses not to intervene in the death of her husband when the rattlesnake he has used against her bites him, and also the much-publicized case of Lorena Bobbitt. Such a combination would surely problematize assumptions about spousal dynamics, medical judgment, ethical conduct, and justice.[6]

I draw on the term genealogy to describe this approach for a couple of rea-sons. One is to underscore Foucault's notion of genealogy as a disruption of those narratives that search for origins, unbroken continuity, and disembod-ied, universal truth — in other words, the assumptions that frame and struc-ture traditional narratives of history, literature, philosophy, and religion.[7] The irony of the use of the term genealogical, associated with the descent of fam-ily lines, to indicate breaks in the hold of official truth and the metaphysics of memory, is worth noting. Reinscribing the term genealogy to signify the countermemories that dispel claims to absolute truth or that uncover out-right lies recorded in "family tree" histories makes visible certain hidden links between sexual matters and the dominant order of history. The decep-tions of this model may be demarcated by at least three erasures that it sys-tematically enforces: (1) the biological paternity that is unacknowledged in favor of a "legitimate" paternity; (2) the denial of paternity within the U.S. slave system, with the white masters' rape and impregnation of enslaved wom-en; and (3) the same-sex intimacies that go unrecorded because of religious and secular law and social norms forbidding or shunning them. Genealogical investigation seeks to discover precisely these kinds of erasures that are inte-gral to dominant claims to truth.

A second reason to draw on the term genealogy is that both Nietzschean and Foucauldian concepts of genealogy prompt us to investigate the cultural con-ditions through which certain ideas and discourses emerge. Applying the term genealogical to American studies promotes a line of descent from the social movements of the past three decades that gave rise to the formalized critiques that we call African-American, feminist, postcolonial, queer, and so on. These critiques have developed as separate fields largely because their respective ar-eas of study were not to be found in either traditional disciplines or in Ameri-can studies, which defined itself initially against the high-art European bias of the humanities and social sciences. By doing so, it brought mass culture is-sues into prominence but remained predominantly white, male, and straight.

Finally, here is the clincher to what is at stake in espousing a genealogical approach. Again, from Foucault: "The purpose of history, guided by genealogy, is not to discover the roots of our identity but to commit itself to its dissipation."[8] That goal transforms not only scholarship and curriculum debates but also classroom dynamics. Disciplinary and interdisciplinary studies remain oriented toward the "discovery" of identity. A genealogical American studies, as an antidisciplinary endeavor, would take as crucial to its practice the dissipation of the nationalism and heterosexism holding up its basic concepts, in particular its founding concepts of "America" and American identity. This point should not be taken to be part of the standard rhetoric of challenging notions of cultural unity. The assumption that national culture is unified and coherent has been roundly disputed, but not all questioning is the same and not all questioning is genealogical.

This gets me back to matters of sex, for sexuality—its pleasures, desires, violences—surely ranks as one of the most complex problems of American society. In the history of the present, sexuality is one of the primary and most intense points of intersection among dramatically different fields of power relations. Genealogical cultural inquiry shows not only that sex matters to literature, law, film, and so on, but also that sex matters them, that is, gives these discourses a particular materiality, one that normalizes, homogenizes, and medicalizes subjectivity. Correspondingly, genealogical inquiry shows that the discourses designated as literature, law, music, film, and so forth, matter sex, that is, inform and define the meaning of sexuality within a given culture. This chapter is entitled "Sex Matters" in order to locate it alongside other recent analyses of the relations of materiality and discourse, including John D'Emilio and Estelle Freedman's history of American sexuality called *Intimate Matters*, Cornel West's *Race Matters*, Toni Morrison's "Black Matters" from *Playing in the Dark*, Ruth Frankenberg's *White Women, Race Matters: The Social Construction of Whiteness*, and Judith Butler's *Bodies That Matter: On the Discursive Limits of "Sex."* My hunch is that this catalog of titles is a response to today's symptomatic refrain that "nothing matters." Genealogy strives to combat such weary indifference by showing precisely how and why things matter—hence its investigations of the material locations of classifications like gene pools, disease, criminality, and desire. The meanings of these designations are traceable in their effects on individual bodies and through the ways that bodies are violently punished or excluded from certain activities and forced into others, disciplined into regularity and docility, ornamented and adored or spurned.

As William Bradford's history of Plymouth Plantation indicates, the matter of sex is a problem that American society has grappled with from the outset. That does not mean that sex has always meant the same thing. Even the abbreviated juxtapositions of the three texts I began with demonstrate that some assumptions about sexuality remain over time while others alter a great deal. A genealogical approach studies what kinds of utterances were and could be made under the precise historical conditions of a given event. It also demonstrates the range of meaning-effects a single word can have over time and in different cultural contexts.

Take sodomy, for example, "that utterly confused category," as Foucault put it.[9] The case of James Porter, the former priest, included six counts of sodomy; these were differentiated from seven counts of unnatural and lascivious acts, and twenty-seven counts of indecent assault and battery. Such differentiation is a recent phenomenon, as Jonathan Goldberg indicates in his book *Sodometries*, and it tells us a great deal about the ways in which the limits of heterosexuality are established.[10] The discursive record of American sodomy, which takes us back to Bradford's history of Plymouth in the infamous year 1642, demonstrates just how undifferentiated the term sodomy was in the seventeenth century. As Bradford reports, 1642 was the year in which "sundry notorious sins" erupted in the colonies, and not just in Plymouth but in Massachusetts Bay as well, as disclosed by the correspondence Bradford includes between Governor Richard Bellingham and himself over how to punish the sinners. Such transgressions as drunkenness, incontinence, and uncleanness had occurred, and "that which is worse, even sodomy and buggery (things fearful to name)" (Bradford, 351). Although Bradford wishes to "forebear particulars," he does name the sinner and the animals in the crime of buggery: Thomas Granger, sixteen or seventeen years old, had confessed to buggery "with a mare, a cow, two goats, five sheep, two calves and a turkey" (355). As Robert Oaks has noted, Puritan magistrates followed Leviticus in declaring death to be the appropriate punishment for both sodomy and buggery. Sometimes mercy was shown, but not in the case of Granger: he was made to identify the animals, which were then "killed before his face." After that, "he himself was executed."[11]

William Bradford discusses sodomy by way of explanation in Thomas Granger's case, linking his acts of buggery to an earlier case involving a man "that had made sodomitical attempts upon another" man. A case of brother-sister incest was also cited as a "sodomitical practice." The two men were whipped in public, as was the sister; her brother was exiled.[12] Under Renaissance and colonial law, sodomy included all of these instances (sex between a man and a "lower" animal, between two men, between a brother and a sister); it also applied to sex between two women and oral or anal sex between various partners. This very lack of coherence allowed and produced arbitrary punishment, ranging from the genocide of indigenous people to no punishment at all.[13]

The term sodomy still connotes acts of abomination, but legal definitions and penalties for sodomy range wildly from state to state and act to act. Long-standing denunciations of sodomy are used to criminalize consenting adult homosexuality, according to the laws of half of the states in the United States and as upheld by the Supreme Court decision in Bowers v. Hardwick in 1986. Yet sodomy has also entered the therapeutic discourse of U.S. society. One of the distinguishing elements deserving careful scrutiny in James Porter's case is the judge's ruling that, following his sentence, Porter must undergo treatment for pedophilia. The early-twentieth-century category of pedophilia and current therapeutic solutions for sexual offenses were simply not part of the discourse or practice of Bradford's time. Puritan concerns focused on procreation and property rather than on psychic health. Along this view, men's sexual abuse of female children was differentiated from abuse of male children. Adult male sex with a girl was regarded as a crime, but it was a crime construed to occur within the realm of the natural, that is, the procreatable. Questions about the mental emotional instability of either the perpetrator or the victim of the crime do not appear in court records or historical accounts.

To understand the history of the present as a therapeutic society, it is useful to contrast current requirements for mental-health treatment with another case that Bradford mentions of "uncleanness" in the Massachusetts Bay colony. This case involved three men who on numerous occasions over a two-year interval had sexually violated two girls, Dorcas and Sara Humfry. When their father, an assistant of the Bay Colony, had returned to England, he left his daughters in the care of one of the men, a former servant, who was married and in good standing in the church. The elder sister (seven to nine years old during this time) was raped by two of the men. The colonial governors found the appropriate punishment for this case more difficult to decide than Granger's was. First, they had no specific law against rape in Massachusetts at that time. Furthermore, they deemed that the girls had consented to the men. They tried to apply the existing sodomy law, but this was problematic because the law required proof of penetration, which the girls attested to but the men denied. Applying the existing sodomy law proved an obstacle for seeking a death penalty in this case, because capital conviction required two witnesses in the absence of clear evidence or confession. The punishment finally arrived at was to have the men confined to Boston and to be severely whipped, with one also having his nostrils mutilated.[14]

The legal confusion surrounding this incident led the governors immediately to specify the death penalty for " 'carnall copulation' with any 'woman child under ten years old,' " regardless of consent. Thus Massachusetts rape law is genealogically related to its sodomy law. Both rape and sodomy were finally deemed capital offenses because, in the words of Reverend Charles Chauncy, "The land is defiled by such sins." Chauncy further provided a rationale based on the equal gravity of sodomy and rape, but differentiated the "unnatural lusts of men with men, or woman with woman, or either with beasts" from the "natural lusts of men towards children under age."[15] As a number of feminist historians have shown, rape law is also related to issues of property, for the death penalty only applied if a man raped a married or engaged woman or a girl under the age of ten; in other words, the violation was seen to be against the property of husbands, fiancés, or fathers.[16]

New England's colonial history of punishment for rape stands in contrast to that administered for sex with animals, in part because the Puritans believed buggery would produce unnatural, monstrous offspring. This anxiety about monstrous birth spilled over in logic to the accusation that a deformed birth might also signify monstrous ideas. Such was the case, for example, made against Anne Hutchinson and her ally in dissent and excommunication, Mary Dyer. As one Puritan man stated about Hutchinson, because she "had vented misshapen opinion, so she must bring forth deformed monsters."[17]

For Puritans, sex between two men or two women was deemed unnatural because it could produce *no* offspring. As Goldberg points out with regard to the sexual abuse of the two girls Dorcas and Sara Humfry, in Puritan logic "raping girls is less criminal than *any* sexual act between men or between a man and an animal."[18] Such a point helps us understand the procedure followed in a sodomy case in 1646 in the New Netherland Colony in which a black man named Jan Creoli was convicted of sodomizing a ten-year-old boy named Mango Congo. Creoli was taken to a "place of public execution, and there choked to death, and then burnt to ashes." What is most notable is that *the boy* was also punished: he was made to witness Creoli's execution, "tied to a stake" with kindling piled around him, and flogged.[19] (This stands in significant contrast to the huge monetary settlement that Michael Jackson's thirteen-year-old accuser was awarded—but that's another essay.)

That nonprocreative sex was an abomination seems to have been the over-riding logic for a statute passed in 1655 in the New Haven Colony that specified death for sex between same-sex partners, for heterosexual anal intercourse, and for masturbation.[20] Part of what William Bradford found so scandalous about John Lyford's sexual behavior was his effort to "hinder conception." Bradford's elliptical and somewhat enigmatic description of Sarah Lyford's having taken her husband "as they lay at their beds' feet" suggests some manner of sodomy according to Puritan interpretation. Until the nineteenth century, reproduction remained a defining feature of male sexuality. The devaluation of reproduction occurred in concert with the rise of biological understanding of women's role in procreation. This shift had various consequences for women, including less emphasis on their sexual pleasure and greater likelihood of courts' granting them custody of their children.[21]

Although *The Scarlet Letter* does not deal with rape, sodomy, or bestiality, its focus on adultery does reveal the movement from the sexual economy of Bradford's time toward the one operating today.[22] To my mind, this novel matters as literature today not because its truths transcend time, though its emotional drama still resonates for many readers, but because its continuities and discontinuities with the colonial past help us understand our own time. *The Scarlet Letter* makes visible the shifts occurring from a predominantly juridical system, in which certain sexual acts are forbidden at risk of bodily punishment or exile, toward a medicalized, therapy-driven system, in which deviant sexual desire and behavior warrant medical treatment.

The call for Hester Prynne to repent by disclosing the name of her partner in sexual crime was generally in keeping with colonial New England practices.[23] As stipulated by Massachusetts law in 1631, adultery was to be punished by the death penalty, and this was at times carried out. In 1644, the Massachusetts court sentenced an eighteen-year-old woman named Mary Latham to death by hanging for having committed adultery with twelve men. In addition to the number of men, which suggests a certain impunity, one of the factors said to contribute to the death penalty in her case was the derision she cast toward her husband to her partners in adultery. One of the latter, James Britton, confessed to his sexual crime and was executed with Latham.[24] The death penalty was not customary for adultery, however; more common were penalties of fines, public whipping, and the wearing of the letters AD on one's clothes or forehead, where the letters were burned into the flesh.[25]

The punishment that Hester Prynne undergoes and that Arthur Dimmesdale struggles to avoid thus adheres to Puritan codes of law. But Hawthorne's portrayal of the personal and community identity of his characters dramatically departs from the earlier period in its emphasis on the adulterer as an aberrant being rather than one who commits sinful acts. Reading *The Scarlet Letter* in relation to both Bradford's history and Porter's court case provides a crystallization of what Foucault theorized as a shift from a system of alliance to the deployment of sexuality. On the one hand, the Puritans viewed adultery as a grave crime because it broke the bonds of the system of alliance, based on principles of kinship. Hester's letter A is simultaneously the sign of the sovereign's display of mercy from the death penalty and of his right of death over his subjects, enacted under the authority of his duly appointed magistrates. On the other hand, as countless critics have noted, over the course of the novel the letter becomes a signifier of Hester's developing sense of moral responsibility. Many critics, feminists and nonfeminists alike, acclaim her as a moral exemplar. Indeed, she does become moral through and through.

From a genealogical perspective, Hester's transformation, not just of the letter's meaning but of her very being, is precisely her entry into the technology of normalization. At the end of the novel, we are told that she realizes that she is not to be the "angel and apostle of the coming revelation" (Hawthorne, 177). But her well-disciplined body *has* become integral to the newly emerging social body — a pivotal subjectivity of the new order of generative and regulative power relations. Sacvan Bercovitch comes closer to this view when he argues that Hester is "the agent of her own domestication."[26] His exploration gets stalled, however, by its emphasis on ideology. I want to focus on this for a moment because Bercovitch's emphasis on systems of ideas and structures of belief helps to differentiate between genealogical and ideological analysis. Put bluntly, ideological analysis operates at the expense of understanding *the matter*, that is, embodied regulation. It loses sight of the everyday practices through which bodies are formed, maintained, disciplined, pleasured, released, and so on.[27] As a result, ideological criticism tends toward all-or-nothing categories, like subversion versus reinforcement of the hegemonic; with Bercovitch, it's either "consensus" or "dissent." Such oppositions require assumptions of textual and cultural unity — a holdover from New Criticism. The consequence of glossing over the ways bodies are materialized is to overlook materialized resistance, which is a condition of power relations but not predictable in its outcome.

A genealogical approach thus looks for regulatory mechanisms in order to mark the conditions for potential destabilization. In literature, destabilization may not be part of the text itself, but can still occur in our responses to it. I do not see *The Scarlet Letter* as an oppositional discourse, but I do read it and teach it as a way of encouraging resistance to the dominant order of sexuality. I want to illustrate this point by showing how the materiality of sex affects the four major characters of *The Scarlet Letter*.[28] Even though they are all sexually abstinent for the entire novel (except for the brief concluding mention of Pearl's rumored marriage and motherhood), their bodies are increasingly invested with the power relations of the deployment of sexuality.[29] Within the novel's logic — not of redemption but of normalization — Pearl, Chillingworth, Hester, and Dimmesdale cannot be fully integrated into the new sexual economy. Yet each one marks its inauguration through processes of heterosexualization and gender stabilization.[30]

The new, normalizing order is officially installed when Hester, Pearl, and Dimmesdale take their place in public *as a family*. This ascension to the scaffold breaks the fraught homosocial bond between Chillingworth and Dimmesdale. Their strange "marriage," as Robert Penn Warren referred to it, may be understood as a homoerotic triangle of the type Eve Sedgwick has discussed, in which a love-hate bond between men is invigorated across the body of a woman.[31] Over the course of the years that they live together, both men are portrayed as becoming somewhat feminine, a gender slippage that is relieved only through the crucial revelation of Dimmesdale's paternity, which establishes a homosexual/heterosexual divide. Chillingworth can never be a proper husband or father within the new order of things, but his death solves that problem. More important, it allows him to bequeath his property to Pearl, a break from the blood logic of the system of kinship and alliance. Thus, in death this physician of the old world affirms the new middle class and increasingly regulatory deployment of sexuality that accentuates identity over act and healthy lineage over aristocratic ancestry.

Just before he dies, Dimmesdale finally gives in to his long-intensifying compulsion to divulge his past sexual desire and guilt as a revelation of the deep truth of himself. Although the novel describes his agony as that of interior soul-torture, genealogical analysis suggests that this is the moment described by Foucault in *Discipline and Punish* as when the soul begins to imprison the body. The process of internalizing normative principles is what feeds the compulsion to confess that proliferates under the deployment of sexuality.[32] This disciplinary power formation retroactively transforms Hester's eroticism into a fertility that is responsible to the community. She can be installed within the new community order only if she has no sex or if she has sex only with a husband. Ultimately, she reembodies herself as the community's Good Mother when she returns to New England, presumably post-

menopausal and still sexually abstinent.[33] She may not be the destined prophet-
ess because of her past stain of sin, but she does become the community's
psychotherapeutic confessor, an able manager of sexual passions.

And what of Pearl? If the rumors are true, she too eventually takes up the
new order of things through marriage and procreation. But it is "little Pearl"
who is really of interest in this discussion, for she represents the sexualization
of children's bodies. This occurs most starkly in the scene by the stream when
she makes an A for herself out of eelgrass. Significantly, she has a fit of hys-
teria — the pathology of the eroticized yet repressed female — when Hester
removes her letter, a "crimson flush" returning to her pale cheek. Hester's
restitution of her letter and cap becalms Pearl for the time being. This poignant
act may be seen as emblematic of the way Hester has learned to control her
passion. Her crimson flush and Pearl's "extravagant contortions" and "piercing shrieks," described as a "fit of passion," provide links between sexualization and bodily heat. According to Thomas Laqueur, the notion that female
bodies had heat emerged only in the nineteenth century; Hawthorne's text
is thus a record of this new linkage. For centuries before, only men's bodies
were seen to have vital heat, and women's bodies, as inverted and inferior
versions of men's bodies, lacked this key feature. The concept of heated female sexuality was not one that brought equality, however, for it was seen to
be an unfortunate alignment with lower animals and in dire need of regulation.[34] Within the logic of normalization, Pearl is invested with demonic or
animalistic eroticism that must be suppressed and rechanneled into a proper
purity.

A genealogical approach strives to understand the history of the present.
By way of this discussion of Pearl as an eroticized child I now return to where
I began, with the case of James Porter. I conclude this essay by referring to
an issue that is taking cultural form reminiscent of the heightened anxieties
around space aliens and communism in the 1950s: pedophile panic. This
panic, I believe, is symptomatic of a changing sexual order of things in the
United States. Changes in the requirements and privileges of normalized heterosexuality get expressed in any number of ways, ranging from gay and lesbian
affirmation to Christian Coalition suppression. For many, sexual rearrange-
ments are quite literally seen as a disorder. One of the leading ways in which
this sense of sexual disorder is currently articulated, especially in the media,
centers on the sexual abuse of children. This is a serious and complex issue,
but it is being obfuscated by the narratives of pedophile panic that are being
circulated within schools, on television, from pulpits, and within families.

The predictable outcome of the panic is the equally charged false memory syndrome, whose proponents strive to prevent abuse investigation.

A genealogical analysis is a more credible way of thinking about this kind of problem. Again, I underscore the value of juxtaposing historical, literary, and current events to help see the complexities of this issue. The sexual molestation of the Puritan girls Sara and Dorcas Humfry provides a point of departure for such inquiry. Literary depictions of eroticized children may be readily found, from Pearl, Huck, Mazie, Flora, and Miles to Holden and Lolita. Cultural anxiety and panic over child molestation seem to be growing in direct proportion to our culture's treatment of children's bodies as media spectacles, simultaneously a figure of innocence and obsession.[35]

The related issue of punishment also warrants genealogical thinking. An examination of the deployments of alliance and sexuality illuminates Porter's peculiar double sentence: first jail time, then therapy time. The judge, in other words, administered *both* the juridical punishment inherited from William Bradford's era *and* the normalizing technology that emerged from Hawthorne's. The judge's sentence is still peculiar, given the demonstrated ineffectuality of prison and therapy for changing the behavior of sexual offenders, but it is less puzzling in light of a genealogical approach. The complicity of church authority in protecting its ministers comes into question here as well. What are the implications of financial compensation as a form of punishment? What new links of surveillance, medicalization, and money are being established? To what extent might demands for monetary compensation be effective as resistance against church-related oppression?

These questions are too rarely asked. It is more typical to draw on the themes of monstrosity and abomination, a legacy of Puritan rhetoric that lends drama but cuts off understanding. This is what James Porter said to the court in a statement read by his lawyer: "It is, I know, a measure of justice that the publicity, this prosecution, and the therapy I have been receiving have brought me to the point where every time I look into the mirror my mind makes me see the monster that I was."[36] Looked at genealogically, this rhetoric of monstrosity is itself a problem, creating and targeting a category of repulsion that masquerades as explanation. Its reductiveness sidesteps investigation about the power/knowledge relations that contribute not only to sexual abuse of children but to other widespread conditions of abuse such as poverty, inadequate health care, and underfunded education. These problems are connected to, not separate from, the sexual order of things. Understanding this order is a crucial task for genealogy today.

Notes

1. "Former Catholic Priest Sentenced to 18 to 20 Years for Sex Crimes," *New York Times*, (7 December 1993): A22.

2. William Bradford, *Of Plymouth Plantation, 1620–1647*, ed. Francis Murphy (New York: Random House, 1981), 164–65. Subsequent page references to this work will be cited parenthetically in the text.

Although Bradford's work follows a year-by-year chronology, as Wayne Franklin indicates, its compressions suggest a retrospective composition. See Wayne Franklin, *Discoverers, Explorers, Settlers: The Diligent Writers of Early America* (Chicago: University of Chicago Press, 1979).

3. Nathaniel Hawthorne, *The Scarlet Letter* (Indianapolis: Bobbs-Merrill Co., 1963), 65, 66. Subsequent page references to this work will be cited parenthetically in the text.

4. Michel Foucault, "Two Lectures," in *Power/Knowledge: Selected Interviews and Other Writings, 1972–1977*, ed. Colin Gordon, trans. Alessandro Fontana and Pasquale Pasquino (New York: Pantheon, 1980), 83.

5. Michel Foucault, "Truth and Power," in *Power/Knowledge*, 109–33. Also, see my discussion of June Jordan as a specific intellectual in my *Freedom, Foucault, and the Subject of America* (Boston: Northeastern University Press, 1991), 150–72.

6. I have tried this technique in American literature classes by assigning students (in groups of three) the task of bringing in both a historical and a contemporary artifact or text with some connection to the text we are reading. The students present their choices to the class and we discuss how the three are mutually illuminating. This has been quite effective and encourages students to think about historical and contemporary artifacts as materialized power relations. I have also found that they make connections I never would have thought about on my own.

7. Michel Foucault, "Nietzsche, Genealogy, History," in *Language, Counter-Memory, Practice*, ed. Donald F. Bouchard (Ithaca: Cornell University Press, 1977), 139–64.

8. Ibid., 162.

9. Michel Foucault, *The History of Sexuality, Volume I: An Introduction*, trans. Robert Hurley (New York: Vintage, 1978), 101.

10. Jonathan Goldberg, *Sodometries: Renaissance Texts, Modern Sexualities* (Stanford: Stanford University Press, 1992), 11–12.

11. Robert Oaks, "'Things Fearful to Name': Sodomy and Buggery in Seventeenth-Century New England," *Journal of Social History* 12 (1978): 268–81.

12. Goldberg, 241.

13. See Goldberg, *Sodometries*, for details of specific incidents.

14. Jonathan Ned Katz, *Gay/Lesbian Almanac* (New York: Harper and Row, 1983), 78–82. Also see Oaks, 274.

15. Chauncy quoted in Katz, 80–82.

16. Oaks, 280, n. 38; Barbara Lindemann, "'To Ravish and Carnally Know': Rape in Eighteenth-Century Massachusetts," *Signs* 10, no. 1 (Autumn 1984): 80.

17. Quoted in Katz, 52. Also see Michael J. Colacurcio, "Footsteps of Ann Hutchinson: The Context of *The Scarlet Letter*," *ELH* 39 (1972): 459–94.

18. Goldberg, 240–41.

19. Katz, 22–23.

20. Jonathan Ned Katz, *Gay American History: Lesbians and Gay Men in the U.S.A.* (New York: Meridian, 1992), 23.

21. Thomas Laqueur, *Making Sex: Body and Gender from the Greeks to Freud* (Cambridge: Harvard University Press, 1990), 8.

22. The importance of focusing specifically on sexuality is made clearer by noting how it gets left out of discussions that purport to be on the politics and power relations of the time in which Hawthorne wrote. See, for example, Jonathan Arac, "The Politics of *The Scarlet Letter*," in Sacvan Bercovitch and Myra Jehlen, eds., *Ideology and Classic American Literature* (New York: Cambridge University Press, 1986), 247–66. Although Arac mentions Foucault in terms of the emergence of "inquisitorial knowledge" depicted in the novel, he does not explore questions of normalization within the deployment of sexuality.

23. There was a relative leniency for cases of fornication that led to premarital pregnancy, especially if marriage was to take place. Following confession and repentance, fornicators were allowed back into the church and the child could be baptized. Fornication was the charge that applied to sex between a married man and a single woman or a single man and a single woman. Adultery was the charge of sex between a married woman and a man.

24. Ernest W. Baughman, "Public Confession and *The Scarlet Letter*," *New England Quarterly* 40 (1967): 532–50; reprinted in the Norton edition of *The Scarlet Letter*, ed. Seymour Gross et al. (New York: Norton, 1988). Also see John D'Emilio and Estelle Freedman, *Intimate Matters: A History of Sexuality in America* (New York: Harper and Row, 1988), 11–12.

25. Charles Boewe and Murray G. Murphey, "Hester Prynne in History," *American Literature* 32 (1960): 202–4; reprinted in the Norton edition of *The Scarlet Letter*. Also see D'Emilio and Freedman, 28.

26. Sacvan Bercovitch, *The Office of "The Scarlet Letter"* (Baltimore: Johns Hopkins University Press, 1991), 11.

27. Judith Butler, in *Bodies That Matter: On the Discursive Limits of "Sex"* (New York: Routledge, 1993), usefully differentiates between this approach and the conception of construction by proposing "a return to the notion of matter, not as site or surface, but as *a process of materialization that stabilizes over time to produce the effect of boundary, fixity, and surface we call matter*" (9; emphasis in the original).

28. For an extended genealogical analysis of *The Scarlet Letter*, focusing on the problematic of national citizenship, see Lauren Berlant, *The Anatomy of National Fantasy: Hawthorne, Utopia, and Everyday Life* (Chicago: University of Chicago Press, 1991).

29. Foucault cites "four great strategic unities" of the deployment of sexuality, namely, a hysterization of women's bodies, a pedagogization of children's sex, a socialization of procreative behavior, and a psychiatrization of perverse pleasure (*History of Sexuality*, 104–5).

30. For an elaboration of the shift into a bipolar model of sex difference accompanied by a stabilization of gender identity, see Thomas Laqueur's argument throughout *Making Sex*. He demonstrates that this shift, which occurs unevenly from the nineteenth century on, replaces a model of one sex and theatrical gender.

31. Eve Kosofsky Sedgwick, *Between Men: English Literature and Male Homosocial Desire* (New York: Columbia University Press, 1985).

32. See Berlant's excellent discussion of Dimmesdale's internalization of the law in the "construction of conscience" (*The Anatomy of National Fantasy*, 126–27).

33. Most critics mark Hester's development into the Good Mother as a moral achievement but fail to see how that achievement is itself a function of the power relations of the deployment of sexuality. This is perhaps most succinctly exemplified in Edwin Haviland Miller's biography of Hawthorne, when he writes that the novel "unfolds a tale in which the participants, having suffered grievous deprivations and rejections, search for roots, love, and nurturing, and a society in which the patriarchal code is humanized by matriarchal values. Mistress Hibbins, the Evil Mother, wants us to believe that witches and demons hover over the land with mad, destructive purposes, but she embodies the nightmare of patriarchy and the debasement of women. Hawthorne's romance focuses not on such aberrations and perversions of human potential and love but on the breast, symbol of fertility, nurturing, and creativity"; see Edwin Haviland Miller,

Salem Is My Dwelling Place: A Life of Nathaniel Hawthorne (Iowa City: University of Iowa Press, 1991), 284.

34. Laqueur, 215–20.

35. See James Kincaid, *Child-Loving: The Erotic Child and Victorian Culture* (New York: Routledge, 1992).

36. "Former Catholic Priest Sentenced to 18 to 20 Years," A22.

10

The Real and the Marvelous in Charleston, South Carolina: Ntozake Shange's *Sassafrass, Cypress & Indigo*

José David Saldívar

It is probably true that critics of African and Afro-American literature were
trained to think of the institution of literature essentially as a set of Western texts.
—Henry Louis Gates Jr. The Signifying Monkey

Ntozake Shange has been widely praised for her oppositional feminist "combat-breathing" poetics in her explosive Broadway choreopoem *For Colored Girls Who Have Considered Suicide/When the Rainbow Is Enuf* (1976) and for her powerful "lyricism" in *Sassafrass, Cypress & Indigo* (1982), but her use of Afro-Caribbean and Latin American magic realism has received little attention, owing to an inadequate understanding of a vast and rich literary and cultural movement in the Americas that began over forty years ago.[1]

The reasons for this state of affairs are complex. Henry Louis Gates correctly claims that critics of African American texts are trained to think of "the institution of literature essentially as a set of Western texts."[2] W. Lawrence Hogue contends that a primary reason for the dearth of comparative cultural pan-American studies is that most critics in the United States are "silent on the production ... of texts."[3] In *Discourse and the Other: The Production of the Afro-American Text* (1986), Hogue critically judges various African American interpretive practices, ranging from Amiri Baraka's "advocacy of a nationalist Afro-American literature" (11) in the 1960s to Robert Stepto's protostructuralist attempts in the 1970s "to isolate an Afro-American cultural myth, the pregeneric myth, and [use] it to define an Afro-American literary tradition" (13). Hogue also analyzes the more recent attempts by Houston Baker Jr. and Barbara Christian, who in their critical practices have created what Hogue calls a powerful but incomplete "theory of the Afro-American literary tradition." Although Hogue is generally sympathetic to Baker's early "anthropology of art," he points out the following problem in Baker's seminal study of African American literature, *The Journey Back*: "He [Baker] ignores the fact that Afro-American myths, stereotypes, and cultural forms are not innocent, that they are bound culturally and historically—even within Afro-American reality—and therefore have political and ideological functions" (15). More important for Hogue, "Baker's anthropology of art is silent on literary production" (16). Hogue's self-conscious analysis is itself silent on Baker's sophisticated and powerful reading of the "blues vernacular" in *Blues, Ideology, and Afro-American Literature* (1984) and his magisterial reading of Caliban's "triple play" in *Modernism and the Harlem Renaissance* (1987).

Hogue turns his Foucauldian hermeneutics of suspicion to Barbara Christian's groundbreaking book, *Black Women Novelists: The Development of a Tradition, 1892–1976*. Although Hogue praises Christian's attempt to account for how "certain ideological and literary forces" produce the image of black women in American society, he finds troubling "gaps" and "silences" in her discourse. He contends: "Without discussing the issue of literary production, Christian's critical practice cannot fully explain how images of black women are tied to the production of literary texts, or why certain black women novelists are published and promoted, others published and excluded, and still others aborted at editors' and publishers' desks" (19). Like the earlier studies of Baraka, Stepto, and Baker, Hogue believes that Christian's analysis of "canon formation" is unconsciously "informed by an external ideological discourse" (20). In contradistinction to Baraka, Stepto, Baker, and Christian, Hogue argues that certain African American writers are published and promoted in the mainstream canon "because they reproduce certain sanctioned ... stereotypes and conventions. Others [are] published and ignored because they fail to reproduce sanctioned literary myths and conventions" (21).

Instructive gaps and silences in Hogue's lucid analysis of contemporary African American women's fiction, however, can be found. In his chapter "Sixties' Social Movements, the Literary Establishment, and the Production of the Afro-American Text," he asserts that the radical "feminist discourse" of the 1970s "produced texts such as Toni Morrison's *The Bluest Eye* and *Sula*, Alice Walker's *The Third Life of Grange Copeland* and *The Color Purple*, Ntozake Shange's *For Colored Girls*, and Gayl Jones's *Corregidora* that produced new myths about black women" (62). Unfortunately, what Hogue's Foucauldian analysis was not in a position to recognize was how some African American writers such as Morrison and Shange were profoundly engaged in a bold cultural conversation with the Afro-Caribbean and Latin American tradition of magic realism. A writer such as Shange thus creates texts that are "double voiced," to use Gates's term, in the sense that her literary antecedents are both black and mestizo (African American and Latin American) novelists.[4] By examining the historical and ideological intertextual forces that produced her magic realism in *Sassafrass, Cypress & Indigo,* we can supplement previous studies of African American literary production. Shange's new narrative is a "mulatta" text, with a two-toned heritage. She speaks in an always distinct and resonant voice, a voice that "signifies" on black male vernacular and mestizo Latin American magic realist traditions.

Shange has been actively engaged during the 1980s and into the 1990s with a group of committed artists and intellectuals associated with the Casa de las Américas. She has traveled extensively throughout the Americas and has read her works in Brazil, Haiti, Cuba, and Nicaragua. Her books *A Daughter's Geography* (1983) and *See No Evil* (1984) speak eloquently of her political interests in Castro's and the Sandinistas' revolutions.

In an interview at the University of Houston in 1985, Shange insists that she moved to Texas "to escape the celebrity status" she received after the successful Broadway production of *For Colored Girls* and to be closer to the Latin American cultures of resistance.[5] In Houston, she tells us, she could "find another version of reality" (2). In *Sassafrass, Cypress & Indigo,* she is directly concerned with this different "version of reality," whose depth and complexity cannot be fully presented by existing U.S. ideological and literary labels and categories. Her novel is concerned with both the Afro-Caribbean and Latin American mythical thought systems outside those appropriated by the dominant official Western society. Before discussing the merits and demerits of magic realism in Shange's new narrative, we must look afresh at the problems, theoretical and historical, involved in *lo real maravilloso* (marvelous realism) and *el realismo mágico* (magic realism).

Some Concepts and Definitions of Magic Realism

What is the history of the Americas but the chronicle of *lo real maravilloso?*
—*Alejo Carpentier*

Magic realism . . . is to be grasped as a possible alternative to the narrative logic of contemporary postmodernism.
—*Fredric Jameson, "On Magic Realism in Film"*

It is generally accepted that the magic realist movement led by Carpentier, García Márquez, Fuentes, and, more recently, Allende has had a powerful influence in the 1980s on a diverse group of U.S. writers: Gary Soto (*The Tale of Sunlight*), Alberto Ríos (*Whispering to Fool the Wind*), Helena María Viramontes (*The Moths*), Paul Theroux (*The Mosquito Coast*), and Dennis Johnson (*Fiskadoro*). The possibility that magic realism functions as a force or as a discursive formation in contemporary African American literature has not been fully explored, however.

As Jameson has noted, "the concept of magic realism raises many problems, both theoretical and historical."[6] We will not retrace here the rich polemical debate among Latin American and U.S. scholars over the concept "magic realism"; Fernando Alegría, Roberto González Echevarría, and Amaryll Beatrice Chanady have written cogent and useful critical surveys of the debate.[7] My task is to make the demanding argument about magic realism available to readers who have heard of its importance but so far have been baffled.

According to González Echevarría, magic realism as a concept appears in "three different moments" in the twentieth century.[8] The first appeared during the avant-garde 1920s in Europe "when the term is used by Franz Roh in his *Nach-Expressionismus: Magischer Realismus* (1925) and when the Surrealists, especially Breton in the first *Manifesto* (1924), proclaim the 'marvelous' (*le merveilleux*) an aesthetic category and even a way of life" (109). The second moment was in the late 1940s when the expressions *el realismo mágico* and *lo real maravilloso* were used by the Latin American writers-intellectuals Arturo Uslar Pietri and Alejo Carpentier to measure, compare, and evaluate indigenous Latin American cultural art forms.[9] Whereas Pietri adopted Roh's term "magic realism," Carpentier, the more influential writer and sophisticated theoretician, adopted in González Echevarría's view "the Surrealists' version and create[d] the term 'marvelous American reality'" (110).

A third period of magic realism began in 1955 when the Latin American scholar Angel Flores published his influential essay "Magical Realism in Spanish American Fiction." For González Echevarría, this third phase continued through the 1960s, "when criticism searches for the Latin American roots of some of the novels produced during the 'boom' and attempts to justify their experimental nature" (111). As will be seen, a "fourth phase" occurred as Ntozake Shange and Arturo Islas, among others, expanded the tradition of magic realism in new and political (often "Signifyin[g]") ways.

Flores argued that what distinguishes magic realism from other realisms is that it attempts to transform "the common and the everyday into the awesome and the unreal."[10] Furthermore, he emphasized the connections between magic realism and examples of European modernist aesthetics practiced by Kafka and Chirico.

In 1967 Luis Leal joined the growing debate by attacking Flores's essay. In "El realismo mágico en la literatura hispanoamericana," he argued that magic realism was, for all intents and purposes, an exclusively New World literary movement. Included in his school of Latin American magic realist writers were Arturo Uslar Pietri, Miguel Angel Asturias, Carpentier, Lino Novas Calvo, Juan Rulfo, Félix Pita Rodríguez, and Nicolás Guillén. According to Leal, the following is the basic difference among the competing schools of "magic realism," "realism," and "surrealism":

> El mágico realista no trata de copiar (como lo hacen los realistas) o de vulnerar (como lo hacen los surrealistas) la realidad circundante, sino de captar el misterio que palpita en las cosas.

> [The magic realist does not attempt to copy (like the realists) or make the real vulnerable (like the surrealists), but attempts to capture the mystery that palpitates in things.][11]

Leal's essay ignores the profound impact surrealism, European modernism, and ethnography had on the generation of writers he analyzes, especially Asturias and Carpentier.[12]

Carpentier made the connections in the famous prologue to his revolutionary Afro-Caribbean novel, El reino de este mundo (1949); an expanded version of this prologue was reprinted in Tientos y diferencias (1964). To the rhetorical question "What is the history of the Americas but the chronicle of lo real maravilloso?," he suggests the ideology that lies at the center of his early magical narratives: how to write in a European language — with its Western systems of thought — about realities and thought structures never before seen in Europe. In the oxymoron lo real maravilloso, Carpentier is concerned not only with African magic (obeah), but with the perceptions and ideas of the world underlying the horizon of Afro-Caribbean magic. For the first time in 1949, he asks these questions: What is the New World African, Amerindian, and mestizo heritage of the Caribbean? How can it function as an ideology, a stylistics, and a point of view?

In Paris, Carpentier was introduced by Desnos to André Breton and began his bold cultural conversation with European modernism and surrealism. Throughout his Parisian stay, Carpentier was concerned with the role of art in revolution, as well as with what constituted surrealism. Not surprisingly, he was attracted to the surrealists' attack on human consciousness, which was part of their larger assault on all forms of bourgeois established order. As we know from their much-quoted maxim, knowledge for these Europeans is the sound "boom," and everyone is entitled to a "boom" of his or her own making.[13] Carpentier was thus initially fascinated by Breton's attempts to break through "the provoking insanities of realism."[14]

He learned much from the surrealists' experiments, which he employed to explore a kind of second reality hidden within the world of dreams and the unconscious. By whatever means, chiefly automatic writing and the imitation of dreams, the individual, according to the surrealists, must strive to achieve "surreality," which Breton saw as the absolute of the unconscious.[15] Surrealism thus led Carpentier to see afresh "aspectos de la vida americana que no había advertido," as he was to confess.[16]

But what caused Carpentier's "break" with Breton's surrealism? Emir Rodríguez Monegal argues convincingly that "political tensions" that arose among the surrealists caused Carpentier to become alienated from them.[17] González Echevarría suggests in *The Pilgrim at Home* that Carpentier went his own way because European surrealism clashed with the Cuban's "Spenglerian conception of man and history he had absorbed through avant-garde journals like the *Revista de Occidente*" (122).

Thus, in spite of his early fascination with surrealism in general, and with Breton in particular, Carpentier never became a committed disciple. Unlike Breton and the surrealists, he argued in his prologue and the essay "De lo real maravilloso" that the "second reality" the surrealists explored in automatic reality is merely part of the everyday world. Further, as a follower of Spengler's *Decline of the West* (in Spengler's universal history there is no fixed "center"), Carpentier eschewed Breton's and the surrealists' Eurocentric doctrines of the marvelous and argued that all things of a truly magical nature are, in fact, found within the reality of the Caribbean Americas — not the "boring" cities of Europe. According to Carpentier, the "discovery," conquest, and colonization of the New World are magical events in themselves:

> Open Bernal Díaz del Castillo's great chronicle [*True History of the Conquest of New Spain* (1552)] and one will encounter the only real and authentic book of chivalry ever written: a book of dust and grime chivalry where the genies who cast evil spells were the visible and palpable *teules*, where the unknown beasts were real, where one actually gazed on unimagined cities and saw dragons in their native rivers and strange mountains swirling with snow and smoke.[18]

For Carpentier, then, Bernal Díaz del Castillo's chronicle of the Spanish Conquest of Mexico is an exemplary magic realist narrative because Díaz (unwittingly) had written about the clash of cultures — Old World and New World —

and had described, in great detail, the superposition of one layer of reality on another. Thus envisaged, in Díaz's narrative armored Spaniards led by Cortés wander over "magical" deserts and cross over barren peaks, some of which burst into flame at their approach. Further, Díaz describes the Aztecs assailing the Spaniards with blood rituals of human sacrifice. At the end of these travels (travails), Cortés enters a great supernatural New World city, heaped with flora, floating in the midst of a blue lake.

Forming a background for Carpentier's theory is what he sees as a "fecundity" of the New World landscape. His concept of "marvelous reality" thus can be summarized in his own words:

> Due to the untouched nature of its landscape, its ontology, the Faustian presence of the Indian and the Black, the revelation inherent in the continent's recent discovery and the fruitful cross-breeding this discovery engendered, America is still very far from exhausting its wealth of mythologies. Indeed, what is the history of America if not the chronicle of marvelous reality? (xiv–xv)

In outlining his theory of lo real maravilloso, Carpentier posits the conditions that must be met for the marvelous to exist (x–xi). Lo real maravilloso unmistakably emerges as such only when it arises from (1) an unexpected alteration of reality (a miracle); (2) a privileged revelation of reality; (3) an unaccustomed or singularly enhancing illumination of the riches of reality that had passed unnoticed; (4) an expansion of the scales and categories of reality, now perceived with a particular intensity by virtue of an exaltation of spirit that leads to a kind of liminal state.

Carpentier thus set up an antithesis between surrealism and magic realism. He unfavorably compares surrealism with a privileged New World aesthetic grounded in a reality that is inherently magical. To be sure, Carpentier's thesis rests on the claims that New World artists and people experience the marvelous in their daily existence and therefore have no need to invent a domain of fantasy. On the basis of local New World privilege, he rejects surrealism as sterile and legitimizes the mode of writing he elects: "a chronicle of the marvelous real."

More recently, Gabriel García Márquez in El olor de la guayaba (The Fragrance of Guava) also anchored his notion of magic realism within a local Afro-Caribbean context:

> I believe that the Caribbean has taught me to see reality in a different way, to accept supernatural elements as something that is part of our daily life. The Caribbean is a distinctive world whose first magic piece of literature is The Diary of Christopher Columbus, a book which speaks of fabulous plants and mythical worlds. Yes, the history of the Caribbean is full of magic.[19]

Although García Márquez's use of magic realism includes Carpentier's familiar tropes of the supernatural—one of the foundation concepts of magic realism—his version differs from Carpentier's in this important way. García
Márquez's concept of magic realism presupposes the narrator's identification
with the oral expression of popular cultures in the Third World *pueblo*. In
other words, the narrative dramatization of magic realism is usually expressed
through a collective voice, inverting, in a jesting manner, the values of the
official culture.

Finally, at a recent PEN conference, Fernando Alegría, the noted Chilean
literary scholar and writer, expanded the debate by arguing audaciously in his
essay "Latin American Fantasy and Reality" (1987) that "reality" in the Caribbean and in Latin America "is neither marvelous nor magical."[20] In reading
Carpentier or Asturias, Alegría contends, "we come to realize [that their real-
ism] is a truthful image of economic injustice and social mockery which passes
off as authoritarian democracy in Latin America." To support his ideological
reading of magic realism, Alegría turns to an interpretation of García
Márquez's "puzzling speech," "The Solitude of Latin America," given at the
Nobel Prize awards in 1982. García Márquez spoke specifically about politics
and economics on a global scale, emphasizing the heated quarrel between the
superpowers, the United States and the Soviet Union. According to Alegría,
García Márquez addressed these issues "to clear up the legend of magical realism in his own fiction." Further, in Alegría's view, García Márquez wanted once
and for all to "acknowledge the basic reality lying at the bottom of the mythical world of Latin America." He used "statistics," Alegría suggests, to give his
audience, "stuffed into their fancy-label penguin suits, an astonishing, brutal
image of a continent torn asunder and bathed in blood" (117–18):

> There have been five wars and seventeen military coups; there emerged a dia-
> bolic dictator who is carrying out, in God's name, the first Latin American eth-
> nocide of our time. In the meantime, twenty million Latin American children
> died before the age of one—more than have been born in Europe since 1970.
> Those missing because of repression number nearly 120,000.... Numerous women
> arrested while pregnant have given birth in Argentine prisons, yet nobody knows
> the whereabouts and identity of their children, who were furtively adopted or
> sent to an orphanage by the order of the military authorities ... Nearly two
> hundred thousand men and women have died throughout the continent, and
> over one hundred thousand have lost their lives in three small and ill-fated
> countries of Central America: Nicaragua, El Salvador, and Guatemala ...
>   I dare to think that it is this outsized reality, and not just its literary expres-
> sion, that has deserved the attention of the Swedish Academy of Letters. A

reality not of paper, but one that lives within us and determines each instance of our countless daily deaths, and that nourishes a source of insatiable creativity, full of sorrow and beauty, of which this roving Colombian is but one cipher more, singled out by fortune.[21]

Alegría is correct when he redefines García Márquez's version of magic realism as a truthful vision of "outsized reality." Perhaps it was "The Solitude of Latin America" that led Jameson in his essay dedicated to Fernández Retamar and the Cuban revolution to theorize and define magic realism as a formal mode "constitutively dependent on a type of historical raw material in which disjunction is structurally present; or, to generalize the hypothesis more starkly, magic realism depends on a content which betrays the overlap or the coexistence of precapitalist with nascent or technological features."[22]

It is precisely this "articulated superposition of whole layers of the past within the present" in Shange's *Sassafrass, Cypress & Indigo* that aligns her with such committed magic realist authors as Carpentier, García Márquez, and Islas.

Feminist Culture and Magic Realism

> Where there is a woman there is magic.
> —*Sassafras, Cypress & Indigo*

What are some of the rules of the black vernacular "Signifyin[g]" formation that produces Shange's radical-feminist text, written in a magic realist style? What are the statements and concepts that inform the author's controversial "mulatta" poetics?[23]

In Claudia Tate's *Black Women Writers at Work* (1983), Shange specifies her concern for a particular African American vernacular and "Signifyin[g]" practice:

My lower case letters, slashes, and spelling [were] influenced by Le Roi Jones's *The Dead Lecturer* and *The System of Dante's Hell* and Ishmael Reed's *Yellow Book Radio*. I like the kinds of diction Ishmael uses, and I like the way Le Roi's poems look on the page ... I like the idea that letters dance, not just that words dance; of course, the words also dance.[24]

Shange's African American tradition is close to music, an insight she thematized in *For Colored Girls*, where she uses popular Motown music, oral speech, feminist poetry, and dance to critique patriarchy in the United States. Therefore, one statement or concept that informs Shange's work in general, and

Sassafrass, Cypress & Indigo in particular, is her attempt to deconstruct traditional modes of representing discourse on the page. Shange's novel does not
always read like a Western traditional novel, but it is designed to challenge
the traditional notions of realism.

Another statement that informs the book's production is the need, according to Shange, for black women to insert themselves into the cultural conversations of U.S. history. As she said in response to the "media blitz" that
followed her Broadway production, *For Colored Girls* "is a record of me once
I left my mother's house. I was raised as if everything was all right. And in
fact, once I got out of my house, everything was not all right."[25] In addition,
Shange believes that her generation of black women was brought up to be
silent in the face of male oppression. Her mother, she suggests, failed to pass on
to her certain truths about male violence. In her work, then, Shange reproduces a version of the black female experience designed to encourage women
of color "to tell their stories." Because she sees herself responsible for letting
others abuse her, she now sees her power as an artist as an attempt to encourage women to refuse victimization.

Sassafrass, Cypress & Indigo represents the author's commitment to radical
feminism: her struggle to articulate the stories and voices of repressed and si-
lenced black females. As Barbara Christian says of the African American
women's fiction of the 1970s and 1980s, Shange, Morrison, Bambara, Walker,
Lorde, and Marshall "explor[ed] these themes — that sexism must be strug-
gled against in black communities and that sexism is integrally connected to
racism."[26] As Hortense Spillers suggests, the novel is structured with "the al-
lusive echoes of the Moirae, the three women of fate in classical mythology,
who weave the thread of human life, or the natural objects and substances to
which the names of the sisters refer."[27] In other words, Shange's narrative attempts to make a new mythos of the black female self. By way of discrete
chapters on each of the three sisters, Sassafrass, Cypress, and Indigo, and
through Hilda Effania's letters, she traces the process of change in the lives
of these women.

Finally, Afro-Caribbean and Latin American magic realism inform significant parts of *Sassafrass, Cypress & Indigo*. When asked about her use of magic
realism in the novel, Shange matter-of-factly responded that her character
Indigo was her attempt to "Signify" on García Márquez's wonderful character Remedios the Beauty in *One Hundred Years of Solitude*.[28] Shange's mulatta
text therefore is double-voiced and talks to other works in a process of intertextual revision. Indigo is a magic realist character with a difference.

Sassafrass, Cypress & Indigo, published in 1982 at the peak of both the "fourth moment" of magic realism in the Americas and the women of color movement, begins:

> Where there is a woman there is magic. If there is a moon falling from her mouth, she is a woman who knows her magic, who can share or not share her powers. A woman with a moon falling from her mouth, roses between her legs and tiaras of Spanish moss, this woman is a consort of the spirits. Indigo seldom spoke. There was a moon in her mouth. Having a moon in her mouth kept her laughing. Whenever her mother tried to pull the moss off her head, or clip the roses round her thighs, Indigo was laughing.
>
> "Mama, if you pull 'em off, they'll just grow back. It's my blood. I've got earth blood, filled up with the Geeches long gone, and the sea."[29]

Not since the first half of Jean Toomer's *Cane,* or García Márquez's descriptions of Remedios the Beauty, have readers seen such an urgently passionate discourse that captures and celebrates female gender. Through etymological wordplay and word associations, Shange introduces the highly charged leitmotivs that characterize Indigo's section in the novel: mouth, moon, blood, spirits, and magic. Throughout the novel's first section, she represents Indigo as in touch with her emergent female sexuality and with the beginning of magic realism, for Indigo "is a consort of the spirits."

Like Carpentier's magical character Mackandal in *El reino de este mundo,* Shange's Indigo can compel the wind to blow a white woman's hat off (71–72); she can "move the razors off the roosters [and] put them in the palms of onlookers" to let them "know the havoc of pain" (44); and she can, in García Márquez's sense, "see reality in a different way, to accept supernatural elements as something that is part of our daily life."

Indigo, as an incarnate of magic realism, thus can see things in Charleston, South Carolina, in ways that her sisters, Sassafrass and Cypress, could not. For example, Shange tells us of Mrs. Yancey's courtship by Uncle John, a local junk man and connoisseur of magic realism in the black community. Although most of their courtship is ordinary, Indigo arrives on the scene and experiences a profound transformation:

> Everybody knew Uncle John lived in his wagon, but nobody had ever seen what Indigo saw. Uncle John went over to his wagon, pulled out a fine easy chair and set it by the curb, then motioned for Mrs. Yancey to have a seat. Next thing Indigo knew, he had spread a Persian rug in the middle of the street, set a formal table, pulled out a wine bucket, and started dinner on the stove at the back of his wagon.... Out of nowhere the guys from the Geechee Capitans, a motorcycle gang of disrepute led by Pretty Man, came speeding down the street. Uncle John

didn't exhibit much concern about these young ruffians ... He looked up, waved
his hand, and the Geechee Capitans, who had never done a good turn by any-
body in the city of Charleston, South Carolina, made road blocks on either side
of Uncle John's parlor....

When Uncle John pulled out a Victrola, played a Fletcher Henderson 78,
and asked Mrs. Yancey to dance, Indigo knew it was time to go home. There
was too much magic out in the night. (13–14)

In this passage we see a characteristic of Shange's magic realism: her new
narrative is informed throughout by an element of the unexpected, of chance,
of the ordinary experience that is not ordinary, and, finally, of the opaque
daily event that must be interpreted (Indigo suggests that there was too much
magic in the night) to be truly seen.

But what accounts for Indigo's "consorting" with the magical, supernatural,
and spiritual worlds? Shange provides the reader with two answers. First, Indigo is initiated into the world of magic realism by Uncle John when he
"tells [her] some matters of the real of the unreal" (26). Specifically, Uncle
John suggests to Indigo that one way of experiencing magic is by understanding the African American vernacular uses of music, especially "the blues":
"What ya think music is, whatchu think the blues be, & them get happy
church music is about, but talkin wit the unreal what's mo' real than most
folks ever gonna know" (27). Thus building on the rich African American
blues tradition, Shange joins Richard Wright, Ralph Ellison, Sherely Anne
Williams, Amiri Baraka, Henry Louis Gates, and Houston Baker in celebrating the strengths and beauties of the blues vernacular tradition that arises, in
LeRoi Jones's term, out of the depth of the black soul.[30] But it must be emphasized that Shange celebrates the blues with a "Signifyin[g]" difference—
the blues constitute "talkin wit the unreal." Throughout *Sassafrass, Cypress
& Indigo*, Shange shows us how Indigo "colored and made the world richer
what was blank & plain. The slaves who were ourselves knew all about Indigo
& Indigo herself" (40).

Shange also posits a second reason for Indigo's intimacy with magic and
the supernatural. Throughout the novel, the author suggests that women in
and of themselves are magical subjects. As Hortense Spillers argues, "There
is a rhetoric appropriate to Shange's realm of women, a set of gestures and desires that distinguishes female from male, even though the latter is ultimately
absorbed by the womb." Indigo grounds it at a more basic gender level when
she has a conversation with one of her dolls about her "Marvelous Menstru-
ating Moments": "When you first realize your blood has come, smile; an hon-
est smile, for you are about to have an intense union with your magic" (19).

Like many contemporary feminist anthropologists such as Carol Delaney and
Emily Martin, Shange criticizes traditional understanding of menstruation
not solely as the negative, polluting phenomenon described by males but as
a magical and potentially positive experience with deep implications for the
spiritual lives and power of women.[31]

The first fifty pages of *Sassafrass, Cypress & Indigo*, then, in magical and
radical feminist rhetoric tell the story of Indigo's creating, nurturing, and
celebrating her feminine essence. Clearly, one aspect of this magic realism is
associated with the author's belief that Indigo is special because her gender
allows her to fully experience her "blood earth." The other element is her
mastery of music, for she captured through her violin "the hum of dusk, the
crescendo of cicadas, swamp in light wind, thunder at high tide, & her mother's
laughter down the hall" (36). It must be stressed, however, that Shange's discussion of what accounts for Indigo's "consorting" with the magical finally
leaves the reader with these questions unanswered: Why should the blues
provide a privileged means of access to the "unreal"? And if the "magical"
somehow inheres in an essentialized notion of femaleness, then how does
Shange explain why the "source" for magic realism within the Latin American grain is emphatically male — Carpentier, García Márquez, and Fuentes?

The other major sections of *Sassafrass, Cypress & Indigo* concentrate on
Hilda Effania's middle daughter, Cypress, a ballerina who uses her training in
traditional dance "to find out the truth about colored people's movements."
Unlike Indigo, who stays with her mother in Charleston, Cypress moves to
San Francisco, and then to New York, using her love for dance to "take on
the struggle of colored Americans" (135).

When Cypress finally settles in New York, she enters into a community of
Third World lesbian dancers called the Azure Bosom. Cypress delights, for
the first time, in female sexuality. Some of these women, Shange writes, "were
super chic and independent ones like Celine ... others rounder than Xchell
and more bangled than Cypress ... [There were] women like Smokey Robin-
son and women like Miriam Makeba" (145). As Barbara Christian has noted
in "No More Buried Lives," the Azure Bosom is "rooted in the image of the
Haitian Voodun, Erzulie."[32] Shange protests the abuse of women's bodies and
allows women collectively "to linger in their own eroticism, to be happy
with loving themselves" (144). Yet her vision of Cypress's world is not idealized; at parties Cypress realizes that the celebrations were "more like a slave
market where everybody is selling herself" (145).

Shange's radical-feminist poetics, at least in this section of the novel, bring
into consideration the issues of race, class, and gender. This is especially true

of Cypress's utopian dream near the end of the novel. In her dream, Cypress survives a nuclear war, and "somehow the men and women are separated." The women survivors are "left to contend with the fruitlessness of the soils, the weight of the skies" (203). In a wonderful narrative of condensation, displacement, and revision, Shange constructs and then deconstructs Cypress's desire for an essentialized and idealist feminist world. To understand clearly Shange's cultural critique of radical feminism, let me quote from most of Cypress's dream:

> Cypress was initiated into the new world—not quite herself. All vestiges of male-dominated culture were to be "rehabilitated" out of her psyche; the true matriarch was to be nurtured ... But here there were no patriarchs, ordering and demanding. Here there were only Mothers and Daughters. "Mothers" were supreme; there was no higher honor than to be deemed "Mother," yet this had nothing to do with biological offspring. Women who had no children were of a higher caste than the "bearers," as they were called. The "bearers" were never seen in public assemblies, nor were they allowed to wear bright colors, because they might bear sons. (203)

On one level, the creation of a new social form is explicitly drawn out in Cypress's dream vision. Women in this world might genuinely learn to love each other. But Shange's narrative is not ahistorical. Throughout Cypress's dream, the author reminds us of the painful lessons of the logic of postmodernist societies—namely, that our postmodernist culture is always a sign of the internal and superstructural expression of class, race, and economic domination.

This explains why Cypress's dream also emphasizes that the underside of postmodernism is always blood, torture, death, and horror. Thus, some of the women in Cypress's dream are "breeders," and they make up an imprisoned class; and the majority of the bearers in Shange's brave new world are Latinas and black. Male babies are murdered, and males captured in the periphery are incarcerated in glass cages. Shange's novel thus represents the African American historical experience not as one continuous development, centered on one object, but as a double-voiced vision of the American historical past made up to different experiences. This is especially true of her sections on Sassafrass, the oldest daughter. Like Indigo and Cypress, Sassafrass is an artist—a weaver of cloth and a poet. Unlike her sisters, she desires to return to social forms and modes of production that are explicitly precapitalist:

> As she passed the shuttle through the claret cotton warp, Sassafrass conjured images of weaving from all time and all places: Toltecas spinning shimmering threads; East Indian women designing intricate patterns for Shatki, the impetus and destruction of creation; and Navajo women working on thick tapestries. (92)

Pervaded with images of weaving and symbols of kinship, the world, as Sassafrass imagines it, assumes a different social form.

Sassafrass attends an expensive boarding school in New England, the Callahan School, but she eschews traditional bourgeois ideologies by moving in with her lover, Roscoe Mitchell, in Los Angeles. Mitch, a black nationalist who shoots heroin and often imagines himself on the same bandstand with John Coltrane, turns out to be given to violence. This section of the novel is the most violent, in which Sassafrass must pay a high price for her independence. After putting up with Mitch's head-bashing for too long, she convinces him to join her in entering the New World Found Collective, a religious Afro-Caribbean commune in Louisiana. Here she is finally free to practice the Bembee religion in a community where social unity and spirituality can be achieved. In illuminating African-oriented religions like *voodoo* in Haiti, *santería* in Cuba, *espiritismo* in Puerto Rico, and Shango and Pocomania (both in Trinidad), Shange attempts, in this final section, to bring the history and cultural identity of black people in the Caribbean, Latin America, and U.S. Southern states closer together. At the end, Sassafrass tries "everything to be a decent *Ibejii*, a Santera. She desperately wanted to make *Ocha*. To wear white with her *elekes*. To keep the company of the priests and priestesses. The New World Found Collective where she and Mitch had been living for over a year offered spiritual redemption, if little else" (213).

Although many readers find Shange's novel depressing (Spillers writes that her "particular strength is the lament, and the lament is an apparently limited, probably even sentimental, form"),[33] its ending is a socially symbolic celebration of the unity of black people in all the Americas. Her emphasis on the Bembee religion, on *santería*, and on other rituals allows for another reading of the African American historical past. In the end, Shange's description of Sassafrass's African-based religious experiences offers an alternative to the Eurocentric understanding of America. Blacks as a people in the Americas, she reminds us, have experienced a history according to different circumstances. This strong understanding of a non-European America in her narratives has helped make her work especially attractive to Cuban and Nicaraguan audiences. In a speech commemorating the fifteenth anniversary of the Bay of Pigs victory, Castro affirms Cuban solidarity with African cultures and acknowledges that Cubans are an Afro-Latin people.[34] Like him, Cuban and Nicaraguan readers of Shange can recognize that Cuba's revolutionary experience and black heritage constitute a bond with African and Caribbean nations.

Finally, because place and territory are crucial in Shange's work, the Caribbean should be understood not as some vague politico-geographic region but as what Wallerstein calls "the extended Caribbean," a coastal and insular region stretching from southern Virginia to easternmost Brazil.[35] The Caribbean social space that Sassafrass desires at the end is the tropical belt defined ecologically or meteorologically. For Shange, then, the extended Caribbean is a historical and magical entity that can offer us a new way of imposing an imaginary coherence on the black experience of dispersal and fragmentation. Only from this position can we properly understand the traumatic character of the New World primal scene — where the fatal encounter was staged between Africa and the West.[36]

Notes

1. For a Fanonian reading of Shange's "combat-breathing" in *For Colored Girls*, see Sandra R. Richards, "Conflicting Impulses in the Plays of Ntozake Shange," in *Black American Literature Forum 17, no. 2* (Summer 1983): 73–78. For a reading of Shange's "lyricism" in *Sassafrass, Cypress & Indigo*, see Hortense J. Spillers's review in *American Book Review 5* (Summer 1983): 13. Although Spillers notes that Shange's narrative style is very similar to Jean Toomer's *Cane*, she fails to mention the cultural conversations among Toomer, Claude McKay, Langston Hughes, and Countee Cullen with African and Caribbean writers living in Paris. Perhaps these dialogues may explain Toomer's lyricism in *Cane* and its subsequent influence on Shange's poetics. Finally, see Michael Awkward, *Inspiriting Influences: Tradition, Revision, and Afro-American Women's Novels* (New York: Columbia University Press, 1989), and Houston Baker Jr., *Working of the Spirit: Afro-American Women's Writing* (Chicago: University of Chicago Press, 1991).

2. See Henry Louis Gates Jr., *The Signifying Monkey: A Theory of Afro-American Literary Criticism* (New York: Oxford University Press, 1988), xxii. Throughout this chapter I rely on Gates's notion of the "Signifyin[g]" vernacular tradition in African American literature and culture. Like Gates, I have elected to write the black term with a bracketed final g to connote that this word is spoken by black people without the final g, as "signifyin." For Gates, to signify is "to engage in certain rhetorical games" (48). More precisely, "Signifyin[g]" is always "black double-voicedness; because it always entails formal revision and an intertextual relation" (51).

3. W. Lawrence Hogue, *Discourse and the Other: The Production of the Afro-American Text* (Durham, N.C.: Duke University Press, 1986), 7. Subsequent page references to this work will be cited parenthetically in the text.

4. Gates's notion of the double-voiced African American text relies on Bakhtin's theory of the double-voiced word. For Bakhtin, a double-voiced word is a sort of palimpsest in which the uppermost inscription is a commentary on the one beneath it. For Gates, however, the African American vernacular tradition of "Signifyin[g]" decolonizes the Western inscriptions beneath it.

5. See *Perspectives*, University of Houston System 6–7 (March 1984): 2.

6. Fredric Jameson, "On Magic Realism in Film," *Critical Inquiry* 12 (Winter 1986): 301.

7. For its new interpretations of García Márquez, Carpentier, and magic realism, see Fernando Alegría, *Nueva historia de la novela hispanoamericana* (Hanover, N.H.: Ediciones Norte, 1986), 186–297. See also Roberto González Echevarría, "Carpentier y el realismo mágico," in Donald Yates, ed., *Otros Mundos, Otros Fuegos*, Congreso Internacional de Literatura Iberoamericana 16 (East Lansing: Michigan State University, Latin American Studies Center, 1975), 221–31; and Amaryll Beatrice Chanady, *Magical Realism and the Fantastic: Resolved versus Unresolved Antinomy* (New York: Garland, 1985).

8. Roberto González Echevarría, *Alejo Carpentier: The Pilgrim at Home* (Ithaca, N.Y.: Cornell University Press, 1977), 107–29. Subsequent page references to this work will be cited parenthetically in the text.

9. Arturo Uslar Pietri used the term *realismo mágico* in his book *Letra y hombres de Venezuela* (Mexico City: Fondo de Cultura Económica, 1948): Alejo Carpentier used the phrase *lo real maravilloso* in his "Prólogo" to *El reino de este mundo* in 1949.

10. Angel Flores, "Magical Realism in Spanish American Fiction," *Hispania* 38, no. 2 (May 1955): 190.

11. Luis Leal, "El realismo mágico en la literatura hispanoamericana," *Cuadernos Americanos* 153, no. 4 (July–August 1967): 234.

12. Echevarría argues in *The Pilgrim at Home* that in the fiction of Asturias and Carpentier there is "a primitivistic orientation" (112).

13. See Tristan Tzara, "Dada Manifesto," in Robert Motherwell, *Dada Painters and Poets* (New York: George Wittenborn Publishers, 1951), 78–79.

14. See André Breton, "What Is Surrealism?" in Richard Ellman and Charles Feidelson Jr., eds., *The Modern Tradition* (New York: Oxford University Press, 1965), 601–16.

15. Ibid.

16. Quoted in Gerald J. Langowski, *El surrealismo en la ficción hispanoamericana* (Madrid: Gredos, 1982), 89.

17. Emir Rodríguez Monegal, "Alejo Carpentier: lo real y lo maravilloso en *El reino de este mundo*," *Revista Iberoamericana* 37 (1971): 619–49.

18. Alejo Carpentier, "Prólogo," *El reino de este mundo* (Santiago: Editorial Universitaria, 1967), xiv-xv. The translation is mine. Subsequent page references to the "Prólogo" will be cited parenthetically in the text.

19. Gabriel García Márquez and Plinio Apuleyo Mendoza, *El olor de la guayaba* (Barcelona: Bruguera, 1982); published in English as *The Fragrance of Guava: Plinio Apuleyo Mendoza in Conversation with Gabriel García Márquez*, trans. T. Nairn (London: Verso, 1983), 54–55.

20. Fernando Alegría, "Latin America: Fantasy and Reality," *Américas Review* 14, nos. 3 4 (Fall-Winter 1986): 117. Subsequent page references to this work will be cited parenthetically in the text.

21. Gabriel García Márquez, "The Solitude of Latin America," *New York Times* (6 February 1982): 17.

22. Jameson, "On Magic Realism in Film," 311.

23. For a reactionary reading of Shange's ethnopoetics, see John Simon's review of *For Colored Girls* in *New Leader* 7, no. 5 (1976), where he states: "What accounts for the ... inordinate praise of too many black plays is not so much black talent as white guilt" (21–22).

24. Claudia Tate, *Black Women Writers at Work* (New York: Continuum, 1983), 163.

25. Ibid.

26. Barbara Christian, "Trajectories of Self-Definition: Placing Contemporary Afro-American Women's Fiction," in Marjorie Pryse and Hortense J. Spillers eds., *Conjuring: Black Women, Fiction, and Literary Tradition* (Bloomington: Indiana University Press, 1985), 242.

27. Spillers, review of *Sassafrass, Cypress & Indigo*, 13.

28. Ntozake Shange, interview with author, 5 May 1985.

29. Ntozake Shange, *Sassafrass, Cypress & Indigo* (New York: St. Martin's Press, 1982), 3. Subsequent page references will be cited parenthetically in the text.

30. LeRoi Jones, quoted in Michael G. Cooke, *Afro-American Literature in the Twentieth Century: The Achievement of Intimacy* (New Haven, Conn.: Yale University Press, 1984), 22.

31. See, for example, the feminist essays by Carol Delaney and Emily Martin in *Blood Magic: The Anthropology of Menstruation*, ed. Thomas Buckley and Alma Gottlieb (Berkeley: University of California Press, 1988).

32. Barbara Christian, "No More Buried Lives: The Theme of Lesbianism in Audre Lorde's *Zami*, Gloria Naylor's *The Women of Brewster Place*, Ntozake Shange's *Sassafrass, Cypress & Indigo*, and Alice Walker's *The Color Purple*," in *Black Feminist Criticism: Perspective on Black Women Writers* (New York: Pergamon Press, 1985), 192.

33. Spillers, review of *Sassafrass, Cypress & Indigo*, 13.

34. See *Foreign Broadcast Information Service, Daily Report* 6, no. 77 (1976): Q-1:8.

35. See Immanuel Wallerstein, *The Modern World System, II: Mercantilism and the Consolidation of the European World-Economy, 1600–1750* (New York: Academic Press, 1980), 103.

36. See Stuart Hall, "Cultural Identity and Diaspora," in Jonathan Rutherford, ed., *Identity: Community, Culture, Difference* (London: Lawrence and Wishart, 1990), 222–37.

11

Body/Talk: Mishima, Masturbation, and Self-Performativity

Donald H. Mengay

The social upheavals caused around the world by western imperialism were also felt in Japan, despite the fact that the west never established a formal colonial bureaucracy there. One of the early outcomes of the western "influence," which began with an act of aggression, the American insistence in the 1860s that Japan open its borders, was the reconfiguration of the terms of a debate about the individual's relation to society. As H. D. Harootonian and Masao Miyoshi point out, this discussion, as well as a more general one related to modernity and modernization, began in Japan well before the invasion by the west.[1] An effect of the western presence, however, was the relabeling of indigenous individualism as "westernism," a semiotic slippage that reveals western attempts to define the terms of the discourse, to take credit for the purported good (human rights, equality, the individual), and to assign the negative to the Japanese (fascism, mindless conformity, ultranationalism, nonrecognition, and even abuse of the individual).[2]

One of the tasks of modern Japanese writers has been to work against such simplistic portrayals. This effort constitutes much of the tension in the work of Yukio Mishima, which when taken as a whole struggles to reconfigure the relations between east/west and individual/society. These become for him and his characters a complex, wrenching, and inescapable conundrum, which he underscores the immediacy and intimate nature of by linking them metonymically to sex, and sexuality generally. More precisely, the mandate and desire to conform to sexual norms is offset by physical urges, desires, and demands that set the individual apart, that have no respect for the collective or for social norms. Sex and sexual acts, particularly masturbation and its attendant upheaval or shaking of the body, both individual and social, constitute the loci of desire and difference and ground a much broader discourse on identity. Drawn into this debate are issues about what it means to be Japanese in an increasingly westernized, or alien, culture; to be a "failed" man, sickly and weak and with (illicit) homosexual desires in a purportedly hetero/patriarchal culture; to write across the gap between east/west and to establish oneself as both international and "uniquely Japanese"; and to hail from a family with (weak) aristocratic links in a strongly class-conscious society.

The time when Mishima began writing, directly after the war, stands out as one of extreme cultural flux in Japan. In placing sexuality at the center of this debate, Mishima locates the quest for self against a historical backdrop that both mandates reproduction and questions the point and even usefulness of it, given the possibilities of mass destruction. This flux is metaphorized mostly in images of fluidity and bodily flow and gets at the impossibility of locating a "solid," essential, definable identity. To employ western, Derridean jargon: the self is established as a process of *differing*—always, through desire, to be found in another place—and *deferral*, ungraspable and without closure in time.

This of course approximates what in the west has come to be called the postmodern condition. "The postmodern identity is frequently theorized as an atomic identity, fractured and disseminated into a field of dispersed energy," writes Diana Fuss, the term "atomic" referring to "multiple identity particles bouncing off each other."[3] For Mishima, these "particles" or coordinates of identity (the entire litany of class, ethnicity, gender, race, sex, and so on) are portrayed as cultural flux occasioned largely by the domineering presence of the west in Japan.

In the works of Japanese writers the referent of this "atomic identity" is perhaps also the atomic bomb, and for them to employ it as metaphor is perhaps also to create a signifier far more immediate, and more vexed, than the use of it as mere figuration, as one finds in the west. It signifies the inversion of the relation of the self to the (epi)center, the negation of the signifier center-as-privileged-space.[4]

Writing as a westerner amid the devastation of the AIDS epidemic, I find Mishima disturbingly relevant, both because of the leveling effect, that is, of hierarchies of power (inside/outside, margin/center), caused by what gets perceived, even mythologized, as an irrational destructive force, and also more generally because of the placement of sex as the central metonym for exploring the effects of this destruction. Sex is portrayed by Mishima as central to an understanding of the self—not to mention that element that is most avoided, occluded, and reviled in social discourse. Positing the centrality of sexuality to modern notions of the (western) self, Eve Kosofsky Sedgwick argues that "many of the major nodes of thought and knowledge in twentieth-century Western culture as a whole are structured—indeed, fractured—by a chronic, now endemic crisis of homo/hetero definition."[5] It is precisely along these lines that Mishima configures a postwar Japanese self, thus effecting a bridge between eastern and western notions of identity.

Without labeling Mishima or his fictional self, Kochan, "gay" in any western sense of the word, the struggle of identity that occurs in his texts (and in *Confessions of a Mask* especially) focuses nevertheless precisely on the issue of (homo)sexuality and gender, expressed in the short-circuiting of relations between language and the body—issues faced uniquely by the contemporary western, queer reader. It is after all the sexed body, and particularly the "gay" diseased body, that constitutes the modern homosexual as inhabitant of both the margins and center, but the center as conceived by Andrew Holleran, as "ground zero."[6]

For all intents and purposes, *Confessions of a Mask* (1949) is the narrative of Mishima's own youth. In this novel he details his experiences as a weak, sickly child forced to live with, and attend to, his equally sickly grandmother. Like André Gide's Michel in *L'immoraliste*, it is through aesthetic/erotic experiences with other men that a desire to live and be strong is planted in Kochan. He quickly discovers not only that his desire to live is intimately linked with homo desire (for example, for the night-soil man and for Omi) but that this desire is also socially unacceptable. He knows instinctually that to fit in is to manifest the "proper" desires, and so he endeavors to suppress his homo urges in order to cultivate hetero ones—specifically, for a young woman named Sonoko. Of course, this leads to disaster, to confusion and self-loathing. Kochan discovers he is capable of hetero desire, but he nevertheless is forced to admit to the persistence and irremediableness of his desire for young men.

Put another way, while Kochan tries to front a stable, culturally approved self, he is troubled by a concomitant, persistent marginalized self, one that threatens to obliterate the respectability that attains through conformity, expressed here in sexual attraction. Central to his struggle is the desire for agency, for the ability to dismantle the regulatory system of sexuality that limits the possibilities of desire.

The tenacity of these sexual norms is revealed in several ways, but most significantly in Kochan's experience of masturbation, with all of its decadent resonances. The latter is *the* subversive act for Kochan, precisely because of the specificity, for him, of its connection to same-sex desire. In this act of privacy he flaunts compulsory demands of heterosexuality in his infatuation with other men. On the one hand his position is rebellious, but on the other he is painfully aware of his investment and his own complicitous reinforcement of the very prescriptive modes he seeks to undermine.

Beauty encompasses the many binarisms marking these regulatory norms. Mishima's notion of beauty, an unusual hybrid of Japanese-samurai, classical Greek and Wildean aesthetics, incorporates both death and sex in such a way that sex appropriates, imitates, and metaphorizes death. Quoting Dostoyevsky's *The Brothers Karamazov* in his epigraph, Mishima asserts an aesthetic in which "Beauty is a terrible and awful thing! It is terrible because it never has and never can be fathomed, for God sets us nothing but riddles. Within beauty both shores meet and all contradictions exist side by side." Not merely a zero-sum game in which binaristic forces cancel one another out, beauty becomes a site in which excess is engaged in for the purpose of baring the nature of binarisms themselves, inherent in societal norms. Beauty's iconography is a pastiche of signifiers in which, for example, "the ideal of Sodom" is metonymically linked with "the ideal of the Madonna" — a connection that both implicates the one in the other and retains its antinomies along the lines of the contestatory/subservient, denaturalized/naturalized, homo/hetero, illicit/licit, male/female, pagan/religious, and profane/sacred. Moreover, vitiation and innocence are contrasted in homo and hetero desire, even if directions for connecting the bilateral set of dots are unclear.

Kochan both reinforces and subverts notions of homosexual desire as degradation, asserting *its* primacy and innocence; hetero desire must be "learned," as in the case of his relationship with Sonoko, but homo desire is decadently cast as "natural." The beautiful, in other words, represents a means of escape from a sanctioned extreme — univocity, lopsidedness. For Mishima, it seems that it is a way out of "normal" (i.e., societal) formulations of the acceptable and the licit, even if the escape is ephemeral.

Mishima metaphorizes beauty in fluidic images that hint at unity and continuity (blood, river, sea, semen, urine), each of which is linked in some way to masturbation. This act molds Kochan's aesthetic, engaging elements of body/language, life/death, and stoppage/flowing, but it also is an expression of his mind-set both as determined subject and agent of resistance. As a performative act masturbation, like beauty, also does not represent a zero-sum game. Opposed to a synchronic perspective in which Kochan experiences only self-negating and warring forces is a diachronic one in which the iteration of the masturbatory act itself accrues, for all of its essentialist resonances, self-knowledge, even if the knowledge gained never seems to serve as a finality. Masturbatory "knowledge" of the self is significant not because the self is an existentialist entity defined merely by the aggregate of its acts, but because through masturbation Kochan discovers the nature of his desire.[7] Through masturbation Kochan scrutinizes his own erotic phantasmatics in order to glean a sense of himself in the broader signifying economy of society; in it he takes stock of his same-sex desire as constitutive of a "real" self.

The groundwork for a problematized thematics of the self is laid at the point the reader learns that Kochan suffers, as a four-year-old child, from "autointoxication" (7).[8] This disease, *jika chudoku* (self-poisoning), signals a somatic dissonance—literally, the body against itself—that foreshadows a cognate mental turning-against-itself, a self-poisoning or psychic nihilism. The illness, typified by a retention or blockage of the flow of bodily wastes (the body here reconstituted as the locus, the bursting receptacle, of conflicting social signifieds) is cured for Kochan through circulation and emission—that is, when he urinates. His uncle declares him alive upon seeing the escape of urine, commenting that "it showed his heart had resumed beating," the pumping prefiguring the significance of blood in Kochan's aesthetic *and* constituting the resignifying process (7). This bout develops, though, into a chronic illness striking about once a month, an indication of a kind of somatic ambivalence. "I encountered many crises," he comments; "I came to be able to sense whether an attack was likely to approach death or not" (7).

Kochan problematizes his body, an entity that assumes greater importance when he begins to see it in contradistinction to that of others. He speaks in comparative terms, indicating for example that he was an underweight baby (5) and that in adolescence he was an abnormally small and frail boy (79–80). His early years were spent in his grandmother's sickroom that was, tellingly, "closed and stifling with odors of sickness and of old age"—the insalubrious atmosphere of the room serving as a metaphor for his oxygen-deprived blood, an effect of the disease but also the body struggling to exist in an atmosphere hostile to it (6). Like Gide's "immoralist" Michel, he decides to fight against physical and mental weakness, remarking in frustration, "now I became obsessed with a single motto—'Be Strong!'" (80). He fetishizes health and puts forth an aesthetic/transgressive model of the body, epitomized in his classmate, Omi:

Life-force — it was the sheer extravagant abundance of life-force that overpowered the boys [at school]. They were overwhelmed by the feeling [Omi] gave of
having too much life, by the feeling of purposeless violence that can be explained
only as life existing for its own sake.... [Omi's] flesh had been put on this earth
for no other reason than to become an insane human-sacrifice, one without any
fear of infection. *Persons who live in terror of infection cannot but regard such flesh
as a bitter reproach....* (78–79; emphasis added)

Kochan becomes preoccupied with, eroticizes, the healthy body, which, as
he says, "exists for its own sake" and which enjoys a certain agency inaccessible to him. The healthy body defines its own fate, serving as a law unto itself. Paradoxically, though, the healthy body is not only expendable but even
developed for the sole purpose of its own destruction. In a world in which
the body is subject to — is "infected" by — strict regulation, the uninfected
body is nothing but an ephemeral anomaly, doomed to early destruction. It
is characterized by circular coursings that must end in emission. The ability
to spill (blood, shit, urine) is a sign of the body's flaunting of norms of con-
tainment, its relish in excess, but also of its moribundity.

Accordingly, Kochan's first physical attraction is to a ladler of excrement
(*funnyuo*: manure/urine), an episode that comes close on the heels of his initial
bout of autointoxication and reinforces his tendency to apotheosize health-
as-reformulation/emission. The ladler collects and circulates waste, disseminates it. Waste is the symbol of a reconstitution process in which initial stages
(i.e., eating) engage one set of norms regulating food consumption, and ter-
minal stages engage another, centered around not just excretion but death as
well. Among humans the entire process is regulated by taboos, all of which
vary in kind and intensity specific to the particular stage in the process. For
example, it appears ludicrous and revelatory to consider the differences in
amount of time allotted to a "proper" experience of eating and shitting. Also,
handlers of food occupy a very different status than handlers of excrement.
A finely articulated hierarchy exists among food preparers that engages an
elaborate industry of culinary schools, market guidelines, rules for presentation and arrangement, nutrition, order of consumption, manners, and so on.
Kochan reconstitutes not just shit-handling but the shit-handler as an object
of desire in a (at this point very unconscious) move to counteract norms of
acceptability and rejection, a move psychodynamically related to what is occurring in his own body.

This ambiguous recognition manifests itself in the first glimmerings of desire. He comments:

The scrutiny I gave the youth was unusually close for a child of four. Although I did not clearly perceive it at the time, for me he represented my first revelation of a certain power, my first summons by a certain strange and secret voice. It is significant that this was first manifested to me in the form of a night-soil man: excrement is a symbol for the earth. (8)

The "summons" and "certain power" to which he is drawn relate in one sense to his own practical need to defecate, which he cannot seem to do. To pass, expel, or disseminate become self-imposed health mandates and, again, emblematic for the need to redirect social limitations on the body. But the connection of excrement to the social *role* of the shit-ladler and the mapping of that role on a sociohierarchic grid—a role that Kochan valorizes and *eroticizes*—indicate the attraction is identificatory as well. In short, Kochan is as much captivated by the stigmatized status of the "manure man" as he is by the act of dissemination.

One effect of Kochan's pairing of recirculation/emission fantasies with the ladler of excrement manifests itself in a homoeroticized coprophilia, in which health and beauty are linked with the collection/dispersal of soil/feces. Compare, for instance, the "invitation" of Omi's footprints in the snow "the color of fresh black soil" (56)—scatological leavings of "coal black earth" that Kochan follows after spotting them from his window (57). These footprints relate to the "traces" Kochan leaves after masturbation and represent a text inscribed by the body, a signature, on the landscape. At the same time, Kochan's interest in them underscores the coprophiliac tendency to play with shit, in the same way Omi does, metaphorically. In a school competition, Kochan notices Omi "[stretch] his hands down leisurely to the ground and [smear] his palms with damp sand from just beneath the surface" (77). The erotic/scatological significance of soil here and in the episode of the excrement ladler is related to other themes, particularly those of beauty and death as they relate to masturbation.

Kochan fetishizes shit as a stigmatized bodily emission by linking it to others, including vomiting (6), sweating (13), bleeding (45), the growth of hair in the armpits (88), disembowelment (93), and ejaculation. These constitute what Mishima would later term, speaking in another context, "the body's loquacity,"[9] its means of articulating (illicit) drives and desires outside of the realm of a sanctioned, verbal signifying order, which becomes an antagonistic force in the text. He contests the linguistic order, implicating it as the mode by which oppression and limitation take place. Agency is not achieved through words; the "free" self that Mishima constitutes is identified with *bodily* acts.[10]

Operating in Mishima's semiotics of the body, Kochan is obsessed in particular with the coursing of blood, which he images in an endless, fatalistic
circularity. "Abundant blood coursing richly throughout [Omi's] body" represents "an untamed soul" (63) eager to escape its endless, goalless meander-
ing like the peripatetic shade of a Noh protagonist. "Life . . . enslaved [Omi]"
(87), Kochan indicates. Blood, the specter of the untamed and untameable,
must escape the body in the same way other wastes must escape — which is
in turn a metaphoric allusion to Kochan's desire to escape the "body politic."
Paradoxically, only in the spilling or passing of blood does "life" become possible. As a result, a central trope in Kochan's erotics is a puncturing of the
imagined object's flesh in order to liberate blood/soul/self.[11] This mythology
reformulates death as the site of freedom; it prefigures Georges Bataille's notion of death as "identified with continuity," as that which "denotes passion"
and is linked to eroticism.[12] Kochan recasts life, by which he means social
life, as an entombing force. Death, that is, of the body, liberates.

This and similar passages elucidate that element in the episode of the night-
soil man (and the general coprophilia of Mishima's text) in which Kochan
comments that it was "Mother Earth that was calling to me" (8). Excrement/
soil/earth beckon Kochan's body not only to divest and "void" itself, but
quite literally to *become* earth, to die and decompose. The synecdochic connection between footprints/scat and Omi works both ways: the part (feces)
represents the whole (the body) to the degree that it is generated *by* the body;
but so is the whole ultimately nothing more than the part. That is, the body
is no more than soil/shit, to the degree that it is nourished and unified with
the earth. Unlike the mind, which is fractured and dichotomous, the body
tends toward unity. Also, while the mind is socially determined, the body offers the potential for freedom.

The greatest possibility of this comes in the moment of orgasm. The experience, including the buildup to it, engages Kochan's aesthetic of death in
which the self is asserted solely in somatic terms (semen), but also annihi-
lated, lost in an emptiness without set boundaries or specificity (in this case,
in "intoxication"). The semiotics of sameness and difference are played out in
orgasm in the sense that the self is distinguished from its erotic object while
it identifies with that object. Describing his first masturbatory experience,
Kochan narrates:

> That day, the instant I looked upon the picture [of Saint Sebastian], my entire
> being trembled with some pagan joy. My blood soared up; my loins swelled as
> though in wrath. The monstrous part of me that was on the point of bursting
> awaited my use of it with unprecedented ardor, upbraiding me for my igno-

rance, panting indignantly. My hands, completely unconsciously, began a motion they had never been taught. I felt a secret, radiant something rise swift-footed to the attack from inside me. Suddenly it burst forth, bringing with it a blinding intoxication.... (40)

The image to which Kochan responds (Guido Reni's painting of Saint Sebastian) is important in that it both accords with Kochan's pattern of fetishizing bodily emission (blood escaping from Sebastian's arrow-wounds) and originates the highly articulated erotic themes that he later associates with Omi: integumental penetration, recircularity, the ebbing of life in the escape of blood, and a well-formed body. In referring to his joy as "pagan" he recognizes his tastes as atavistic, recalling ancient aesthetic formulations, as well as transgressive, in that his fantasy object is not only male but western. The unconscious aspect of his masturbatory movements foreshadows Kochan's realizations toward the end of the text, in which he recognizes his "selves" to have been less freely determined than he expected. Again, although this self may be unconsciously generated, it is also obliterated in a state of intoxication (*meitei*).

The Japanese term for intoxication refers literally to drunkenness, a word that reinforces the notion of circularity by metaphorizing semen as urine, an effect of drinking, but also invokes other more archaic meanings that evoke the decadence of a Shinto festival in which Kochan reads in the faces of the young men carrying a shrine "an expression of the most obscene and undisguised drunkenness in the world" (33). After this first experience he frames his erotic narratives in similar secular/religious terms, calling the act of masturbation a "pagan ceremony" and the masturbatory image—"victim"—a "ritual sacrifice" (175).

In the first ejaculatory episode, semen, like feces, is disseminated, and in this case dots the top of his worktable "leadenly" (40). "My blood soared up," Kochan remarks, and then, significantly, "my loins swelled as though in wrath." "The monstrous part" approaches the point of bursting if it doesn't soon, like Kochan's four-year-old, autointoxicated body, relieve itself (40). This "something" (*mono*) that the body releases is troublesome in its indeterminacy. As it is here contextualized, one way it signifies is as a kind of artillery of the body. "I felt a secret, radiant something rise swift-footed to the attack from inside me," the Japanese word for attack (*seme*) used primarily in the military sense. This "aggression" may imply several things, including the strength of Kochan's healthy resolve; a long-overdue—and therefore overcompensated—effort to assert a (homo) self; a violent attack against the restrictions that society places on the body; and even a carryover of Japanese-western hostilities, which had "ended" only three years before Mishima began writing. In the original text, Mishima employs the Latin term *ejaclatio* (37), which evokes the valence of not merely ejection/discharge but, literally, the hurling of a spear (or in the Sebastinian context, an arrow), the word *ejaclatio* meaning to throw away (a javelin, for example). Fixated on the image of Sebastian, whose body is riddled with arrows, Kochan objectifies him, even "attacks" him, but so does he identify with him as a symbol of salubrity. Evoking the samurai tradition of *shinju* or double suicide, Kochan's "little death" signifies a dying *with* Sebastian.[13]

Kochan's first ejaculation also serves as a complex interchange between body and text — or it reconfigures the body as a (censored) *urtext*. The body in effect rewrites itself:

> I looked around the desk I was facing. A maple tree at the window was casting a bright reflection over everything — over the ink bottle, my schoolbooks and notes, the dictionary, the picture of St. Sebastian. There were cloudy white splashes about — on the gold-imprinted title of a textbook, on a shoulder of the ink bottle, on one corner of the dictionary.... Fortunately, a reflex motion of my hand to protect the picture had saved the book from being soiled. (40–41)

The juxtaposition of the ink bottle — the covering of it — with semen foregrounds the nonverbal "loquacity" of the body to that of the verbal signifying order. Through his somatic "speech act" he attacks the social hegemony of this order, signified in the dictionary, schoolbooks, notes. Twenty years after the writing of *Confessions of a Mask*, in *Sun and Steel*, Mishima would refer to the way words corrode and destroy the body (82). The notion of *ejaclatio* as an "attack" (*seme*), therefore, also relates to the desire to go against the prevalent foregrounding of the written, verbal text, insofar as it is a culturally privileged medium, one that constitutes the body-text as inferior, governable, colonizable.

Kochan protects only the image of Sebastian from being "soiled," the term signaling his own ability now to disseminate "shit." This recalls Gide's protagonist Michel, who in the throes of tuberculosis coughs up blood and mucus, which marks a turning point in his fight against the disease. "J'en étais extraordinairement soulagé," Michel remarks. "C'est le fin du rhume" ("I was extraordinarily relieved.... It was the end of the [disease]").[14] Similar to Kochan, illness for Michel is dispelled through the emission of blood/phlegm: "je crachais," Michel says, the verb *cracher* meaning to spit/come out with/splash. His masturbatory expectorations work in harmony with the carriage in which he is riding, *les cahots* (the jerks) of which mimic the motions of his body.[15]

For Kochan, too, ejaculation represents a significant triumph, a telling moment in his struggle to "express" himself, achieve health, construct a self as agent.

This liberatory moment, however, lasts only for the duration of the orgasm itself. No sooner does he experience it than he undergoes an intensification of guilt. "This was my first ejaculation," he explains at the end of the episode. "It was also the beginning, clumsy and completely unpremeditated, of my 'bad habit'" (*akushu*) (40–41). This negative characterization (the Japanese *aku*: bad, evil) of the repetitive act that masturbation represents, both in a single masturbatory moment and in its temporal constitution as "habit" (*shu*) over time, indicates just how inescapable the norms are of which Kochan seeks to divest himself. Identifying generally with his schoolmates, for instance, he is nonetheless aware of a key difference:

> Suffice it to say, then, that—*always excepting the one shameful difference I am describing*—in that most colorless phase of the bashful student I was exactly like the other boys, that I had sworn unconditional loyalty to the stage manager of the play called adolescence. (122; emphasis added)

Awareness of difference between himself and his (putatively hetero) classmates in both desire and its complicated thematics affects him negatively and leads him to, in short, an epistemology of the closet. This locution, formulated by Sedgwick, posits silence as being "as pointed and performative as speech"[16]— a posture Kochan adopts while privately resorting to masturbation as the means of achieving "utterance." He can do it, he learns, but at the price of guilt and remorse. He finds the regime of compulsory heterosexuality indomitable and indelibly "written" on him; all he can do is mask or outwardly silence the prohibited, (what he takes to be) "real," self.

In her article "Imitation and Gender Insubordination," Judith Butler, speaking of her own self-constitution as a "lesbian," articulates a dynamic similar to that promulgated by Mishima:

> How and where I play at being [a lesbian] is the way in which that "being" gets established, instituted, circulated, and confirmed. This is not a performance from which I can take radical distance, for this is deep-seated play, psychically entrenched play, *and the "I" does not play its lesbianism as a role*. Rather, it is through the repeated play of this sexuality that the "I" is insistently reconstituted as a lesbian "I"; paradoxically, it is precisely the *repetition* of that play that establishes as well the *instability* of the very category that it constitutes. For it the "I" is a site of repetition, that is, if the "I" only achieves the semblance of identity through a certain repetition of itself, then the I is always displaced by the very repetition that sustains it.[17]

This rather masturbatory iteration of an "I" at once engenders and destabilizes it; in Derridean terms, both repeats *and* alters it.[18] Again, it is the diachronic experience of masturbation that works toward granting Kochan some sense of knowledge about the self. Reinforced patterns, even if contestatory or "illicit," get taken for the "true" self while deviations from these repetitions appear to him artificial. Taking hetero desire as utterly foreign — and therefore immoral in Kochan's ethics — he comments, "I mastered the art of delusion until I could regard myself as a truly lewd-minded person" (115). Linking homo desire to physical passion and hetero to another form, he complains:

> In order to delude myself that [heterosexual] desire was animal passion, I had to undertake an elaborate disguise of my true self. The unconscious feeling of guilt resulting from this false pretense stubbornly insisted that I play a conscious and false role. (116)

The early, essentialist notion of the self mapped along an axis the termini of which constitute the true/counterfeit, normal/anomalous, licit/illicit informs Kochan's self-understanding and induces bouts of self-reproach (172, 173, 203, 206). This stems from his consciousness of what he considers to be cross-gendered sexual desire as a conscious "masquerade" (100–101), a "counterfeit" (106), "a machine of falsehood" (108), "the art of delusion" (115), a "camouflage" (120), "the machinery of deception" (201), and the "playing [of] a part" (229).

But this repetition — of albeit a "false" self — both reinforces its falseness and calls it into question, in the same way Butler's "I" is both constituted and called into question by its "deep-seated play." "My 'act' has ended by becoming an integral part of my nature," Kochan comments. What he has assumed to be a conscious performance has been "psychically entrenched play."[19] That is, no play at all. Kochan remarks:

> My "act" has ended by becoming an integral part of my nature ... It's no longer an act. My knowledge that I am masquerading as a normal person has even corroded whatever of normality I originally possessed, ending by making me tell myself over and over again that it too was nothing but a pretense at normality. (153)

The degree to which "play" is meant in neither the ludic nor western-histrionic senses inheres in the Japanese word for play, *engi*. It carries the notion of a staged performance, but one in which the requirements for "acting" are different from those in the west. As Donald Keene points out, Japanese stage actors (here, of Noh) begin their training in infancy and continue until the "last tottering appearances on the stage."[20] They live the subtle nuances and intonations they "perform" on stage until the movements — each of which are encoded with gender valences — become "unconscious." The main *kabuki* actor, the *onnagata*, must repeatedly enact his "role" as well. As Mishima writes in his short story "Onnagata," "unless the *onnagata* lives as a woman in his daily life, he is unlikely ever to be considered accomplished."[21] The "performed" self and the "real" self, then, become in a sense conflated, but they are also called seriously into question. The *onnagata* is an appropriate metaphor for Kochan in that he inhabits stereotypically male and female roles, and in so doing proliferates another possibility. The "counterfeit" and the "real" become in part moot categories, because the *onnagata* represents both.

Prefiguring the western notion of the postmodern condition, the "unified" or "normal" I becomes impossible for Kochan. He finds only tension, and a strong measure of guilt. After proclaiming his love for Sonoko, he comments (assuming his [male] reader shares his early essentialist demands for a continuity of self):

> The reader who has followed me this far will probably refuse to believe anything I am saying. He will doubt me because there will seem to be no difference between my artificial and unrequited love of [Sonoko] and the throbbing of the breast of which I am now speaking, because there will seem to be no apparent reason why on this occasion alone I should not have subjected my emotions to that merciless analysis I had used in the former case.... He will think that I say a thing simply because I want to say it so, *without any regard for truth*, and anything I say will be all right so long as I make my story consistent. (143; emphasis added)

This notion of truth-as-consistency foils Kochan in his early attempts at self-knowledge. He solicits the reader to accept the possibility of a self, other than the norm-flaunting one with which he has identified early on, a gesture that exposes as problematic the binarisms artificial/real and foreign/naturalized. "What appeared to be the inside was the outside," Kochan comments, "and what appeared the outside was the inside" (177). This destabilization of the self as a single pattern of desire, so contrary to culturally bound (and I would add western as well as eastern) notions of the self, is difficult for Kochan to accept. "Even the strength of a Samson would not have been sufficient to make me adopt a *manly and unequivocal* attitude toward Sonoko," he admits, assuming that a "manly" attitude is a rigidly consistent one. It is this socialized assumption, outside of the realm of his understanding, that, he says, "aroused my disgust" (203; emphasis added).

Worse, however, is the possibility that equivocal desire equals no desire. Deciding not to marry Sonoko, who is interested in marrying him, Kochan considers how to bow out:

> Even though my heart was filled with uneasiness and unspeakable grief, I put a brazen, cynical smile upon my lips. I told myself that all I had to do was clear one small hurdle. All I had to do was to regard all the past few months as absurd; to decide that from the beginning I'd never been in love with a girl called Sonoko, not with such a chit of a girl; to believe that I'd been prompted by a trifling passion (liar!) and had deceived her. (212)

He surprises himself to discover that the mask he has assumed is not a role now but another identification. Formerly having concretized the "true" as the homo "I" of his masturbatory fantasies, Kochan now realizes despite himself that this "I" is not the only one, that there is another axis along which his now-split self is mapped. The hetero, "masked," identity becomes a habit paralleling the self of Kochan's "bad habit," and in this way also becomes naturalized.

Both the complicitous hetero self and the transgressive homo self are all of a rather tattered piece: two possibilities engendered by a prohibitive, heterosexist economy. If he realizes the potential for either identification, he nevertheless comes to discern the limitations of agency as well. The homo-transgressive, if no longer constituted as the real or only self possible, nevertheless represents the more "immutable" and consistent for him. In a series of several meetings with Sonoko, who has now married another man, he repeats his early, now-formulaic, homonarrative fantasy. Standing next to Sonoko he is "drawn to ... a youth of twenty-one or -two [who] ... had taken his shirt off and stood there half-naked, rewinding a belly-band around his middle" (251). This belly-band recalls for him the samurai ritual of *seppuku*, again reiterating his antiregulatory, aesthetic thematics:

> I was beset by sexual desire. My fervent gaze was fixed upon that rough and savage, but incomparably *beautiful*, body.... I had forgotten Sonoko's existence. I was thinking of but one thing: Of his going out onto the streets of high summer just as he was, half-naked, and getting into a fight with a rival gang. Of a sharp dagger cutting through the belly-band, piercing that torso. Of that soiled belly-band beautifully dyed with blood. Of his gory corpse being put on an improvised stretcher ... (252; emphasis added)

This fantasy is followed by an orgasmic moment marked again by martial rhetoric. "I felt as though I had witnessed the instant in which my existence had been turned into some sort of fearful non-being," he remarks, referring to the state of intoxication and orgasm/melding of the self that we saw earlier

(253). This orgasmic moment is also marked by "some sort of beverage [that] had been spilled on the table top and was throwing back glittering, threatening reflections" (254). As is his pattern, this moment is followed by yet another awareness of regulatory sex norms, which he refers to as his "icy-cold sense of duty" (253).

The experience of masturbation remains for Kochan a temporary escape from the force field of compulsory heterosexuality. His desire and unconscious pull toward subverting heterosexist injunctions engage him in the masturbatory act that is apotheosized in the moment of orgasm/death, arrived at through beauty and its attendant thematics. The moment of fusion that beauty/death represents, though, the stepping "outside," is a fleeting one, followed by the reinforcement, the relaying of the prohibitive grid on the subject as it returns to "sobriety," to its social prison.

This same circularity characterized the act of writing for Mishima, which, like masturbation for Kochan, became a self-revelatory act in which the text became "seminal," both physical proof and a search for the self. "What I have written departs from me," Mishima remarked a short time before his death by suicide, underscoring the importance for him of expelling that which was inside.[22] But the text as ejaculation/iteration, Mishima realized, was not enough finally to constitute a stable self; the notion of a fixed self itself is problematic. Writing "never [nourished] my void," he explains in his notes for the Tobu Exhibition. Self-solace (with all of the masturbatory connotations of the Japanese *jii*) achieves only in the (repetitive/masturbatory) act of writing itself: "I still have no way to survive but to keep on writing one line, one more line, one more line ..."[23] This is the same principle at work in Mishima's presentation of body building as he discusses it in *Sun and Steel*, which is also effected through repetitive motions.[24] In accordance with his nihilistic aesthetic, the construction of a "pumped up" body served as a preparation for (his own) death through *seppuku*, a process in which emission is achieved in the form of a slitting of the abdomen in order for the viscera to escape, as well as in the form of beheading.[25]

If Kochan is incapable of actually escaping the heterosexist signifying order in which he himself has been constituted, he nevertheless achieves a certain kind of agency through a fantasy of excess.[26] The formulation in particular of death as excess—whether in the temporary "death" of desire/passion/orgasm, the unifying death of decomposition/defecation, or the obliterating death in the physical act of *seppuku*—seems to have been one in currency among mid-twentieth-century Japanese writers. Several, including Ryuunosuke Akutagawa, Osamu Dazai, Yasunari Kawabata, and Mishima himself, committed suicide.

Confessions of a Mask represents for Mishima a deliberate writing against the social grain, against what Jakobson referred to as the "stagnating slime" that caused many Russian poets to take their own lives.[27] Mishima's case is complicated in that the forces he bucked were the same ones he would find provided him a privileged status. His death fantasies, and by extension those of Kochan, appear to be an admission of the immutability of these forces, as well as their limitation. His familiarity with "the deadly absence of fresh air" that Jakobson speaks of is metaphorized in the "closed and stifling" sickroom — that is, the broader cultural sphere — in which his protagonist is forced to stay (6).

As civil-rights-minded people in the United States have learned, windows of change open and shut quickly. The potential for *appreciable* change remains limited at any time, given entrenched social patterns. Tragic scenarios of mass destruction (the slave trade, the holocaust, the bomb, AIDS), which Mishima metaphorized in the "destroyed" or shaken orgasmic body, are often avoided, occluded, or even denied rather than occasioning soul-searching and self-knowledge. If in his later works Mishima would revert to a more traditional, atavistic, and even reactionary conceptualization of Japanese identity, one rejected by and large by the Japanese themselves, the subversive questioning — directive — of the early text remains.

Notes

I would like to thank Professor Seigo Nakao for his assistance with the original Japanese.

1. H. D. Harootonian and Masao Miyoshi, *Postmodernism and Japan* (Durham, N.C.: Duke University Press, 1989), x.

2. There is great irony and even hypocrisy in this when one considers that at the height of U.S. intervention in Japan, the postwar occupation during the forties and early fifties, the United States was enforcing Jim Crow laws, treating women as the legal property of their husbands, holding Japanese-Americans in internment camps, imprisoning and "treating" homosexuals, and denying legal land rights to Native Americans.

For western views of the American relationship with Japan, see Meiron and Susie Harres, *Sheathing the Sword: The Demilitarization of Postwar Japan* (New York: MacMillan, 1987); Edwin O. Reischauer, *The Japanese* (Cambridge: Harvard University Press, 1979); Peter Tasker, *The Japanese: A Major Exploration of Modern Japan* (New York: E. P. Dutton, 1987). Reischauer in particular stands out as one who avoids giving credit to the United States for what was indigenous to Japan, before the western intrusion.

3. Diana Fuss, *Essentially Speaking: Feminism, Nature and Difference* (New York: Routledge, 1989), 103.

4. For a disturbing portrayal of the physical and cultural effects of the bomb, see Ibuse Masuji, *Black Rain*, trans. John Bester (New York: Kodansha, 1979).

5. Eve Kosofsky Sedgwick, *Epistemology of the Closet* (Berkeley: University of California Press, 1990), 1.

6. For Holleran's employment of the bomb as metaphor for AIDS destruction, see his *Ground Zero* (New York: New American Library, 1989).

7. For a discussion of the existentialist model of identity, see Judith Butler, *Gender Trouble: Feminism and the Subversion of Identity* (New York: Routledge, 1990).

8. Page references in this section are to Yukio Mishima *Confessions of a Mask*, trans. Meredith Weatherby (New York: New Directions, 1963).

9. Yukio Mishima, *Sun and Steel* (New York: Kodansha, 1970), 18.

10. See Mishima, *Sun and Steel*, 50, 64–65, 66.

11. Among the many such fantasies are the following: the killing of Wilde's knight (11–12); the Rose Elf being stabbed to death (21); Kochan imagines Andersen's prince being torn apart by dragon's teeth, then dying: Kochan rewrites the story (23); the plaintive melody of a chant "piercing through" the confused tumult of the festival, mating humanity with eternity (30); dueling scenes/hard-ons (35); death by bullets (36); Sebastian (39–40); Sebastian pierced by countless arrows (42); Omi's fingers in game, like weapons about to run through Kochan (69); Kochan's ritual sacrifice of youth in his imagination during masturbation (175); penetration of the ephebe and delight in seeing blood flow trace ephebe's curves when running down (177); the twenty-one- or twenty-two-year old man on the street (252).

12. Georges Bataille, *Erotism: Death and Sensuality*, trans. Mary Dalwood (San Francisco: City Lights Books, 1986), 13, 20, 59.

13. The notion of *shinju* is an element of the samurai code of honor, *bushido*, which is limned in the eighteenth-century book *Hagakure* (A life hidden behind the leaves). As Tsuneo Watanabe points out, the text "teaches how one may be 'beautiful' in death." This beauty is both ethical, militating a preparedness and even eagerness for one's own death, and aesthetic, suggesting that the samurai "should always carry rouge and powder" with him in order to preserve an appealing aspect at the moment of mortality. Sebastian, according to legend a martyr for the Christian cause, approximates many of the requirements of honor encoded in the term *bushido*. See Tsuneo Watanabe, *The Love of the Samurai: A Thousand Years of Japanese Homosexuality*, trans. D. R. Roberts (London: GMP, 1989), 116.

14. André Gide, *L'immoraliste* (Paris: Mercure de France, 1902), 25.

15. Ibid.

16. Sedgwick, *Epistemology of the Closet*, 4.

17. Judith Butler, "Imitation and Gender Insubordination," in Diana Fuss, ed., *Inside/Out: Lesbian Theories, Gay Theories* (New York: Routledge, 1991), 18; emphasis in original.

18. See Jacques Derrida, *Limited, Inc.*, trans. Samuel Weber (Evanston: Northwestern University Press, 1988), 53, 61–65, 70, 76, 92, 100, 102, 105, 119.

19. In her book *Bodies That Matter: On the Discursive Limits of "Sex"* (New York: Routledge, 1993), Judith Butler further explains the notion of performativity: "Performativity is thus not a singular 'act,' for it is always a reiteration of a norm or set of norms, and to the extent that it acquires an act-like status in the present, it conceals or dissimulates the conventions of which it is a repetition. Moreover, this act is not primarily theatrical; indeed, its apparent theatricality is produced to the extent that its historicity remains dissimulated (and, conversely, its theatricality gains a certain inevitability given the impossibility of a full disclosure of its historicity" (12–13). The discovery of a personal-historic dimension to his "performance" indicates to Kochan his actions are not merely "acts," but something "deeper." This personal dimension is in turn related to the social norms of contestation and, in Foucauldian terms, reverse discourse, revealing the fractured nature of dominant discourse of (hetero)sexuality. Kochan's "performance" exposes the hidden flaws in purportedly rigid or univocal, social ideal.

20. Donald Keene, *Noh and Bunraku: Two Forms of Japanese Theater* (New York: Columbia University Press, 1990), 57.

21. Yukio Mishima, "Onnagata," in *Death in Midsummer and Other Stories* (New York: New Directions, 1966), 144.

22. Henry Scott-Stokes, *The Life and Death of Yukio Mishima* (Tokyo: Tuttle, 1990), 124.

23. Ibid.

24. Mishima, *Sun and Steel*, 25.

25. For Mishima's characterization of body building, see *Sun and Steel*, 25. For an elaborate and graphic portrayal of *seppuku*, see Mishima's short story "Patriotism," in *Death in Midsummer and Other Stories*, 93–118.

26. This notion of excess as a means of subversion is based on one suggested by Judith Butler during a workshop at the CUNY Graduate Center, December 7, 1991.

27. Roman Jakobson, *Language in Literature*, eds. Krystyna Pomorska and Stephen Rudy (Cambridge: Harvard University Press, 1987), 227.

12

"Dreadful Dioramas": Guibert's Countermemories

Kate Mehuron

In the most secret recesses of these vessels lurked, like dreadful dioramas, two or three indelible images.

Hervé Guibert[1]

Diorama: A mode of scenic representation in which a picture, some portions of which are translucent, is viewed through an aperture.... The name has also been used to include the building in which dioramic views are exhibited; and in later times has been transferred to exhibitions of dissolving views, etc.

Oxford English Dictionary

Imagine yourself at the portal of a life-size exhibition that features your friend dying. The details of his dying mime your own death, which you know is shortly to follow, based on an expert's diagnosis of your case as HIV positive. You are only a quasi-spectator, for your presence at this dioramic exhibit guarantees that you are inducted into a unique mimesis. Your friend is performing the gestures of an anguish that also overtakes you. In spite of this, you do not desert him. Rather, you attend to his drama and thus enact for the first time a partial rendition of your own.

This is the scene confronting Hervé Guibert as recounted in his novel *To the Friend Who Did Not Save My Life*. He narrates other such scenic representations in his earlier essay "A Man's Secrets."[2] All of these scenes announce Guibert's friend as the featured player, himself as spectator at the portal of the scene. Guibert's fictional use of dioramic representation powerfully deconstructs the static variables of his photographer's aesthetic. He photographs and tints with words his dioramic scenes. His prose then sets these scenes into motion and establishes various sorts of distance between his scenic portrayals and the narrative voice of his text. The spectator's induction into mimetic participation and the extent of the mimetic production of the actual are sorceries whose compelling effects are dependent on these fictive gaps.

Most significant for this essay, Guibert's dioramic representations sketch countermemories of the philosopher's process of becoming-a-genealogist. As countermemories, his dioramas stage certain spatialized dispersions of thought from which this process emerged. Guibert's countermemories desacralize certain idols enshrined by philosophy's gravity and further demonized or idealized by contemporary scholars: the open secrets of the philosopher's queer subjectivity, HIV positivity, the famous name itself.

Countermemories and Delirium

In a passage that describes the wake he kept with his friend, Guibert asks,

> What right did I have to record all that? What right did I have to use friendship in such a mean fashion? And with someone I adored with all my heart? And then I sensed—it's extraordinary—a kind of vision ... that I was completely entitled to do this since it wasn't so much my friend's last agony I was describing as it was my own, which was waiting for me and would be just like his, for it was now clear that besides being bound by friendship, we would share the same fate in death. (*To the Friend*, 91)

Is there a privileged access to the pure space of experience, intimacy, or likeness that entitles someone to scavenge the remains of the dead? Guibert's aesthetic scavenging at the wake of his friend and his subsequent explanation establishes an affinity, or constructed resemblance, between his fate and Muzil's own. This resemblance entitles him to use the remains of his friend for the fictive construction of his dioramas. Such animate portraits have the chance of remaining after him in perpetuity. The remains of Guibert's diorama signify his ethical experiment, an experiment in which he fashions the possibility of his own death through his fictional reinscription of the death of his friend.

Simon During argues that within the acategoriality of anti-Platonic thought, representation and mimesis are "unstable" or delirious categories.[3] On his account, both the photographer's free variation of the image and the philosopher's resolutely anti-Platonic genealogical expeditions into the events that fragment historical continuity exemplify a kind of delirious acategoriality.

The presumed acategoriality of aesthetic production perforates any sense of authenticity, hence any sense of entitlement based on a presumed authentic access to an event. An anti-Platonic account of Guibert's dioramic access to his friend's death indicates that no one, neither Guibert nor his readers, can move closer to an authentic experience of such a friendship, wake, and death. Although the notion of delirium dispenses with authenticity as a trait of the wake kept with one's friend, delirium does not rule out the community of loss that is occasionally induced by representations of such scenes.

Here is part of Guibert's narration of his visit to Muzil in the hospital before Muzil's death:

> Muzil was sitting in front of the sunny window in a white imitation-leather reclining chair.... He avoided meeting my eyes, and said, "You always think that in a certain kind of situation you'll find something to say about it, and now it turns out there's nothing to say after all." He wasn't wearing his glasses, and along with the discovery of his young man's torso, with its delicately crepey skin, came that of his face without glasses: I don't know how to describe it because I don't remember it, for the image of Muzil I try to keep from recalling is still engraved in my heart and memory with glasses, except for those brief moments when he'd take them off to rub his eyes. (*To the Friend*, 84–85)

The vertigo of yearning and sadness induced by such scenic portrayals is part of a delirium of mimesis presupposed by both the photographer and the philosopher. I suggest that such a mimesis fractures privileged representation and thus supplementarily displaces the voyeurism that might otherwise frame the scene. The vertigo of my own yearning displaces the distance needed for voyeuristic appropriation and tempts me to evoke Eve Sedgwick's "White Glasses." Her delirious meditation offers another, perpetually dissolving view that sadly fixates on the glasses of her loved one, lost to the plague.[4] Sedgwick's, Guibert's, my own yearning seek correspondences, affinities, differences, immaterial principles that connect one freeze-frame of our friend's glasses to another. Mimetic delirium seeks yet rejects the comforts of nostalgia. It retrieves only the artifice of such correspondences and it manufactures fictive rather than actual closures, closures that might quell sadness's infinite digressions. Perhaps the word "community" is better than most words to name the evanescent, passionate intersubjectivity achieved by the shared vertigo of loss in this epidemic. This is an intersubjectivity whose form implodes by the dispersals of singular stories recounted, the scenic representations of brief affinities of body surface, memory fetishes, and raw feeling. This implosion constructs an infinity of absences, and is partially inscribed by the scenes in

Guibert's text. Also inscribed by his fiction is the philosopher's work: an ironic witness to the delirium at the center of any memoir's "authenticity."

Which philosopher? In *To the Friend Who Did Not Save My Life*, Guibert depicts the death of Muzil, and in "A Man's Secrets" he sketches the "dreadful dioramas" of "the philosopher's" childhood secrets. Guibert's masked references to the philosopher's famous name, his narrativizing of the philosopher's quotidian life and extraordinary mind, have not avoided scathing critique. Guibert has been accused of violating the uniquely French value of discretion and the secrets of the philosopher himself by his fiction.[5] The grievances against Guibert's fiction are piled high: his literary opportunism at the scenes of his friend's death, the ideologically laden nostalgia of his literary vehicle, the betrayal of his friend's ontological allegiances and political strategy, and the violation of the philosopher's discretionary maneuvers against public appropriations and transformations of his own identity. None of these grievances is easily substantiated, for Guibert's masks, candor, and dioramic perspectives are far too mobile, pleasurable, and laden with instruction to bury by condemnation. Guibert's countermemories of Michel Foucault solicit a replay of his friend's laughter: a resounding peal that dispenses with transcendental viewpoints and the ancien régime of sovereignty over one's assets, blood lineage, and royal name.

In the interview "The Masked Philosopher" in 1980, Foucault dispenses with the condemnation leveled by certain critics and celebrates the underestimated virtue of curiosity: "I can't help thinking of the critic who would not try to judge, but bring into existence a work, a book, a phrase, an idea."[6] Curiosity, he asserts, is a vice that has been stigmatized within certain overlapping disciplinary games of truth. Rather than being considered a vice, curiosity is praised by Foucault as "the readiness to find strange and singular what surrounds us; a certain relentlessness to break up our familiarities and to regard otherwise the same things."[7] In this interview, Foucault refuses the use of his proper name, thus notating his resistance to the critics' oversimplifications and distortions of the works associated with his name. Not only does this refusal thwart the critics' unwelcome judgments, it also operates as a tactic by which to subvert the identity referenced by the proper name, an identity solidified by the circle of critics who interpret his work.[8] His refusal tactically reinstalls his thought in the world as a curiosity that, in its readable anonymity, will wreak strange and singular effects. This dissociative gesture is a Nietzschean hallmark of countermemory, committed as an effective use of history to dissipate identity, reveal the multiple and discontinuous mortal selves that inhabit one's persona, and counter antiquarian history's nostalgic preservations of soil, language, and polis.[9]

Foucault's experimentation with himself as a subject of knowledge enlists Nietzsche's buffoonery of masks and his notion of the will to knowledge, as well as the somber documentary work of genealogy. The latter form of countermemory labors to discover the heterogeneous forces that, through administrative and governmental processes of subjugation, produce the "truths" of the self in the present.[10] Guibert's mimicry at the site of his death and funeral produces countermemories in another way: by the effective use of history in its parodic or farcical mode. This mode uses the ephemeral, discretionary props of a dioramic aesthetic to battle against the conservatism of nostalgia. In Guibert's case, the conservatism of nostalgia is toxic. It poisons the curiosity requisite for the aestheticization of his own impending painful and courageous death. Guibert's antisentimental buffoonery in the production of the countermemories of his friendship is presciently described by Foucault as a sort of genealogical inquiry. He writes that genealogy must

> record the singularity of events outside of any monotonous finality; it must seek them in the most unpromising places, in what we tend to feel is without history — in sentiments, love, conscience, instincts; it must be sensitive to their recurrence, not in order to trace the gradual curve of their evolution, but to isolate the different scenes where they engaged in different roles.[11]

Foucault's description can be taken to condone the "ruthless erudition" required of Guibert as he filches the remains of their friendship. At the scene of his friend's anguish, Guibert acquires the ephemeral props with which he will be able to stage, through countermemory, his confrontation with AIDS-related pain, stigmatization, and isolation.

Filching the Remains

The theme of filching and thievery is ubiquitous in Guibert's novel, and is also the topic of his comedic novel *The Gangsters*.[12] Although confessing torment over the possible betrayal of trust inflicted by his descriptions of Foucault, Guibert candidly notes the difference between the discretionary thievery of his prose and the horror with which he views the betrayals of discretion by actors in the French biomedical establishment.[13] Guibert's prose illustrates the tensions between the customary partnership of general physicians and their patients, and the hierarchies of subordination between physicians and the biomedical institutions that control the drugs and specialized technologies required for the treatment of AIDS. This subordination is portrayed by Guibert to be replicated by the subjugation of those who are HIV positive to the covert research agendas and technologized, quantitative mechanisms of the biomedical institution.

Guibert reports that he switched doctors after a certain "Dr. Nacier" proved himself guilty of indiscretion, revealing the HIV positive status of celebrities in his care. The same doctor, a failed male model and actor, invited Guibert to surreptitiously photograph individuals in an elderly hospice in which he worked at the time. "Dr. Nacier" assumed that Guibert would enjoy filching images at the hospice for his photo essays, one of which had been published about his two aging aunts.[14] Guibert takes revenge on Nacier in *To the Friend Who Did Not Save My Life*, recounting the "shame and horror" with which Nacier's callousness had filled him, and then portrays Foucault and himself poking fun at the opportunist. Nacier's attempts to create a "designer death resort complete with registered trademark" and to recruit Muzil as his moral authority is met with glee:

> Muzil never laughed so heartily as when he was dying.... "This is what I told your little buddy: that nursing home of his, it shouldn't be a place where people go to die, but a place where they pretend to die. Everything there should be luxurious, with fancy paintings and soothing music, but it would all be just camouflage for the real mystery, because there'd be a little door hidden away in a corner of the clinic, perhaps behind one of those dreamily exotic pictures, and to the torpid melody of a hypodermic nirvana, you'd secretly slip behind the painting, and presto, you'd vanish, quite dead in the eyes of the world, since no one would see you reappear on the other side of the wall, in the alley, with no baggage, no nothing, forced to invent a new identity for yourself." (*To the Friend*, 16–17)

This scenario, comedically narrated in Guibert's novel, reemerges with intellectual gravity in Foucault's interview "Social Security" in 1983. At the close of the interview, which examines the administrative power wielded by the social welfare systems in France and the United States, Foucault wryly remarks that if only he could win a few billion francs in the national lottery, he'd set up an institute where people who wanted to die could spend the weekend enjoying themselves, and then disappear, "as if by obliteration."[15]

The discretionary filching on the part of both friends from their friendship's economy of gossip, humor, and experiences is staged by Guibert's dioramic representations in which the grievous betrayals by other friends and doctors are revenged, or at least fictively lent to posterity for future judgment. The gravity of such betrayals is determined by the ways that certain friends and medical personnel cold-bloodedly manipulate Guibert's and Muzil's life and death. The comedic, farcical stage of Guibert's dioramas avoids the morality play, however. In sections 15 and 16 of *To the Friend Who Did Not Save My Life*, Guibert parodies the histrionics of his own body in the biomedical regimes to which he is forced to submit, contrasting his own style in the examining room with Muzil's stoic and muscled endurance of the indignities of AIDS-related symptoms. The friendship itself seems to enact a shadow play of Foucault's account of how Platonism's moralizing legacy can be disrupted through the uses of countermemory. Guibert shows us how one can pervert the morality tale that stages those who betray the trust of others in the biomedically extreme circumstances of a plague. Foucault writes that such a perversion would "search out the smallest details, to descend (with the natural gravitation of humor) as far as its crop of hair or the dirt under its fingernails — those things that were never hallowed by an idea." Or, one can follow Foucault's appropriation of the joke in this instance through irony, subverting the Platonic tendencies toward morality plays by the sideways glance of his irreverent parenthetical remarks.[16]

The Nietzschean battle of masked subterfuge that Muzil wages against the coerced identities of publicly acclaimed authorship, homosexuality, and HIV positivity is a war conducted with the weaponry of the "open secret." Guibert witnesses the thievery of Muzil's physical autonomy, words, mental lucidity, and memory itself by the predatory incursions of opportunistic infections and hospitalization. This is an insidious thievery that threatens to turn his friend's own weaponry against himself. Guibert's journal will strike the first blow of this reversal and will bear witness to a truth that Muzil may have preferred erased in order to "leave only the well-polished bare bones enclosing the black diamond — gleaming and impenetrable, closely guarding its secrets — that seemed destined to form his biography, a real conundrum chock-full of errors from end to end" (*To the Friend*, 88). Before the sententious critics have a whack at that skull, stealing its remains with their interpretive probes, Guibert dioramically stages the biomedical filching of the "gleaming and self-contained enigma" of his friend's skull. The flagrancy of surfaces in these dioramic portrayals insists, by reiterative staging, upon the infinite impossibility of positivist or interpretive reductions of those enigmatic scenes.

The most devastating instances of thievery are those toward which Guibert's dioramas seem designed to exert psychic damage control. These instances feature the stripping away of bodily boundaries experienced by those whose very blood is pathologized within the heteronormative regime of the family; this pathology is decisively literalized by HIV contamination and the biomedical mechanisms that "steal" the truths of the flesh from the deceased. Guibert describes the sense of violation and exposure that presaged his diagnosis: "From that moment on, I would have to live with this exposed and denuded blood, like an unclothed body that must make its way through a nightmare" (*To the Friend*, 6). The onset of AIDS assails Guibert's skin surfaces, robbing him of bodily intactness, further exposing him to the shaming purview of the public eye; shingles fastens like succubi to his torso, thrush invades his tongue, an abcess tortures the back of his throat.

The containing function of the skin envelope in its fundamental role of mediating affect, imagination, and well-being is provocatively developed by Didier Anzieu, Guibert's psychoanalytic contemporary and Foucault's early mentor. Anzieu's psychoanalytic contribution *The Skin Ego* provides an analytic of the skin and the testaments of his analysands for substantiation. With the assistance of Anzieu's account, readers can begin to apprehend the psychical sense of disenfranchisement that accompanies the violations of AIDS, and the restorative necessity of writing as a secondary envelopment of flesh and bodily boundary.[17] Anzieu does not critique the heteronormativity that pervades psychoanalytic theory and practice, however. The sociosymbolic pathologization of queer blood is theorized by Guibert's friend in *The History of Sexuality*, and by his other queer contemporaries who also battle the plague with oppositional theory and queer-affective literatures and practices.[18]

Emily Apter observes that Guibert's portrayals of his own disease occasionally adopt the historically established French genre of the "pornography of death."[19] The effect, she argues, conflates the pain recounted with exhibitions of voluptuous sexual encounters. There are moments in *To the Friend Who Did Not Save My Life* in which Guibert applies a voyeuristic photographic gaze toward his own symptomatic body, conflating sex and death in certain scenes (141). I suggest that the transgressiveness of such gestures ought to be understood to take aim at the coercively imposed, heteronormative symbolic pathologization of his disease. Even in its transgressive register, Guibert's adaptation of this genre is readable on Anzieu's terms as recuperative: a healing tactic of cloaking himself in a literary tradition that counters the "deadly radiation" of the homophobic lights trained upon those targeted by the plague. Guibert's conflations of sex and death function to displace heteronormative assumptions about the nuclear family. His graphic accounts of lovemaking with his friend Jules are inflected by the tenderness of his attachments to Jules's family and his friendship with Jules's wife Berthe. This "family unit" reappears with similar emotive complexity in his novel *The Gangsters*. I use quotation marks to reference these attachments, because Guibert's representations disrupt heteronormative reductions of homoerotic affiliations. Voyeurism is only a partial technique within his tactic of portraying the heterofamilial thievery of queer attachments in his prose. To this end, I believe, Guibert filches all the scenes of touch and exposure that he can recall or fabricate for his aesthetic productions.

"Dreadful Dioramas"

Historically, the diorama has functioned as a dreadful pedagogical tool by imperialist processes of colonization. Susan Stewart mentions the European circus as a site in which dioramas spatialize and temporize class hierarchies, exposing and reinscribing the exotic "others" within the colonizing gaze of European views.[20] Cynthia Enloe has remarked the role of the diorama in the Euro-American pedagogy of the World's Fair, which specializes in the reiteration by scenic representation of imperialist legitimations of specific nationalist, gendered, and ethnic hierarchies.[21] The dioramic exhibits mobilized by the technologies of Western natural history museums are shown by Donna Haraway to naturalize Euro-American perceptions of intercultural and interspecies hierarchies, disciplining common apprehensions of natural rights, boundaries, and humanist identity itself.[22] And Michael Warner has pointed to NASA's launching of a dioramic spaceship scene of the paradigmatic heterosexual couple, which anticipates that extraterrestrials will become participants in the reiterative naturalization of humanist heterosexuality, relayed to the cosmos.[23] All of these instances require the complicit presence of the quasi-spectator. The spectator's pedagogical induction into the scene mobilizes its implicit values into virtual, dioramic motion. Finally, the dreadful manipulation of the power effects of such spatialized representations are elucidated in genealogical detail by Foucault. The spatialization of power by such feats as Bentham's panopticon attests to an emergent modern deployment of representation that is administrative, regulative, and interconnected with the representations of power deployed by earlier, perduring sovereign regimes.[24]

Given the grisly disciplines and subjugations disclosed by these genealogical analyses of institutions, what are we to make of Guibert's literary use of this tool, especially as it is deployed to survey the surfaces of his friend's secrets? In "A Man's Secrets," Guibert's parodic gesture targets the biomedical regime that would colonize the contents of his friend's skull by positivist, surgical means. Guibert begins by mocking the surgeon's hypocritical reverence for the philosopher's soul ("A Man's Secrets," 67–68). He depicts the surgical blade that opens the "luminous, teeming principality" of Foucault's mind. Thus Guibert appropriates the surgeon's weapon and wields his literary blade to "dispel the chimeras of origin."[25] His phantasmic reversal of voyeuristic appropriations of Foucault's life and death produces a second skin, or what his friend would have called a "thin membrane" or "incorporeal materiality."[26] Here is Guibert's fictional exegesis of the lesioned surfaces of his friend's memories:

> Three turrets had collapsed—that much was obvious—but from nearby furrows golden thoughts continued to flow, and with them laughter. More pronounced crevices carried off the debris of wretched old things of all sorts, prison towers and torture devices. Yet certain whips seemed to gleam like royal scepters, and there were gags made of the finest cloth. The surface shimmered with unmasked discourses, exposed to mockery. ("A Man's Secrets," 68)

This dioramic exhibition beats the critics in their heteromoralistic race to Foucault's grave to filch the remains for their lucrative scandal. In advance, this animate phantasm perverts these secrets, the possession for which the critics would otherwise vie.

Guibert's dioramic rendition in "A Man's Secrets" of the most deeply buried secrets of his friend's childhood resurrects the memory of the sovereign father's surgical/symbolic disciplining of his son's hetero-masculinist virility. Guibert then goes on to animate other figures of childhood shame:

> In the second, the young philosopher passes through an ordinary backyard. ... it was there, on a straw mattress in a sort of garage, that the woman the newspapers called the prisoner of Poitiers had lived for decades. In the third, ... the child philosopher is seized by hatred, cursing the intruders and calling down all sorts of maledictions on their heads. And the Jewish children, refugees in the provinces, did in fact disappear. ("A Man's Secrets," 68–69)

The dreadful dioramas of Foucault's childhood secrets instruct spectators about the puzzles that awaited decoding in his subsequent development as a genealogist of power relations. But Guibert's scenic representations are less a pedagogical induction into the "truth" of Foucault's motives than a surface event that parodically imitates the confession. This spectacle of a simulated confession incites readers to engage with fake depths and mechanical players. Simulation reiterates the absolute absence of the author behind the narration, the infinite distance between the spectators and the "meaning" of the scene. For some readers, these dreadful dioramas may be the occasion for the more gentle vertigo of tender regard or curiosity. For all, these simulated distances are real infinities of absence, and they arrest the nostalgic promise of the discovery of Foucault's "real" self or the verity of his "real" memories. There is fool's gold here, and Guibert has seen to it that there are plenty of props to seduce those who will try to steal the confessional "truths" behind the scenes of his friend's death.

Sorceries

Guibert's prose is described by Emily Apter as instigating the "fantasmatic contagion" of blurred boundaries between self and other, memory and reality. She writes that his prose ushers readers into perilous proximity to the "netherworld of metempsychosis" of dead souls.[27] In the preceding discussion I have claimed more for Guibert's use of countermemory than this contagion. Additionally, Foucault demands more for the role of countermemory than the phantasmic play of ghosts or the pornography of death. Subjugated knowledges are necessary not only to dispel the chimeras of origin but to anchor chimeric countermemories into strategies that counter biopower with oppositional practices. His calculated risk of authorial anonymity was less a surrender to the netherworld of ghosts than a risk of self-experimentation in the work of "truth-telling" in relation to specific power formations.

The zero degree point of countermemory is, as During has argued, the non-representational field of practice, struggle, strategy, and demand. To be sure, the field of practice in this plague is delirious by virtue of the metempsychosis of the souls of the deceased into the living present of those living with HIV. If you attend the local scenes of AIDS activism, you will sense the heavy burden of this collective delirium on the souls of the living. Yet, to declare activism dead in this second decade of the epidemic is to yield to the delirium of melancholia and pornographic death.

Nietzsche reminds us that the archives of one's aesthetics of existence will encounter a certain futility:

> And has it ever been different? What things do we copy, writing and painting, we mandarins with Chinese brushes, we immortalizers of things that *can* be written—what are the only things we are able to paint? Alas, always only what is on the verge of withering and losing its fragrance! Alas, always only storms that are passing, exhausted, and feelings that are autumnal and yellow![28]

To sidestep either melancholia or futility, practices of resistance must perform a sorcery of today's commodity exchange relations pertinent to health care and heteronormative regimes. The exercise of power in relation to specific formations of power involves an antimetaphysical shamanism: the experimental will to knowledge that descends to the local, the practical, and to the resources of subjugated knowledges.

I dub this descent a sorcery or genealogical trick of the trade, because it is the most difficult for philosophers or critics to cognitively fathom. Foucault asserts that the work of struggle that preserves the "rude memory" of historical conflicts is neither empiricism, Marxism, positivism, nor scientism.[29] Rather, strategists need the phantasmic to exorcize the metaphysical, hence to proceed with the sorcery of the insurrection at hand. Now imagine that you are a sorcerer, and turn away from these painted thoughts to begin your dreadful, recurrent descent. This sorcery travels the axis of many infinities: between practices and their sociopolitical ends, the violences of institutions and their overthrow, the analysis of power and practical deliberation, "truth-telling" and the constitution of the subject in the telling. Traveling these axes, the shaman overthrows exhausted representations with the desacralizing sword of countermemory.

Notes

1. Hervé Guibert, To the Friend Who Did Not Save My Life, trans. Linda Coverdale (New York: Macmillan, 1991), 84–94. The original French publication was A l'ami qui ne m'a pas sauvé la vie (Paris: Gallimard, 1990).

2. Hervé Guibert, "A Man's Secrets," trans. Arthur Goldhammer, Grand Street 39: (1991) 67–71. The essay originally appeared in French as "Les Secrets d'un homme," Mauve le Vierge (Paris: Gallimard, 1988).

3. Simon During, "Post-Foucauldian Criticism: Government, Death, Mimesis," reprinted as chapter 5 of this volume.

4. Eve Sedgwick, "White Glasses," Tendencies (Durham, N.C.: Duke University Press, 1993), 252–66.

5. Paul Keegan, "The Lesson of the Master," Times Literary Supplement 4565 (28 September 1990): 1038.

6. Michel Foucault, "The Masked Philosopher," Foucault Live, ed. Sylvere Lotringer, trans. John Johnston (New York: Semiotext(e), 1989), 196.

7. Ibid., 198.

8. Foucault remarks, "This knowledge of the author's name has no real use. It serves only as a screen." See Michel Foucault, "Aesthetics of Existence," Foucault Live, 315.

9. Michel Foucault, "Nietzsche, Genealogy, History," in Language, Counter-Memory, Practice, ed. Donald Bouchard (Ithaca, N.Y.: Cornell University Press, 1977), 161–62.

10. Michel Foucault, "Two Lectures," Power/Knowledge: Selected Interviews and Other Writings 1972–1977, ed. Colin Gordon, trans. Colin Gordon et al. (New York: Pantheon, 1980), 97.

11. Foucault, "Nietzsche, Genealogy, History," 160.

12. For example, in To the Friend Who Did Not Save My Life, Guibert refers to his own blood, stolen by biopower's institutional incursions on his body boundaries. Also, he recounts his filching of his friend Marine's life for drama, and to the thievery of Muzil's bone marrow and life secrets by Muzil's family, the medical establishment, and the press (40, 70–72, 89, 97). The thievery of Muzil's death, name, and nature of illness by his family is also reiterated in "A Man's Secrets." See Hervé Guibert, The Gangsters, trans. Ian White (London: Serpent's Tail, 1991).

13. Medical anthropologists attest to the significance of the values of trust and discretion in the doctor-patient relationship in the French nationalized health care system, a relationship lacking exact parallel in the United States. See Jamie Feldman, "The French Are Different: French and American Medicine in the Context of AIDS," in "Cross-Cultural Medicine — A Decade Later," special issue of the *Western Journal of Medicine* 157 (September 1992): 345–49.

14. See also Guibert's comedic portrayal of the infiltration of his aging aunts' home by gangsters in *The Gangsters*. This book reads as an allegory of the self-deception of the general public in its nationalistic projections of the fear of contamination onto the immigrant "other." See too Guibert's video documentary of his own self-care as AIDS-related opportunistic infections invade his life: "La Pudere ou l'impudeur," directed by Hervé Guibert, produced by Pascale Breugnot (TFI/Banco Productions, March 1991). This video features candid interviews with Guibert's Aunt Louise, whose conversation demonstrates that she is undeceived about Guibert's life and health.

15. Michel Foucault, "Social Security," *Politics, Philosophy, Culture: Interviews and Other Writings 1977–1984*, ed. Lawrence D. Kritzman, trans. Alan Sheridan et al. (New York: Routledge, 1988), 176. My thanks to Lee Quinby for referring me to this passage.

16. Michel Foucault, "Theatrum Philosophicum," *Language, Counter-Memory, Practice*, 168.

17. Didier Anzieu, *The Skin Ego*, trans. Chris Turner (New Haven: Yale University Press, 1989). For an account of Anzieu's mentorship of Foucault, see Didier Eribon, *Michel Foucault*, trans. Betsy Wing (Cambridge: Harvard University Press, 1991), 195–96.

18. Michel Foucault, "The Deployment of Sexuality," *The History of Sexuality, Volume I: An Introduction*, trans. Robert Hurley (New York: Random House, 1980), 75–132; Guy Hocquenghem, *Homosexual Desire*, trans. Daniella Dangoor (Durham, N.C.: Duke University Press, 1993). See also Hocquenghem's novels written during the last years of his life spent fighting AIDS: *The Wrath of the Lamb* (1985), *Eve* (1987), and *The Travels and Extraordinary Adventures of Brother Angelo* (1988). These novels are discussed in detail by David Wetzel, "The Best of Times, the Worst of Times: The Emerging Literature of AIDS in France," in *AIDS: The Literary Response*, ed. Emmanuel S. Nelson (New York: Twayne Publishers, 1992), 95–113.

19. Emily Apter, "Fantom Images: Hervé Guibert and the Writing of 'sida' in France," in *Writing AIDS: Gay Literature, Language, and Analysis*, ed. Timothy Murphy and Susanne Poirier (New York: Columbia University Press, 1993), 93. Apter connects Guibert's pornographic gestures in his book *Le protocole compassionel* (Paris: Gallimard, 1991) with Alphonse Daudet, *La Doulou* (Paris: Fasquelle, 1931), which chronicles the onset of syphilis in his body.

20. Susan Stewart, *On Longing: Narratives of the Miniature, the Gigantic, the Souvenir, the Collection* (Durham, N.C.: Duke University Press, 1993), 12–13.

21. Cynthia Enloe, *Bananas, Beaches, and Bases: Making Feminist Sense of International Politics* (Berkeley: University of California Press, 1990), 25–28, 161–62.

22. Donna Haraway, "Teddy Bear Patriarchy, Taxidermy in the Garden of Eden, New York City, 1908–36," *Primate Visions: Gender, Race, and Nature in the World of Modern Science* (New York: Routledge, 1989), 26–58.

23. Michael Warner, "Introduction," *Fear of a Queer Planet: Queer Politics and Social Theory* (Minneapolis: University of Minnesota Press, 1993), xxi–xxiii.

24. Michel Foucault, "Panopticism," *Discipline and Punish: The Birth of the Prison*, trans. Alan Sheridan (New York: Random House, 1977).

25. Foucault, "Nietzsche, Genealogy, History," 144.

26. Foucault, "Theatrum Philosophicum," 169.

27. Apter, "Fantom Images," 88.

28. Friedrich Nietzsche, "What Is Noble," *Beyond Good and Evil: Prelude to a Philosophy of the Future*, trans. Walter Kaufmann (New York: Random House, 1966), section 296.

29. Foucault, "Two Lectures," 83–84.

Contributors

Claudette Kemper Columbus is professor of English and comparative literature at Hobart and William Smith Colleges and has been the recipient of two Fulbright research grants to Peru. She is the author of *José María Arguedas: Mythological Consciousness and the Future* as well as numerous articles on the relationship between colonizing practices and pre-Columbian rites, tales, myths, and terrain, particularly as these affect twentieth-century authors.

Lennard J. Davis teaches literature and cultural studies at Binghamton University (SUNY). He is the author of *Factual Fiction: The Origins of the English Novel, Resisting Novels: Fiction and Ideology*, and the forthcoming *Theorizing Disability: Embodiment in the Realm of the Senses*. He is coeditor of *Left Politics and the Literary Profession* and editor of *The Disability Studies Reader* (forthcoming), as well as editor of the journal *Early Modern Culture*.

Simon During holds the Robert Wallace chair in English and cultural studies at the University of Melbourne. He is the author of *Foucault and Literature* and editor of *The Cultural Studies Reader*.

Michel Foucault, internationally known philosopher and lecturer, held a chair at the College de France until his death in 1984. His books include *Madness and Civilization, The Order of Things, The Archaeology of Knowledge,*

The Birth of the Clinic, Discipline and Punish, and the three volumes of *The History of Sexuality*.

Ellen J. Goldner teaches literature at Syracuse University. She has published articles on Edith Wharton and Mark Twain, and is currently working on a book about global capitalism and early signs of the dissolution of the subject in nineteenth-century American and British fiction.

Tom Hayes teaches English and cultural studies at Baruch College and the Graduate Center of the City University of New York. He is the author of *Winstanley the Digger* and *The Birth of Popular Culture: Ben Jonson, Maid Marian and Robin Hood*. He has edited a forthcoming collection of essays on the work of Robert Mapplethorpe entitled *Mapping Mapplethorpe: A New Erotics, A New Ethics*.

Kate Mehuron is associate professor of philosophy and women's studies at Eastern Michigan University. She is the coeditor of *Free Spirits: Feminist Philosophers on Culture* and the author of numerous articles on postmodernism, feminism, and cultural analysis. Her forthcoming book *Epidemic Reflections* applies postmodernist and feminist analysis to contemporary AIDS-related cultural productions.

Donald H. Mengay teaches literature and theory at Baruch College, CUNY. He is currently writing a book on homosexual travel narratives entitled *Male Crossings*.

Imafedia Okhamafe holds a double Ph.D. from Purdue University and teaches philosophy and English at the University of Nebraska at Omaha. His current research interests include intercultural communication in philosophy and English literature. His publications have appeared in such journals as *Research in African Literatures* and *Soundings: An Interdisciplinary Journal*.

Lee Quinby is professor of English and American studies at Hobart and William Smith Colleges. She is the coeditor, with Irene Diamond, of *Feminism and Foucault: Reflections on Resistance* and the author of *Freedom, Foucault and the Subject of America* and *Anti-Apocalypse: Exercises in Genealogical Criticism* (Minnesota, 1994).

José David Saldivar is professor of comparative ethnic studies at the University of California at Berkeley. He is the author of several books, including *Criticism and the Borderlands* and *The Dialectics of Our America*.

Malini Johar Schueller is associate professor of English at the University of Florida. She is the author of a book on personal narratives, *The Politics of Voice: Liberalism and Social Criticism from Franklin to Kingston* and has published numerous essays on race, ethnicity, and colonialism in U.S. literature. She is currently writing a book, *U.S. Orientalisms, 1780–1890*, and is editing a special issue of *Prose Studies* titled *U.S. Personal Narratives and the Subject of Multiculturalism*.

Index

Compiled by Eileen Quam and Theresa Wolner

229